Contents

Preface

The intention of this book is to detail, as factually as possible, the history of British deaf people, including the development of education for the deaf and the growth of the Deaf Community.

There are enough books in existence that detail the achievements of hearing people who have participated in the deaf world, such as Bulwer, Wallis, Arnold. It is not the intention of this book to add to the record. It is also the view of this author that some of these 'achievements' have no parity with what was actually achieved (e.g. Wallis and Whalley,q.v.)

The main drawback with many books about hearing people was that the deaf subjects who made them so famous scarcely got a mention: sometimes there was no mention at all.

In other cases, hearing people have in the past been guilty of embellishing events so that they 'saw' things as they wanted to see them, not what was reality. Into this category falls the story of St. John of Beverley.

In the Venerable Bede's *Chronicles* written about 685 A.D. St. John took a paternal interest in a number of sorely-afflicted persons so that he might minister to their wants. One of these was a youth who was unable to speak. On one occasion, John is said to have ordered the youth to thrust forth his tongue and show it to him (John) upon which John made the sign of the cross. This having been done, the youth was told to draw his tongue back and say 'Gae' (an old Saxon equivalent of Yeah). Immediately the youth's tongue was loosened and he said what he had been ordered to say. St. John then added the names of the letters, 'say A', he said A: 'say B', he said this too, and so on through the alphabet, then some syllables and words. All through that day and the following night, the youth is said to have not ceased talking.

On the basis of this story St. John of Beverley is claimed to be the first teacher of the deaf: indeed, he is regarded as the Patron Saint of deaf people and there have been schools and deaf clubs called after him. In the years between the two Wars there existed an organisation of clergymen called the Guild of St. John of Beverley which severely retarded the status and the development of the British Deaf Community.

However, if we care to examine the Venerable Bede's chronicles closely, at no time did Bede ever use the word 'surdus' (Latin for deaf). The word that Bede did use was 'mutus' (Latin for mute/dumb). This youth was never deaf at all; what he had was, in present day terminology, a speech impediment. One does not have to be deaf to have a speech impediment.

So right at the beginning the scene was set for centuries of misunderstanding about deaf people and deafness which has persisted to the present day.

Inaccuracies in deaf folklore and emotive reporting in magazines for deaf people added to the difficulty in trying to be factual. Taken together all these made the research for this book extremely difficult in the interests of accuracy.

The following three instances illustrate this.

Dumb Dyott

The story of Dumb Dyott has been well-known in deaf folklore for centuries, and also in the city of Lichfield. What was not known was his proper name and what he was. Even Greasley's well-known book, *The Siege of Lichfield*, does not give Dumb Dyott his proper name or any background detail.

Several visits to Lichfield and Stafford were needed to confirm the story of Dumb Dyott and trace his background.

Daniel Whalley

I came across many articles which referred to 'a little boy' who was presented before King Charles II in May 1662 by Dr. John Wallis.

Only Thomas Arnold in his book updated by Farrar: *Arnold's Education of the Deaf got it correct. Presumably because his school was based in that town, Arnold did the same as I did. That was to spend several days going through the numerous manuscripts and documents about the Whalley family held in Northampton County Records Office.*

Daniel Whalley was aged 25 in May 1662 - hardly a little boy.

The Sinking of the Schooner *Chrisean.*

A number of articles in deaf literature around 1904 spoke of an award bestowed upon a deaf person who was a member of the Gorleston lifeboat crew that took part in the rescue of a number of survivors from the wreck of a Swedish schooner called the *Chrisean.* No name was given in any of the articles. (This was not unusual - it frequently happened.)

Because it sounded like a good story, some considerable time and effort was spent in trying to get to the heart of the matter.

Enquiries at the headquarters of the Royal National Lifeboat Institution showed no record of the sinking of the *Chrisean.* However, these enquiries brought to light the fact there had been two lifeboats based at Gorleston - one was the official RNLI lifeboat, the other was privately owned: sometimes the same people crewed both lifeboats. (Presumably, this depended whether there was any salvage value). It had been the private lifeboat which had attended the sinking of the *Chrisean.* A list of crew members frequently on call around that time was obtained: indeed, there was one person called Dummy Harris listed as a sometime crew member. However, his name was not listed as one of the crew called out to that wreck. Neither was there any record of any award being made to any crew member for attending that wreck in the local press or in the lifeboat station's records.

This story was obviously false or incorrect.

These three instances illustrate the meticulous detail which had to be given to each and every story, and I have tried to do this wherever possible. A number of possible stories have therefore been excluded because there was no proof to substantiate them. This included tracing two families with records of deafness who could be linked to the descendants of Martha's Vineyard, U.S.A.

Acknowledgements

A book of this nature inevitably takes up a considerable amount of time, not only of the author's but those of other people who may either willingly help or be cajoled into doing so. Countless favours are called upon, many begging letters sent, telephone bills are run up regardless of cost.

There was never really enough time to do proper justice to the search for the deaf Britain story, but it is thanks to so many who either put themselves out to help, or had their arms twisted, that the book has taken the shape that it has. In an Utopian World, I could have taken five years full-time research, and had unlimited time and money to write the story, but we do not live in an Utopian World.

Foremost of all the thanks I have to give is to the British Deaf Association for the honour and the opportunity of writing the book.

The time spent on this book was a long and difficult period for my partner, Maureen Cox and Emma, who lives with us, and our other children who do not, Nancy and Wayne. The cumulation of months and months of research meant that the house was often full of newspaper cuttings, books, photographs, and other miscellanea which filled many boxes; the dining room was often an area where absolutely no admittance was allowed lest the carefully positioned piles got disturbed. The inconvenience often extended to time spent away from home, and in lieu of holidays, I would take my family on some of the trips where the children would be sometimes compelled to accompany me to records offices, libraries, museums, and art galleries - all of which they bore with patience. The debt I owe to Maureen extends to the point where she typed most of the manuscript.

I also owe so much to Mary Plackett and her staff in the library of the Royal National Institute for the Deaf, and to the staffs of Northwich and Warrington county libraries for the numerous queries and tasks that I set them to find, most of which they coped with admirably.

Members of the staff in countless county records offices, museums, art galleries and other libraries must also be thanked for the time and effort taken to satisfy my very demanding requests for information - in particular, those at Cornwall, Norfolk and Northampton for tracing old documents.

I also wish to thank:

Lillian Lawson, Head of Administration, British Deaf Association, for her confidence and support with the book.

John A. Hay for his assistance with the research, especially in connection with Old Edinburgh. His contribution was most invaluable.

P.D. Hingley, Librarian at the Royal Astronomical Society, London, for his interest and contribution in respect of John Goodricke.

The Duchess of Devonshire for allowing me and Maureen to visit Chatsworth out of season, and rendering us every assistance in connection with the 6th Duke of Devonshire.

Richard A. Goulden for his assistance with research, and contribution with computer print-outs of literature through his employment.

Richard A. Belsten, Social Worker with Deaf People, Somerset County Council, for his time and contribution in investigating several stories on my behalf in his area.

M. Seton, Librarian, Moray District Council, Elgin, for his assistance with the research on Stotfield.

Major A.J. Dickinson of the Royal Humane Society for his time and patience during my enquiries about deaf holders of the Society's awards.

Gordon Chapman and his staff at the Glasgow and West of Scotland Society for the Deaf for their help and contribution during my researches in Glasgow, and for providing rare photographs of the 1890s.

Melinda Napier and Betty Shrine for providing photographs of the National Deaf Club and British sports activities of the 1930s and 1940s.

The Principals and staff of the following Schools for the Deaf who allowed me access to their archives: Northern Counties School for the Deaf, Newcastle; Donaldson's School, Edinburgh; Royal School for the Deaf, Derby; Royal School for Deaf Children, Margate; Royal West of England School for the Deaf, Exeter; Royal Cross School, Preston.

Anthony J. Boyce, Head of Applied Technology, Doncaster College for the Deaf, who allowed me access to his book and the records of the Yorkshire School for the Deaf, Doncaster.

Jack R. Gannon, author of *Deaf Heritage, A Narrative History of Deaf America*, who gave me valuable assistance whilst I was researching at Gallaudet University, Washington, D.C., U.S.A.

Mrs. J.A. O'Rourke, Royal Air Force, for running down a missing detail which made the story being researched complete in every respect.

Mr. S.C. Whitbread for permission to include the first known painting of a deaf person.

Caroline Taylor of the Ely Diocesan Association for the Deaf for obtaining on my behalf old and rare photographs.

Bob Duncan, producer of Channel Four's *Listening Eye* programme for his support and interest in the book.

Lt.Col. A.A. Fairrie of the Queen's Own Highlanders who arranged for me to take photographs of Francis Humberstone Mackenzie, Lord Seaforth, at the end of what was a long, exhaustive search for a most elusive portrait.

And individuals listed below who contributed in a variety of ways too numerous to mention:

*Doug Alker; *Peter Allen; *Bernard Allery; *Bobby Bailey; *David Bromwich; *David Bullock; *Peter Collins; *Martin

Colville; *Wendy Daunt; *Mike Davis; *Clark Denmark; *Sally Ellis; *T.K. Faragher; *Mrs. M. Ford; *William Gilbert; *Peter Gosse; *Joe Goulding; *Sheila Gregory; *Irene Hall; *W. Hallett; *J. Hammond; *Carole Harris; *Dennis Harris; *Mrs. A. Humphrey; *David Hyslop; *Jane Kilgour; *Margaret Lawrie; *Ronald Lee; *Rev. C. Lowndes; *Catrina Lucas; *Edith McEwen; *Mrs. L. McGrath; *Jimmy McGregor; *Canon A.F. Mackenzie; *Dorothy Miles; *Bernard Quinn; *Terry Riley; *George Scott; *Sarah Scott; *Keith Simmons; *Ian Stewart; *Teddy Webb; *Maureen Wood; *John A. Woods; *Mrs. P.K. Wrighton.

I feel this book in some areas only scratches the surface of the history of one of Britain's most overlooked minority groups, but I hope that it will influence others to explore the history in more detail. May those who do so experience the same tough and fascinating research as I did, and become a much prouder Deaf Person.

Peter W. Jackson,
Northwich,
Cheshire,
December 1989

Prologue

It is *circa* 1595, and the scene is the old market town of Truro, Cornwall.

The young man had a sharp instinct for news, and having learnt that someone was going to speak in the market place, he made his way there quickly, and shoved aside other townsfolk until he was firmly in front of the speaker. The townsfolk were used to him and let him have his way.

While the preacher spoke, the young man watched him intently and steadfastly, taking in what was said.

Once the speaker had finished, the young man would leave and hurry to his master, who was the Member of Parliament for the county, and repeat to him in very effective sign language what had been said idn the marketplace. In this manner, his master was kept well-informed of the goings-on in his constituency.

When his master no longer needed his immediate services, the young man would go to a nearby village and seek out another young man.

Together they would exchange such passionate gestures, such hearty laughter that their lack of speech was of no importance to them, so well did they understand each other in sign language.

So wrote Richard Carew (1555-1620), a rich resident of Cornwall who spent from 1580 to 1602 writing his *Survey of Cornwall*. His disinterested observation, mentioned in passing and occupying less than a full page of his book, is in fact the first recorded independent observation in Britain of how a deaf person could lipread, communicate with his hearing employer by signs, and seek out another deaf person and communicate in a sign language not readily understood by most hearing people.

John Young
Chair British Deaf Association

BRITAIN'S DEAF HERITAGE

As Chair of The British Deaf Association and a profoundly deaf person, I am well aware how important Deaf Heritage is to deaf people. It is part of our culture.

The book Britain's Deaf Heritage not only gives an opportunity for deaf people to learn about their own heritage but also an opportunity for hearing people to become aware of how rich deaf people's heritage truly is.

I sincerely believe that Britain's Deaf Heritage should become essential reading for every deaf child. Furthermore, that Britain's Deaf Heritage should be included in the curriculum of every deaf child.

John Young
Chair,
British Deaf Association

Chapter 1
The Early Years

The Will of Framlingham Gaudy
The First known ever to be written by a
Deaf Person - dated 1672
Reproduced by the kind permission of Norfolk County Records Office

CHAPTER 1

The Early Years

A heritage that relies largely on the visual does not have a long history unless it is written about, or painted, or built as a permanent structure, and herein lies the greatest difficulty in looking at the history of deaf people, for their language, British Sign Language, is a visual gestural language where no written form exists like Ancient Greek, Latin or any other ancient language.

Thus, we come to rely on the writings of other people, like Richard Carew's *Survey of Cornwall*, John Bulwer's *Deafe and Dumbe Man's Friende* published in 1648, or even further back, the Hebrew book *Talmud*, to learn something about the existence of deaf people and the kind of lives they led. In this, we are also helped by stories of deaf persons that have been passed down in legend, like Dyott, Princess Katherine Plantagenet and Princess Jean, and in families where deafness was hereditary.

The picture that history has always painted for us of deaf people living in Britain - or indeed Europe - up to the beginnings of deaf education in the eighteenth century with the founding of schools in Paris (Charles Michel de l'Epee), Germany (Samuel Heiniecke) and Edinburgh (Thomas Braidwood) is that most deaf people were feeble-minded, legally incompetent and leading lives of isolation within their own communities.

This was probably correct for *some* deaf people in distant times: there are still *some* deaf people feeble-minded and unable to look after themselves even now in the 1980s, but then there are also *some* hearing people in the same category so this classification is meaningless.

1

What is probably more accurate is that in distant times, *most* deaf people had a sharp sense of highly*undeveloped* intellect which they were mostly unable to express by writing or speaking but which they could do so through sign language, a factor which went unrecognised until the 17th century in Britain when a number of people like Richard Carew, John Bulwer, and George Dalgarno wrote about it, and which the first teachers like Levold Watts, Dr.Holder and Dr.Wallis tried to develop.

Were deaf people truly feeble-minded imbeciles, it is highly unlikely that Princess Jean of Scotland would have become betrothed to James Douglas, Earl of Angus, no matter how beautiful she was; it is highly unlikely that Edward Bone, the man whom Carew wrote about, would have been able to lipread so well, to communicate with his master so well, and to engage in hearty sign language conversation with another deaf person. To be able to lipread as expertly as Bone did presupposes that the lipreader had language to begin with. It is also highly unlikely that Sir Edward Gostwicke and his brother William would have been such womanisers, that John Dyott could not understand the difference between an ermine- coated Parliamentary general and a common Roundhead soldier (or indeed, who were the enemies of his King).

When John Bulwer wrote his *Deafe and Dumbe Man's Friende* in 1648, he mentioned the existence of over twenty-five deaf persons in various parts of the country, mostly in London, Essex and in the South-east, but some in Cheshire as well. Many of those he mentioned were deaf siblings. In his book, Bulwer makes a dedication to Sir Edward Gostwicke which is more of a treatise on lipreading, but there is no doubt that Sir Edward was also a fluent user of British Sign Language - we know that from independent sources - and with Sir Edward known to be a regular traveller, it was probably Sir Edward who gave Bulwer the names of the deaf persons mentioned in the book.

This factor, together with an account written by the diarist

Samuel Pepys on 9th November 1666, and the fact that British Sign Language was discovered to be in common usage in Martha's Vineyard, off the Massachusetts shore, U.S.A. in the late nineteenth century and early twentieth century which could be traced back to the first settlers to come to Martha's Vineyard in the 1670-1690s, which in turn could be traced back to English immigrants who had come to New England between 1634 and 1644, all point to a thriving interaction between deaf people and deaf families using B.S.L.

The instances are too numerous, too coincidental, to dismiss as isolated cases - in Britain, King James I even tried to establish a Professor of Signs. B.S.L. was in common usage among deaf people, and some hearing people, by the early 1630s, and had probably been in existence for centuries before that as well, and not only in Britain.

We should be aware that in the Middle Ages there was some considerable trade between Southern England, especially Kent where the first settlers of Martha's Vineyard originated from between 1634 and 1644, and Europe and the possibility has to be considered that some form of two-handed system similiar to that in use in Britain was also being used in some parts of Europe before the one-handed alphabet system became more universal through the establishment of education for the deaf.

Jacob de Gheyn, a Flemish painter (1565-1629), painted a picture titled 'Master & Pupil' in 1599 which clearly shows the two-handed alphabet being used by the Master to the Pupil.

Edward Bone (c.1570- ?) John Kempe (c.1578- ?)
Edward Bone was a manservant of Peter Courtney (1559-1605), who was at one time the Member of Parliament for Cornwall, living at Ladoc, near Truro.

Bone, who had a retarded deaf brother, is described by Richard Carew as being a very religious and clean-living deaf man, so alert that he would be one of the first to learn of any news that was stirring in the county which he would immediately report to his master with whom he could communicate well by signs. He was also probably unpopular with Peter Courtney's other servants because he would report any lewd behaviour and would not rest until the offending servant had corrected his behaviour, or his master told off the servant. Bone was said to be 'assisted with so firme a memorie, that hee would not onely know any partie, whome hee had once seene, for ever after, but also make him knowne to any other by some speciall observation, and difference.'

Master and Pupil By Jacob de Gheyn
Reproduced by the kind permission of Manchester Art Galleries

This phrase suggests that Bone gave people signed names in the same way deaf people do to-day.

Edward Bone's great friend was a John Kempe, also deaf, whose family was related to the Courtneys by marriage. Kempe came from the nearby village of Merther and every so often, the two would meet, and engage in sign language conversation which Carew refered to as 'strange and often earnest tokenings' which were not understood by hearing people. Carew himself could not understand the conversation between the two deaf men, although he could understand Bone's effective signs to Courtney and the other servants. This would suggest that Bone was intelligent enough to adapt his communication systems according to the capabilities of the people he was communicating with to understand him. Carew had earlier mentioned Bone's ability to lipread, so in this observation we can see that in Edward Bone, an ordinary manservant, there was language and intelligence enough to enable a deaf person to provide three effective communication systems.

Sir Edward Gostwicke, 3rd Bart., (1620-1671): William Gostwicke (1630-1696)

Sir Edward Gostwicke was the sixth child of Sir Edward Gostwicke, 2nd Baronet of Willington, Bedfordshire, and his wife, Anne Wentworth, and became the heir when his elder brother William died as a child.

Born deaf, he succeeded to the baronetcy when aged 10 on the death of his father a few months before the birth of his youngest brother - also named William, and also deaf.

Sir Edward was described by John Hacket, Archdeacon of Bedford between 1631 and 1637, as a 'sweet creature of rare perspicuity of nature whose behaviour, gestures and zealous signs have procured and allowed him admittance to sermons, prayers, the Lords Supper and to the marriage of a lady of a great and prudent family, his understanding speaking as much in all his motions as if his tongue could articulately deliver his mind.'

Sir Edward, and his brother William, were both given to pursuing women of their fancy, even after marriages (Sir Edward to a Mary Lytton, and William to a Joanna Wharton). Sir Edward for many years pursued the affections of Dorothy Osborne who was later to complain: 'Just now, I was called away to entertain two dumb gentlemen... They have made such a tedious visit and I am tired of making signs and tokens for everything I had to say! Good God! how do those

that always live with them? They are brothers; and the eldest
is a baronet, has a good estate, a wife and three or four
children. He was my servant (suitor) heretofore and comes to
see me still for old love's sake but if he could have made me
mistress of the world I could not have had him. And yet I'll
swear he has nothing to be disliked in him except for his
want of tongue.'

Sir Edward Gostwicke
by an unknown artist
Reproduced by the kind permission of the
Owner: S.C. Whitbread

It is a pity, perhaps, that Dorothy Osborne rejected Sir
Edward - her family was ruined by the Civil War whereas Sir
Edward's deafness prevented his being involved and his
estate came through unscathed, and he was quite a rich man.

Bulwer dedicated *Philocophus, or the Deafe and Dumbe Man's
Friende* to the Gostwicke brothers for their lip reading

abilities, yet we can see from Hacket's and Dorothy Osborne's letters that they used sign language. Because Sir Edward was rich, and could travel, he undoubtly met many other deaf people, and gave their names to Bulwer.

The English Civil War also created a legend of one deaf man in another city, Lichfield.

John Dyott (1606-1664)

John Dyott, well-known locally as 'Dumb Dyott', was 37 years old when the Civil War between King Charles I's Royalists and Oliver Cromwell's Parliamentarians reached the town of Lichfield in March 1643, and laid siege to it.

Lichfield was being held for the Royalists by Captain Sir Richard Dyott, the father of John Dyott (not the brother as some historians have said). Sir Richard had been Stafford's M.P. since 1638, and was a strong Royalist supporter.

The Royalist garrison at Lichfield was small and weak, but they were determined to deny access to Lichfield to the Commanding Officer of the Parliamentary Army, General Robert Greville, Lord Brooke, who had vowed to reduce Lichfield Cathedral to rubble.

John Dyott was one of only three men who were up on the battlements when the Parliamentarians began their assault on the morning of 2nd March 1643. Those three men caused such havoc to the Parliamentarians that the assault was held up.

During a lull, a horseman expensively clad in ermine rode into view. It was Lord Brooke, who had come to see for himself what was holding up what should have been an easy assault. Almost immediately, John Dyott fired his gun, and the bullet went through Lord Brooke's right eye into the brain and the General fell dead from his horse.

The assault died away with the death of Lord Brooke, and John 'Dumb' Dyott was led down from the battlements to a hero's reception from the townsfolk of Lichfield.

Despite this setback, however, the Parliamentary forces captured Lichfield three days later on 5th March 1643 with a renewed assault, but the Cathedral was spared destruction.

Very little is known of John Dyott after this incident which earned him fame, as he seems to have been ignored by the rest of his wealthy family. He is not mentioned in his father's will, or in any other family wills. He is not buried in the family vault in the Dyott Chapel in Lichfield, but is stated to have been buried in Temple Church, London in 1664. What we do know, however, is that he married a deaf and dumb girl called Katherine after the Civil War who bore him four daughters and a son. This must be one of the earliest ever recorded marriages between two born-deaf people

Freeford Manor, Lichfield
Photo: Author's collection

Despite what seems to have been shabby treatment by his illustrious family, who include a number of descendents achieving high- rank in the British Army, there is one memento of John Dyott which exists. The gun with which John 'Dumb' Dyott felled Lord Brooke is still in possession of the family at the ancestral home, Freeford Manor in Lichfield. Typically of a family that glories in their military history, it occupies pride of place on the mantlepiece in a room adorned by family portraits of long-dead soldiers.

The Gun used by John Dyott at Freefold Manor
Photo: Author's collection

Samuel Pepys and the Martha's Vineyard Link

The great diarist, Samuel Pepys, had a close encounter with a deaf boy whom he met in a visit on 9th November 1666 to the home of a Mrs Pierce where the guests were alarmed by the news of a fire near Whitehall not long after the Great Fire of London.

'By and by comes news that the fire is slackened; so then we were a little cheered up again, and to supper and pretty merry. But above all, there comes in that Dumb boy that I knew in Oliver's time, who is mightily acquainted here and with Downing, and he made strange signs of the fire and how the King was abroad, and many things they understood but I could not - which I am wondering at, and discoursing with Downing about it, "Why" says he, "it is only a little use, and you will understand him and make him understand you with as much ease as may be". So I prayed him to tell him that I was afeared my coach would be gone and that he should go down and steal one of the seats out of the coach and keep it, and that

would make the coachman stay. He *(Downing)* did this
so that the Dumb boy did go down, and like a
cunning roague went into the coach, pretending to
sleep; and by and by fell to his work, but finds the
seats nailed to the coach; so he did all he could, but
could not do it; however, stayed there and stayed the
coach, till the coachman's patience was quite spent,
and beat the Dumb boy with force, and so went away.
So the Dumb boy came up and told him *(Downing)* all
the story, which they below could see all that had
passed and knew it to be true.'

Clearly, the boy's 'strange signs' were not just gestures or
mime, but proper sign language, and equally clearly, Downing was an expert at interpreting as well as communicating
directly with the boy. What is really interesting is that Sir
George Downing, the man referred to in Pepy's diary and
after whom Downing Street is named, grew up in Maidstone
in the 1630s. It was from this area that the first settlers in
Martha's Vineyard left to go to America between 1634 and
1644, which eventually led to B.S.L. being used for centuries
on Martha's Vineyard Island. In the Maidstone area, therefore, use of sign language must have been quite commonplace in the 1630s for George Downing to become so familiar
with it that in 1666 as a politican, he was to communicate
with a deaf boy with the greatest ease.

The Early Teachers of the Deaf
By the middle of the seventeenth century, following Bulwer's
two publications, there was some interest in the theories of
the learning of speech and language in deaf people which led
to two different men to experiment with deaf subjects. They
were a Dr. William Holder, and Dr. John Wallis. Dr. Holder,
the brother-in-law of Christopher Wren, concentrated his
efforts on speech teaching whilst Dr. Wallis made use of
a manual alphabet taken from a Spanish source to teach
English words.

An Example of Sign Language
An illustration from *The Chirologia* by John Bulwer
British Museum, London

Both Dr. Holder and Dr. Wallis may be said to be the first teachers of speech to the deaf, but neither were really as successful as they made themselves out to be, as a study of their subjects Alexander Popham and Daniel Whalley shows. At least Dr. Wallis did succeed in showing the Royal Society as well as the King and his court in 1662 what could be done with the speech of deaf people, and by their feud with each other, Holder and Wallis laid the groundwork for the future of education of the deaf. This groundwork was followed up by George Dalgarno of Aberdeen (who - as far as is known - never taught a deaf person, but nonetheless published in 1680 an account of how it could be done, using a manual alphabet as well as speech training), and by Henry Baker who from 1720 to 1729 taught a Miss Jane Forster to read, write, speak and understand the English language. He is also said to have taught a number of deaf people (this is recorded in Defoe's *Life and Times of Duncan Campbell*) but left no indication of his methods.

Though the two eminent and feuding Doctors of Divinity are regarded as the first to teach deaf people in Britain to speak, there was in fact an earlier teacher of the deaf who taught two deaf brothers to read and write in immaculate English. He was not a learned man of letters with a keen desire to create fame for himself like Holder or Wallis; he was secretary and estate factotum to the Gaudy family, and very little is known of him except where he is mentioned in wills and family correspondence. His name was Levold Watts, and his legacy to deaf heritage is that many of the letters written by the deaf brothers between 1658 and 1703 still exist.

Alexander Popham (1649-1708)
Alexander Popham shares with Daniel Whaley, *q.v.*, the dubious distinction of being the first born-deaf person in Britain to have supposedly been taught to speak.

Alexander was the second-born son of Colonel Edward Popham, a Member of Parliament for Minehead,

Somerset, and Anne Wharton. (For centuries, in deaf folklore, Alexander's father was mistakenly named as Admiral Alexander Popham. This confusion may have arisen due to the fact that the Popham brothers Alexander and Edward were staunch Parliamentarians who served in Cromwell's forces in the Civil War. Both brothers were Colonels, but Edward had naval experience and had the distinction of of becoming one of Cromwell's so-called 'Three Generals-at- Sea,' responsible for Cromwell's fledgling navy.)

Colonel Edward Popham died at sea of a fever in 1651, and young Alexander was thus brought up amongst his uncle's household which must have been confusing as Colonel Alexander Popham also had a son called Alexander.

Alexander was sent at the age of 11 to Dr. William Holder, F.R.S. (1616-1698) at Oxford after this eminent gentleman had undertaken to teach the boy how to speak.

This appears to have had some success for Dr. Holder explained at length in his *Elements of Speech etc. with an Appendix concerning persons Deaf and Dumb*, published in 1669.

In 1661, Alexander was sent to Dr. John Wallis (1616-1703) who had already been teaching Whaley for about a year, his family not apparently happy with the progress made by Dr. Holder. Evidently, Alexander did not like Dr. Wallis very much and forgot much of what he had learnt through Dr. Holder's instruction.

Nonetheless, Dr.Wallis took the opportunity to present both Popham, then aged 14, and Whaley, then aged 25, before the Court of King Charles II in May 1662 where both young deaf men were said to have spoken before the king.

However, Alexander apparently uttered only one or two words and was taciturn and ill-disposed towards the occasion. It may be that the young lad still had strong feelings towards Royalty given his family's strong Parliamentary links.

After this event, nothing more is heard of Alexander until 1679 when he married Brilliana Harley, the daughter of Sir Edward Harley of Hereford, and went to live with her at Bourton Manor, Bourton-on-the-Hill, Gloucestershire which his family purchased for him.

He had three daughters and one son, Francis, by Brilliana. Family documents do not record whether Brilliana or any of the four children were deaf, only that one daughter died in infancy, the other two daughters remaining unmarried throughout their lives, and Francis dying without any male issue.

It is a pity that of all the Popham family, Alexander is the one where there is very little by way of family documents, apart from land deeds and a will which is rather undecipherable. The latter however gives credence to the fact that Alexander was indeed taught to read and write, and had an education of sorts which enabled him to get married to a presumably hearing person and manage a Manor House. (Daniel Whaley's life subsequent to the presentation before the king in 1662 is poor in comparison.)

Alexander Popham died in early 1708 and was buried on 9th February 1708 aged 59.

Daniel Whalley (1636-1695)

Daniel Whalley has a special place in British Deaf History as being one of the first two *named* prelingually deaf persons to be taught to speak.

Daniel Whalley was taught by Dr. John Wallis, who subsequently wrote about these experiences. Dr. Wallis took the opportunity to present Daniel, together with another youth he was teaching, Alexander Popham, to a special gathering in Whitehall in May 1662 of the court of King Charles II.

Daniel Whalley was then 25 years old.

The king was reported to have asked both young men their names, which were mouthed by Dr. Wallis, and the two youths told their names and where they lived.

Daniel Whalley was the sixth child of Peter and Hannah Whaley** of Northampton who had a total of 13 children, four of whom died in infancy. His father was a wealthy stationer and bookbinder who was a freeman of the town of Northampton, and served as Mayor in 1646-7 and again in

1655-6, during which term he died in office. At the time of his death, Peter Whaley was also M.P. for Northampton.

Peter Whaley's wealth is evident by the bequests in his will. Apart from the third-born son, also named Peter, who evidently fell out with his father and only received £20, all the other surviving children*with the exception of Daniel himself* received handsome legacies. Samuel, the eldest, and Nathaniel, the seventh child, were left land and houses; William, Hannah and John were each left £200 whilst Elizabeth, the youngest daughter, was left £300. In contrast, Daniel was left an annuity of £15 per annum out of the rents of Tower House (which still stands in Northampton today).

In the will of Hannah Whaley, his mother, who died in 1671, all children also receive handsome bequests and legacies except Daniel, who only received a silver spoon and one of his mother's little silver cups, plus a burial plot.

Hannah's will concludes with this injunction -

'..And I charge you all my children with whom I have travailed in birth that you take especial care of your poor brother Daniel, and if any affliction befall him, that you succour and comforte him all the daies of his life..'

For all that Dr.Wallis is supposed to have taught Daniel Whalley to read, write and to speak, it is evident that this education was insufficient to enable Daniel to support and look after himself (unlike Alexander Popham).

Daniel Whalley never married, and died at Cogenhoe, Northampton, in March 1695 and was buried in his brother's, the Rev. Peter Whaley, church.

**The family name was spelt Whaley with one l up to the deaths of Peter and Hannah Whaley. Some of their children spelt the family name Whalley, including Daniel - others retained the original spelling.

Sir John (1639-1708) and Framlingham Gaudy (1642-1673)

The deaf brothers Sir John and Framlingham Gaudy came from a wealthy family residing in Norfolk, with ancestors who were at times Members of Parliament or High Sheriffs of Norfolk.

Sir John and Framlingham were the second and fourth of four sons of Sir William Gaudy, 2nd Baronet and his wife Elizabeth who also had a daughter Mary, but the eldest and third brothers both died in the smallpox epidemic of 1660 that also claimed the life of Henry, Duke of Gloucester, brother of King Charles II, so that the second eldest son, John inherited the baronetcy.

All four brothers received an excellent education at home, and in the case of the two hearing brothers (and possibly also the deaf brothers) at the Bury St. Edmunds Grammar School.

While the two hearing brothers went on to university, both deaf brothers went to study art in the school run by Sir Peter Lely intending to become professional artists. However, the death of his elder brother in 1660 followed by his father in 1669 caused Sir John to paint for amusement only whilst Framlingham Gaudy got such a severe attack of smallpox at the height of his excellent academic progress that he retired to the family home, and after a lingering illness, died unmarried aged only 31.

Framlingham Gaudy's will, proved at Norwich on 5th September 1673, is interesting in that it is the first *known* will written by a deaf person, and contains a certificate to validate this, which says 'These instructions for a Will were written with the proper handwriting of the said Framlingham Gaudy, who is a person both deafe and dumbe and soe not able otherwise to expresse his minde and this was written of his proper motion, the second day of May 1672, in the presence of William Smyth, Preb. Norv. B. Gibson.' The will is reproduced on the frontspiece to this chapter and shows the excellent quality of Framlingham Gaudy's handwriting and English grammar.

Sir John Gaudy married a Anne de Grey and had by her four children, and in a visit to Bury St. Edmunds in 1677, the diarist John Evelyn reported that 'there dined this day at my Lord's one Sir John Gaudy, a very handsome person but quite dumb, yet very intelligent by signs and a very fine painter; he was so civil and well-bred, as it was not possible to discern any imperfection in him. His lady and children were also there, and he was at church in the morning with us.'

By this, we see that Sir John, and presumably his deceased brother as well, used sign language. In fact, they were acquainted with a family named Lukes, mentioned more than once in Sir John's correspondence, who were in turn acquainted with Sir Edward Gostwicke. It is therefore probable that the two baronets had known, and perhaps, met each other.

It is also interesting to note that William Gostwicke's wife, Joanna Wharton, was the niece of Anne Wharton, mother of Alexander Popham, so there is another link in relationships and social intercourse between deaf people of the 1660s.

Sir John and Framlingham Gaudy were given to writing a lot of letters to their father from London, to their invalid sister, and to friends. The letters, although written in a quaint Old English style, show excellent command of the English language and are rich in vocabulary. They also show that Sir John in particular - after his brother's death - used to travel up to London quite a lot, so he was well-known. Some of the correspondence also refers to the financial debts that the family was burdened with, perhaps as a result of the Civil War, and from appearances, Sir John Gaudy was not a rich man.

Benjamin Ferrers (c. 1670-1732) The Father of Deaf Art

Notwithstanding the fact that both Sir John and Framlingham Gaudy were painters before him, it is Benjamin Ferrers who is our earliest recognised British deaf artist.

The date of his birth is uncertain, and the extent of his education is unknown although he could certainly read and write.

Although his earliest known painting is titled *Plant in a China Pot* and dated 1695, he was mainly a portrait painter who specialised in Chancery Court scenes around Westminister where he lived for many years until his death.

Court of Chancery By Ben Ferrers
*Reproduced by the kind permission of the
National Portrait Gallery, London*

One of the Gaudy Letters, written about 1685
Reproduced by the kind permission of the British Museum, London

Chapter 2
The Late Eighteenth Century

Himself as a Deaf Man
Self-portrait by Sir Joshua Reynolds
Reproduced by the kind permission of the Tate Gallery, London

CHAPTER 2

The Late Eighteenth Century
1750 - 1800

The second half of the eighteenth century saw some remarkable developments in the deaf world. Not only did this period see the birth of deaf education, it was also the era of the first deaf Member of Parliament, the first (and only) deaf painter to be given a royal appointment, the first deaf person to be made a Fellow of the Royal Society. It was also in this period that the world-famous Royal Academy was founded in 1760, and a deaf man was its first President.

The First School for the Deaf

In 1760, a wealthy Edinburgh merchant, Alexander Shirreff, approached Thomas Braidwood (1715 - 1806) the owner of a mathematical school and asked him to educate his ten-year old deaf son with a view to his learning to write.

Thus the first school for the deaf in Britain was started.

Braidwood abandoned any further aspirations at teaching only mathematics, and devoted the remainder of his life to the teaching of deaf children. These children were mostly those of wealthy parents.

The school was known as Braidwood's Academy for the Deaf and Dumb, and is mentioned in Sir Walter Scott's novel, *The Heart of Midlothian*.

In October 1773, Dr. Samuel Johnson visited the school on his way to the Western Isles of Scotland and was moved to write as follows: 'There is one subject of philosophical curiosity in Edinburgh which no other city has to show; a College for the Deaf and Dumb, who are taught to speak, to read and to write, and to practise arithmetic, by a gentleman whose name is Braidwood. It was pleasing to see one of the most desperate of human calamities capable of so much help: whatever enlarges hope will exalt courage. After having seen the deaf taught arithmetic, who would be afraid to cultivate the Hebrides.'

Braidwood never published any account of his teaching methods, but we can gather enough from authentic sources to know that Braidwood used a form of total communication.

Braidwood had a number of pupils who went on to make remarkable achievements after they had left his Academy: Shirreff, John Goodricke, Francis MacKenzie. None of these people had any understandable speech in later life, and had to rely on sign language or writing for communication purposes.

Craigside House, Edinburgh
Formerly Braidwood's Academy for the Deaf

The father of another pupil, Francis Green, however published *Vox Oculis Subjecta: A Dissertation on the most curious and important art of imparting speech, and the knowledge of language, to the naturally deaf, and (consequently) dumb; With a particular account of the Academy of Messrs. Braidwood of Edinburgh.* The Latin title was the Academy's motto, and in this account, we learn that Braidwood included a fair amount of oral teaching.

Incidently, the pupil referred to above, Charles Green, was the first deaf American to receive an education.

In 1783, the Braidwoods moved their school to Hackney, London where it was carried on by Thomas Braidwood's widow and son after his death in 1806.

The Asylum for the Deaf and Dumb

The first *public* school for the deaf was established in Grange Road, Bermondsey, London with Dr. Joseph Watson, a nephew of Thomas Braidwood, as Principal following the efforts of a distinguished Congregational minister, Rev. John Townsend. The Rev. Townsend, minister of Bermondsey, had become acquainted with a Mrs. Creasy whose deaf son had been a pupil of the Braidwoods.

Mrs Creasy so interested Mr. Townsend in the subject of the education of the deaf that he resolved to found a charitable institution for the indigent deaf. He succeeded in securing the interest of a wealthy man named Henry Thornton, and obtained subscriptions from a number of other people.

In November 1792, the new school was opened with six children and grew rapidly until it had 70 children in 1809, when the school moved to Old Kent Road.

Charles Shirreff (1750 - 1831)

The name of Charles Shirreff (at times spelt variously as Sherrif, Sherriff and Shirref) has a special niche in British Deaf history.

He was the first deaf pupil of Thomas Braidwood, and his progress was such that Braidwood forsook his previous calling as a mathematical teacher, and devoted the rest of his life to the education of deaf children.

The son of Alexander Shirreff, a wealthy merchant of South Leith, Edinburgh, Charles left Braidwood's Academy at the age of 18 to go to the Royal Academy Schools in August 1769 from which he graduated with a silver medal in 1772 to make a career as a miniature painter.

He successfully exhibited at the Free Society of Artists and at the Royal Academy, as well as others, and built up a clientele that was mainly theatrical.

He worked from London after graduating from the Royal Academy, and applied to go to India in 1778. In his application to the East India Company, he stated that he had no speech but was able to make himself understood by signs and requested that he be accompanied by his father and his sister Mary to act as interpreters. However, the failure of Fordyce's Bank ruined his father; his plan to visit India was abandoned and Charles had to stay to support his family.

He lived and worked from Bath from 1791 to 1795 where he was undoubtly acquainted with no other deaf miniaturists, Sampson Towgood Roche and Richard Crosse, *qq.v.* Certainly, all three shared at various times the same people whom they painted.

In 1795, he renewed his application to go to India, and left England in the *Lord Hawkesbury* which reached Madras in January 1797. He painted in Madras for some years before moving to Calcutta, where he worked on his *Illustrations of Signs*. In 1807, he announced it was nearly completed and would be available to subscribers as soon as possible. This work has never been traced and is presumed lost *en passage* from India.

He returned from India in 1809, and after painting in London for a number of years, retired to Bath where he died, unmarried, in 1831.

Other British Artists: 1750 - 1800
Richard Crosse (1742 - 1810)

The last three decades of the eighteenth century were a golden age in the history of British miniature portrait painting. Some of the best miniature painters flourished at this time, and deaf art produced three such painters - Shirreff,

Roche and Crosse. Of these three, Richard Crosse was regarded as one of the best of the second rank of British miniature portrait painters.

Richard Crosse: Self portrait
Reproduced by the kind permission of the
Royal Albert Memorial Museum, Exter

He was the second son of John Crosse and his wife Mary and was born at Knowle, near Cullompton, Devon on 24th April 1742.

He had a deaf sister, Alice, and it is evident that both of them were fairly well-educated although neither could speak. It is not known who educated them as a large part of the family records perished when the ancestral manor home of the Crosse family was destroyed by fire in the 1870's when a servant set alight some straw in the kennels where the Crosse hounds were kept. One of the manuscripts which survived the fire, however, was a well-written letter by Alice to her brother James complaining about a portrait that Richard Crosse had painted of her husband on wood instead of on canvas!

Bearing in mind some of the family were lawyers, it would appear that the deaf siblings shared the same tutor(s) as the other children at the family home.

When aged 16, Richard Crosse won a premium at the Society of Arts in 1758 and went to study in London at Sibley's Drawing School and the Duke of Richmond's Gallery.

Richard Crosse was a profilic painter, painting hundreds of miniatures between 1½ inches and 6 inches high. He kept a ledger in which he meticulously recorded every painting done and sold. In the space between 13th September 1776 and 30th January 1777, he painted and sold 56 small miniatures for eight guineas each, two of a medium size for ten and twelve guineas, a half-size portrait for fifteen guineas, and two large size portraits for thirty guineas each - a total of 61 works for £572, an excellent income for those days. This ledger can be seen in the Victoria and Albert Museum, London.

Many of his paintings and miniatures were unsigned, which resulted in his not getting the credit he deserved in latter years. Those which he did sign were either with his initials R.C. or in four different ways in full in careful handwriting as shown below.

In 1789, he was appointed Court Painter in Enamel to King George III.

He fell in love with his cousin, Miss Sarah Cobley, who refused his offer of marriage and instead married a Mr.

Haydon, the father of B.R. Haydon, the painter. This left him embittered and turned him into a recluse in his later years, causing him to retire from painting in 1798 already a wealthy man - and go to live with Miss Cobley's brother, the Prebendary Cobley, at Wells, Somerset for a number of years.

In his *Memoirs*, B.R.Haydon describes the final meeting between Richard Crosse and his mother.

'My dear Mother felt her approaching end so clearly that she made every arrangement with reference to her death.

I went to Exeter to get her apartments ready at the hotel, the day before she left home. She had passed a great part of her life with a brother (the prebend of Wells), who took care of a Mr. Cross [SIC],a dumb miniature painter. Cross (who in early life had made a fortune by his miniatures) loved my mother, and proposed to her, but she being at that time engaged to my father, refused him, and they had never seen each other since. He retired from society, deeply affected at his disappointment. The day after leaving Exeter, we stopped at Wells, as my mother wished to see my uncle once more.

The meeting was very touching. As I left the room and crossed the hall, I met a tall handsome, old man; his eyes seemed to look me through; muttering hasty unintelligible sounds he opened the door, saw my mother, and rushed over to her, as if inspired of a sudden with youthful vigour. Then pressing her to his heart he wept, uttering sounds of joy not human! This was Cross. They had not met for thirty years. We came so suddenly to my uncle's they had never thought of getting him out of the way. It seemed as if the great sympathising Spirit once again brought them together, before their souls took flight.

He was in agony of joy and pain, smoothing her hair and pointing first to her cheek and then to his own, as if to say "how altered!" The moment he darted his eyes upon my sister and me, he looked as if he *felt* we were her children, but did not notice us much beyond this.

My sister, hanging over my poor mother, wept painfully. She, Cross, my uncle and aunt were all sobbing and much touched; for my part my chest hove up and down, as I struggled with emotions at this singular and affecting meeting. What a combination of human feelings and suffering!

Disappointment in love, where the character is amiable gives a pathetic interest to woman or man. But how much more than ordinary sympathies must he excite, who, dumb by nature, can only express his feeling by the lightings of his eye; who wondering at the convulsions of his own heart, when the beloved approaches him, can but mutter unintelligible sounds in the struggle to convey his unaccountable emotions? Thus had this man been left for thirty years, brooded over affections wounded as for the mere pleasure of torture. For many months after my mother married, he was frantic and ungovernable at her continued absence, and then sank into sullen sorrow.

His relations and friends endeavoured to explain to him the cause of her going away, but he was never satisfied and never believed them; now when the recollection of her, young and beautiful, might occasionally have soothed his imagination, like a melancholy dream, she suddenly burst on his with two children, the offspring of her marriage with his rival - and so altered, bowed, weakened, as to root out the association of her youthful beauty with the days of his happy thoughts.

There are great moments of suffering or joy when all thought of human frailties is swept away in the gush of sympathy.

Such a moment was this. His anger, his frantic indignation, and his sullen silence at her long absence, all passed away before her worn and sickly face. He saw her before him broken and dying; he felt all his affection return, and flinging himself forward on the table, he burst into a paroxysm of tears, as if his very heart-strings would crack. By degrees we calmed him, for nature had been relieved by this agonising grief, and they parted in a few moments for the last time.'

Mrs. Haydon died the next day.

Richard Crosse himself lived out his final days at Knowle, and died there in May 1810.

Sampson Towgood Roche (1759 - 1847)

Sampson Roche was born deaf in Youghal, Ireland and began to show an aptitude for art, and was sent to Dublin to study under painters who were practising there, and also in Bath between between 1784 and 1788.

It is not known if he was educated, but he could write his name. His pictures were usually signed simply Roch or Roche, followed by a date. The letters were always separate and simple.

He married a Miss Roch (probably a cousin) in Cork in June 1788, then returned to live in Bath in 1792 where he and Charles Shirreff were contemporaries.

He had a flourishing practice painting miniatures, and lived in Bath until 1830, when he retired as a miniaturist and returned to Ireland where he died at Waterford in 1847.

Sir Joshua Reynolds (1723 - 1792)

A portrait and history painter and the dominant artistic personality in the reign of George III, Reynolds was born at Plympton, Devon on 16th July 1723.

Whereas other deaf painters of the same era such as Crosse, Shirreff and Roche had been born deaf or had become so in early childhood, Reynolds did not lose his hearing until he was 26 years old as a result of a riding accident in Rome. Even so, he did not lose his hearing completely; he was able to hear shouted conversation with the aid of an ear trumpet.

By then, however, he was already an accomplished painter although his main work and fame was to come after he had lost his hearing and his ear trumpet had become a familiar sight.

When they judged without skill, he was hard of hearing,
When they talked of their Raphaels, Corregios and stuff,
He shifted his trumpet and only took snuff.'
     Goldsmith c 1730 - 1774

Well before the first ever public exhibition of art was held in 1760, Reynolds had established himself as the leading portrait painter in London, and when George III established the Royal Academy in 1768, Reynolds was the only possible candidate for the presidency even though the King found his style and personality unsympathetic. Indeed, Reynolds was not well-liked by London society of the time. A lot of this may have been due to his deafness which caused him to remain aloof

In 1769, he was knighted and became Sir Joshua Reynolds. Now he was at his zenith, earning £6000 a year, and in 1773, he become mayor of Plympton, his native place.

In 1789, Reynolds became blind and resigned as the President of the Royal Academy. In the following years up to his death in 1792, he was a lonely man.

He never married.

A Deaf Astronomer
John Goodricke (1764 - 1786)

In November and December 1782, a young man of 18 made a significant discovery in the study of variable stars that laid the foundations of an important branch of stellar astronomy.

His name was John Goodricke, and had been born in Groningen, Netherlands, to an English diplomat and his Dutch wife on 17th September 1764.

Deaf Art

1750-1800

Man in Dark Coat and White Cravat: Sampson Roche

Man in Blue Coat: Sampson Roche

Lady in Blue: Richard Crosse

Officer in Red Coat: Richard Crosse

Thomas Wilkes of Overseal: Charles Sherriff

31

In infancy, Goodricke became deaf as a result of a severe illness, and at the age of 8 in 1772 he was sent from the Netherlands to Edinburgh to be educated at Thomas Braidwood's school.

John Goodricke
Reproduced by the kind permission of the
Royal Astronomical Society, London

Although school records do not show the state of his progress, it must have been satisfactory because in 1778 he was allowed to enter Warrington Academy. It was at that time a well-known educational institution in Cheshire which made no special provision for handicapped pupils. Goodricke may thus be said to have been one of the first, if not the first, successfully *integrated* pupils.

John Goodricke became an excellent mathematician during his stay at the Academy. He had for a teacher William Enfield, a mathematician of some renown. Bearing in mind, however, that Braidwood was himself a teacher of mathematics before he devoted his career to the deaf, there is no doubt that Goodricke developed his love of mathematics first through Braidwood, and went to Warrington Academy to further his knowledge of the subject.

It was probably Enfield, whose hobby was astronomy, who set Goodricke on his subsequent career, though this interest may already have been in Goodricke through his grandfather, Sir John Goodricke, who was said to have amused himself with astronomy.

On leaving Warrington Academy, Goodricke returned to his family who had settled in York. At that time, in York, there was already an accomplished astronomer, Edward Pigott (who had just discovered a comet).

From a window in Treasurer's House near this tablet, the young deaf and dumb astronomer

JOHN GOODRICKE
1764 - 1786

who was elected a Fellow of the Royal Society at the age of 21, observed the periodicity of the star ALGOL and discovered the variation of δ CEPHEI and other stars thus laying the foundation of modern measurement of the Universe.

A plaque on the wall of the Treasurer's House in York, from where Goodricke observed the stars.
Photo: Author's collection

Pigott and Goodricke were to form an astronomical alliance that began initially as instructor and pupil, but which later evolved into a close partnership. Pigott had fine instruments and a network of scientific contacts that Goodricke was to make good use of. Isolated in provincial York, Pigott had yearned for companionship in astronomy, and welcomed his new pupil eagerly. Even so, he was to complain in 1783 that 'there is not a soul here to converse with on astronomy' because he and Goodricke communicated almost entirely by pencilled notes. Because of this, only once was there any clash between the two men, and their working relationship remained excellent throughout the brief life that was left to Goodricke.

On 12th November 1782, Goodricke recorded the message that was to make him famous:

'This night I looked at Beta Persei and was much amazed to find its brightness altered - it now appears to be of about the 4th magnitude...'

Goodricke was not the first to notice the variability of Beta Persei (or Algol as it is more commonly known), but he was the first to establish that these light changes were periodic. For these observations, Goodricke was awarded one of the two Copley Medals for 1783.

Goodricke went on to discover the variability of two other naked-eye stars, Beta Lyrae (1785) and Delta Cephei (1786).

For his work, the Royal Society elected him to a fellowship, but Goodricke died at York only two weeks later, supposedly due to a cold from exposure to the night air in astronomical observations.

He was only 21 years old.

No stone over his tomb at Hunsingore, near York, commemorates his final resting place, but the University of York has named a lecture hall after him.

Deaf Parliamentarian and Governor of Barbados.
Francis Humberstone MacKenzie, Lord Seaforth (1754 - 1815)

Francis MacKenzie was born a deaf-mute, the second son of Major William MacKenzie, nephew of the 5th Earl of Seaforth.

He was placed with Thomas Braidwood at his Academy in Edinburgh where he learnt to some extent to speak. However, for the major part of his life, Francis MacKenzie used sign language to communicate with his peers. He was a very fluent fingerspeller, and many of his associates such as Lord Melville, Lord Guildford acquired fluent fingerspelling skills.

He was a highly intelligent and articulate man, given to writing numerous letters.

On 22nd April 1782, he married Mary Proby, daughter of the Dean of Lichfield, who bore him 4 sons and 6 daughters.

In 1783, his elder brother Thomas, who had succeeded his second cousin Lord Seaforth in 1781 as chief of the clan MacKenzie died, and Francis succeeded his brother as chief of the clan and inherited the considerable Seaforth estates which were in a neglected state.

Because of his interest in his Scottish estates, MacKenzie stood in 1784 against all expectation for Parliament against Lord Macleod, the sitting member for Ross-shire, and was elected, it is said, with a number of fictitious votes.

Francis Humberstone Mackenzie, 6th Lord Seaforth
Reproduced by the kind permission of the Queen's Own Highlanders Regiment Museum, Fort George, Inverness

He served as M.P. from 1784 to 1790 when he resigned because of his financial problems and gave his interest in the seat to a friend, William Adams.

On the outbreak of war with France, MacKenzie raised the 78th Regiment of Foot, Ross-shire Militia, with himself as Lieutenant-Colonel Commanding. In 1794, he added a second battalion. Although he rose to the rank of Lieutenant-General of the Army by 1808, he never joined his, or any other regiment, on active service.

The impact of events in France on domestic politics drew him out of policitical retirement, and upon his friend Adams being offerred a seat at Banbury, he stood again for Ross-shire, and was handsomely re- elected. On his return to the House, he gave silent support to the government as a result of which the Seaforth peerage was revived, and he was created 6th Lord Seaforth.

He was appointed Governor of Barbados in 1800, and during his governorship up to 1806 he strove to improve the conditions of slaves. He was reported to have been an able and vigorous governor.

On his return to Britain in 1806, Lord Seaforth played no further significant part in national politics, and his later years were blighted by misfortune. His financial embarrassments caused him to sell the 'gift land' of his house, as well as much of his estates. In addition, the only survivor of his four sons died unmarried in 1814, and MacKenzie himself died a few months later a physically and mentally broken man.

These last tragic events fulfilled the words of a seer, Kenneth MacKenzie prior to his execution by the 3rd Lady Seaforth in the 1660s:-

'In the days of a deaf and dumb caberfeidh, the gift land would be sold and the male line of Seaforth will cease.'

Chapter 3
More Schools 1800 - 1850

The School at Old Kent Road in 1816
From an Original Engraving at the
Royal School for Deaf Children, Margate.

More Schools 1800 - 1850

The first half of the nineteenth century was what could be called the Golden Age of Philanthropy. There was an abundance of people willing to embrace charitable causes, and education for the deaf was one such cause to benefit.

Between 1800 and 1850, fifteen schools for the deaf were started. Although one or two fell by the wayside during the latter part of the century, the majority of them grew into great institutions with hundreds of pupils in their heydays, and some still remain to the present day.

Asylum for the Deaf and Dumb.

The establishment of the Asylum for the Deaf and Dumb Poor at Grange Road, Bermondsey, was such a success that even with the addition of a training centre for the instruction of tailoring and shoemaking for boys, staymaking and shoebinding for girls, and a hospital for sick children, the demand for places was outstripping capacity.

This led the governors of the school to purchase a freehold piece of ground in Old Kent Road for £1,800 in 1803, and building work commenced on a new school that could accommodate 120 pupils.

The new school was opened in 1809 at a cost of £21,000 and the premises at Grange Road were disposed of.

Queen Charlotte visited the school in 1817 with Princess Elizabeth, and presented the institution with fifty guineas and twenty guineas respectively. The Queen accepted the title of 'Protectress of the Asylum for the Deaf and Dumb'.

The school was enlarged in 1819 to accommodate 200

pupils, and had on the total roll 219 pupils with 4 hearing and 8 deaf teachers.

The first headteacher of the school was Dr. Joseph Watson whose publication, *Instruction of the Deaf and Dumb* (1809) was the first of its kind since Dalgarno's in 1661. The school taught trades such as shoemaking, tailoring, printing, book-binding, cotton and twine spinning, sackmaking and rope making.

The School at Old Kent Road in 1819
From an Original Engraving at the
Royal School for Deaf Children, Margate.

In 1830, the first link with Margate was made with the establishment of four beds at the Sea-Bathing Hospital for the benefit of pupils of the school.

In 1860 the first branch school was opened in Margate and this saw such tremendous strides in the development of healthly deaf children that by 1873 it had been decided to transfer the whole school to Margate. This transfer was to take a number of years, and it was not until 1903 that the final transference of pupils from the Old Kent Road premises took place. (The building at Old Kent Road was incidently taken over by the London Schools Board and continued as a deaf school until 1968).

The Original Foundation Stone of the Old Kent Road School
Photo: Author's collection

In 1910, King George V and Queen Mary became Patrons, and an Act of Parliament was passed in 1915 to enable the Asylum to change its title to the 'Royal School for the Deaf & Dumb Children, Margate'. In 1975-6, the school was rebuilt on the same site with modern classrooms and accommodation and the old buildings were demolished.

Edinburgh: Institution for the Deaf and Dumb

For a period of just over twenty years from 1760 the rich of Scotland had the means of obtaining education for their deaf children through Braidwood's Academy, while for the poor no provision was made.

With the removal of the Academy to Hackney, London, in 1783 there was no education available in Scotland for deaf children, but during the first eighteen years of the London Asylum's existence a few individuals from Scotland were admitted to receive its benefits. However, the difficulty of gaining admission, together with the expense of removal to so great a distance and the disinclination of parents to have their children so far separated from them showed the necessity of having a similiar institution in Scotland.

In June 1810, an institution was established for the education of the deaf and dumb poor belonging to Scotland. A grandson of Thomas Braidwood, John Braidwood, was engaged as the first teacher while an assistant, Robert Kinniburgh, was admitted to Braidwood's Academy at Hackney to acquire a competent knowledge of the method of instructing the deaf.

The Deaf and Dumb Institution, Canongate, Edinburgh
Photo: John Hay

INSTITUTION FOR DEAF AND DUMB,
EDINBURGH.

41

Robert Kinniburgh was bound by a bond under a penalty of £1000 that he would not communicate his teaching methods to anyone for 7 years, and that he would for the same period confine his teaching only to the poor. Having acquired a competent knowledge of the art of instruction, Kinniburgh returned to Edinbough in December 1811 and took charge of the pupils, John Braidwood having departed to America where he began teaching a private class of deaf children at Bolling Hall in Cobbs, Virginia.

At the time of Robert Kinniburgh's return to Edinburgh, there were 10 pupils on the roll, and as a result of an increase of pupils under instruction the school moved annually during the first four years into larger premises until it settled in Chessels Court, Canongate, where it remained for ten years until that also became too small.

In 1824, the school moved to premises in Henderson Row where it remained until it closed in 1977.

A little-known and interesting account of a pupil's education at the Chessels Court premises is contained in a book called *Memoirs of My Youth* by Alexander Atkinson published in 1865.

Birmingham: General Institution for Deaf and Dumb Children, Edgbaston

The origins of education for the deaf in Birmingham date from 1812 and the interest that two men, a Dr. De Lys and his friend Alex Blair, showed in a girl deaf from birth named Jane Williams. In their spare time they had undertaken some instruction which enabled her to read and write and by means of signs, communicate with and understand other people. In the autumn of that year, Dr. De Lys gave a lecture in the rooms of the Birmingham Philosophical Institution and introduced Jane Williams to the assembly.

As a result of that lecture a more general meeting was held in December and a Committee appointed. One of the members of this Committee went to the private school in Hackney run by Thomas Braidwood, grandson of the original founder of the Academy at Edinburgh, and his mother. The Committee succeeded in persuading Thomas Braidwood to come to Birmingham (thus effectively closing the school at Hackney and over 50 years of private instruction by the Braidwood family).

Institution for the Deaf and Dumb, Birmingham
From an engraving at the School, 1852

The first school was a day school with 15 pupils, and one year later, a building on the Calthorpe estate was obtained, and the school removed there and became a boarding school. The school remained on the same site with various extensions and alterations until its sad closure in 1985.

The school was granted royal patronage in 1901, and changed its title to the Royal School for Deaf and Dumb Children.

Following its closure in 1985, the school premises could not be sold because of the nature of the covenant by which the then Lord Calthorpe had transferred some of his property to enable the school to be established in 1814, and the premises were taken over by SENSE, the National Deaf-Blind Rubella Association.

Glasgow: Society for the Education of the Deaf and Dumb

The first institution in Glasgow for the instruction of deaf and dumb children was established in 1819 at Barony Glebe with a Mr. Anderson as headmaster.

However, in 1822, Anderson had a dispute with the directors of the institution, and he resigned as headmaster to open a private school in St. Andrew's Square. Many of his students followed him there.

The Glasgow Institution, Barony Glebe, 1820
Photo: Robert Cormac

In 1825, following the closure of Anderson's private school - Anderson having gone to Liverpool - the institution began to prosper, and established itself at Langside where it remained for many years into the present century, when it moved to Maryhill and was renamed Glasgow School for the Deaf.

Aberdeen Institution for the Deaf and Dumb

In 1817, the Principal of the Edinburgh Institution of the Deaf and Dumb paid a visit to Aberdeen, and as a result of his encouragement, a young man named Robert Taylor was sent to Paris to train under the renowned Abbe Sicard in 1818. On his return in 1819 the Aberdeen Institution for the Deaf and Dumb was established which led to premises being secured in a house in Schoolhill which belonged to the Trustees of a John Gordon.

Glasgow Deaf and Dumb Institution, Langside
Photo: Glasgow & West of Scotland Society for the Deaf

The school remained here until 1904, when it was rehoused in a building known as the Beech Lodge Public School (this building is now known as the View Terrace Health Clinic and incorporates the Deafness Diagnosis Clinic).

It was not based in Beech Lodge for long - only for six short years before it was transferred to Westburn Road.

In 1944, a large house in Polmuir Road was acquired and the school relocated there. This building now provides the present Boarding Hostel, and the school itself, after a period in Linksfield Road, is now housed in Regent Walk, the first purpose-built school for the deaf in Aberdeen's history at a cost of £1 million.

It is now known as the Aberdeen School for the Deaf.

Manchester: Institution for the Deaf and Dumb
In 1823, a wealthy Manchester merchant, Mr. Robert Philips,

was intrigued by the brightness and intelligence of a girl in his neighbourhood, and discovered that she was not receiving any education, because she was deaf and without speech. He knew of another merchant, a William Bateman, who had two deaf children, and inquired of him where the girl could obtain an education.

Institution for the Deaf and Dumb, Manchester
Photo: Author's Collection

Mr. Philips discovered to his dismay that deaf children in England could only be educated at two schools, the Asylum in Old Kent Road, and the Institution at Edgbaston, Birmingham. He further discovered that both these institutions were full and that there was a long waiting list for admission.

He decided to do a survey at one large cotton factory, and found that there were 19 deaf children without speech of various ages belonging to the workers in that factory alone!

A meeting was therefore called on 11th June 1823 where Mr. Philips laid before the collection of influential citizens the case for the establishment of an institution for the education of the deaf and dumb in the city of, or in the vicinity of, Manchester. There was sufficient financial help at the disposal of a Committee formed at that meeting to rent a building adjoining the Lying-In Hospital in Stanley Street, Salford, at an annual rental of £68 for a fixed term of three years.

Great difficulty was experienced in the appointment of a schoolmaster well-versed in the tuition of deaf children, but eventually, Dr. Watson of the Asylum for the Deaf and Dumb Poor in London, anxious to see the establishment of such a school in the area, suggested that his principal assistant, a William Vaughan, be appointed.

The school was opened on 29th February 1825 with 14 children, eight boys and six girls.

In the early years, financial restraints meant that the Committee could only afford to admit a few children at a time. In addition, the absence of a playground affected the children's health, and epidemic fevers were frequent.

This led the Committee to look for a more suitable site, and eventually after viewing many plots of land, it was decided that a plot of land adjoining the Royal Botanical Gardens at Old Trafford was the most suitable; this was purchased, and plans drawn up for the new building.

A contract was entered into with a Richard Lane, but before building could commence, an approach was received from the Trustees of the proposed Henshaws' Asylum for the Blind that they join in with the Committee for the Deaf and Dumb to use the site for the erection of a joint building.

The Committee regarded this proposal with favour, and the design of the building was extended to provide for the two institutions, with a chapel in the centre to provide for both - this agreement was to have unfortunate results for the deaf half of the land in that the buildings became popularly known as 'Henshaws', and many donations and legacies were received by the Trustees for the Blind which should have gone either to the Deaf, or been shared by both. It also meant that as the school population grew it was necessary to purchase other properties to accommodate the children. By

1923, besides the main school, there were four 'branches' housing the Infants, Juniors and the training establishments dotted around various parts of Old Trafford, all of which could have been comfortably accommodated on the land given away to the Blind.

The new school premises were opened on 21st June 1837, the day Queen Victoria ascended to the Throne, and remained in continuous occupation until the final transfer of the Secondary Department to the new premises in Cheshire was completed in 1966.

The title was changed to the Royal Residential Schools for the Deaf and Dumb in 1897 by decree by Queen Victoria, and is now known as the Royal Schools for the Deaf (Manchester).

The present-day Schools are now almost entirely geared to the needs of multiple-handicapped hearing-impaired children.

Liverpool

Rivalry between Manchester and Liverpool as important and prosperous cities in the North West of England was as high in the 1820s as it still is today. This, together with an assertion uttered by the Principal of the Institution near Dublin, that it was possible to educate deaf and dumb children to a considerable extent if sent to a common school led a Liverpool businessman named Edward Comer to place and pay for four deaf children to be educated in a Liverpool Day School in 1824, but after six months it was apparent that this method was unsatisfactory.

A special school was then organised for these children and others in premises in Wood Street which were opened in January 1825. The first Headmaster was John Anderson who had previously been Headmaster of the Glasgow Institution before he had a difference with the Committee of that school.

Anderson was well paid (for that time) with a salary of £250 per annum, and this soon ate into funds, and economy measures had to be introduced. The next Headmaster to be appointed, J.C. Scott in 1830, had a salary of £110 per annum, and all local children were compelled to become day children. However, these children were given both free education and a free daily dinner, perhaps one of the earliest examples of free education.

Institution for the Deaf and Dumb, Oxford Street, Liverpool
From an Engraving

J.C. Scott was soon succeeded by James Rhind who introduced evening classes for the deaf - probably the first of their kind in the world.

By 1839 the school had outgrown its Wood Street premises, and the Old Botanical Gardens were presented to the institution by the City of Liverpool Corporation, and a new school built on the site. The new school, called Oxford Street School for the Deaf, was opened in 1840 with 48 boarders, and enlarged in 1860 to accommodate 120 children.

In 1904 the school was transferred to new buildings in Crown Street where it remained until, in the 1960s, it became apparent that the area in which it was situated was becoming very run-down and creating an unsuitable environment in which to educate deaf children.

In 1968, the Alice Elliott School for the Deaf was opened in Childwall, a Liverpool suburb, where it remains to this day.

Exeter: West of England School for the Deaf and Dumb
In 1824, a Mrs. Hippisley Tuckfield and her friend Miss Grace Fursdon were impressed by the intelligence of an uneducated deaf child of a farm labourer living at Fursdon, near Exeter, and became aware that there was nothing that could officially be done for this or any other deaf child living in the region.

West of England Institution for the Deaf and Dumb
Exeter, 1827
Photo: School Archives

The following year, 1825, she made a visit to the National Royal Institution for the Deaf in Paris, the first free school for the deaf in the world established by Charles Michael de l'Epee in 1760.

Inspired by what she saw on this visit, she returned to Exeter and found two other deaf children, and took them into her home at Little Fulford where she began to educate them using the methods she saw in Paris.

As a result of this perseverance, she was able to impress a public meeting held on 6th April 1826 in Exeter as to the educational potential of deaf children. This meeting was so successful that it raised £883 in donations.

In January 1827 the Governors rented a house in Alphington Causeway, and appointed after interviews a Henry Brothers Bingham, an assistant master at the Edgbaston, Birmingham, Institution as the first Headmaster.

The school opened with six pupils, four boys and two girls, and within months had a rollcall of twenty-six pupils, and already the rented premises at Alphington Causeway were too small.

Drawing upon the considerable public donations they received, the Governors purchased on 29th November 1827, 3½ acres of land on the Topsham Road, and in the remarkable space of 13 months, the new school premises were ready for Christmas 1828 after which the children moved in. The total cost was £2,147.

This building remained in continuous use until 1969, and within a few months of its opening, it contained 50 pupils of which 9 were private fee-paying pupils.

Cholera struck Exeter in the summer of 1832, and there were 440 deaths in the city, but in spite of the prevalence of the disease the school kept free from any attack. This expression of relief was premature - a second wave of the disease affected the school, and there were 40 cases of cholera, of which three were fatal.

The school was completely rebuilt on the same site between 1967 and 1969, the old buildings being demolished, and is now known as the Royal West of England School for the Deaf, Exeter - the prefix 'Royal' having been granted by King Edward VII in 1902.

Doncaster: The Yorkshire Institution for the Deaf and Dumb
In 1828 a clergyman named William Carr-Fenton who was also employed as a school inspector visited a poor labourer called Field in Brookhouse, near Rotherham, and found that

he had five children, two of whom were already attending the Asylum for the Deaf and Dumb in Old Kent Road, London. The other three were all under seven years of age and considered too young to go to school. The long distance and expenses involved in sending these children to London, allied with the lengthy periods of removal away from their parents during their period of schooling convinced the Rev. Fenton of the need for a similiar institution in Yorkshire.

Eastfield House, Doncaster
Photo: Yorkshire School for the Deaf Archives

After a visit to the National Royal Institution for the Deaf and Dumb in Paris, the Rev. Fenton saw Mr. Bingham, the headmaster of the newly-established Exeter Institution, and was convinced of the feasibility of educating the deaf. He also visited the schools in Birmingham and Manchester.

Back in Doncaster, he called a public meeting towards the end of 1828 which was attended by Mr. Vaughan, the headmaster of the Manchester Institution, and Mr. Field with his three youngest children.

After the meeting, it was moved that *an institution be formed at Doncaster for the benefit of deaf & dumb children of the poor in the county of York and it be called the 'Yorkshire Institution for the Deaf & Dumb Poor'.*

A rented property, Eastfield House, was found opposite the Doncaster Racecourse in Leger Way, and an advertisement sent out for a suitable Headmaster.

Mr. Charles Baker, aged 26, a teacher of the deaf at Edgbaston for 3 years, applied and was appointed Headmaster. Charles Baker was to be a leading influence on the education of the deaf for the next 50 years, and did much to improve the status of deaf people, and sign language. He engaged a number of deaf people as assistant teachers. He had little patience with attempts to teach speechtraining, taking the view that the time spent doing this was better used in giving the deaf an acquisition of language.

One of his profound observations uttered at a conference in 1852 is still relevant these days :-

Do such educated deaf persons converse orally among themselves? On the contrary, do they not invariably converse with each other by signs and spelling?

On 2nd November 1829, the school was formally opened with 11 boys, to which were added 10 girls during 1830.

In 1831, the Committee purchased Eastfield House, influenced by the many acres available at the back for future development.

In 1865, the Eastfield House was extended.

Today, the schools still occupy the same site, and are known as the Yorkshire Schools for the Deaf. With the decline of the numbers of deaf children in special education, much of the establishment is given over to further education, and known as Doncaster College for the Deaf.

Across the Irish Sea
At this stage, it is necessary to take a look at the develop-

ments in the education of deaf children in Ireland.

The first school for the deaf was established, after a great deal of difficulty in obtaining a teacher, by the National Association for the Education of the Deaf and Dumb at Claremont in Dublin in 1816. This made it the fifth school to be opened in the British Isles.

For a number of years, this school took in such pupils from all over Ireland as could pay the fees and who could travel to Dublin.

Not all deaf children in Ireland could, however, travel to Dublin, so the Headmaster at Claremont sent his 17-year-old brother, George Gordon, to Belfast where a room was taken in the Congregational Church building, Donegal Street, in 1831, to serve as a classroom and there, the first attempts were made to educate Belfast's deaf children.

Two years later, in 1833, the Belfast class was moved to a room in King Street to cater for a number of children attending from outside the city who were lodged in a small dwelling house owned by the person from whom the school classroom was rented.

These unsatisfactory arrangements, coupled with the increasing difficulty in attracting sufficient financial support from the public, caused the Committee to call a public meeting on 26th Feburary 1835 to discuss the closing of the school. During that meeting, a conversation arose regarding the admission of blind children. No attempts had hitherto been made in Belfast to provide for the education of blind children.

The Ulster Society for Promoting the Education of The Deaf and The Dumb and The Blind.

As a result of the February 1835 public meeting, a decision was made to appeal to the public for support in setting up a school for blind children as well as deaf children. Such was the response to this appeal that another public meeting was held and it was resolved to build a school as quickly as possible.

Circular to Parents: 1856
Yorkshire Institution for the Deaf and Dumb, Doncaster
School Archives

The Belfast Charitable Society made available a site on College Street on which a school was erected at a cost of £800 and completed in 1836. The new building was named The Ulster Institute for the Deaf and Dumb and The Blind, with the Committee and supporting members calling themselves the 'Ulster Society for Promoting the Education of The Deaf and The Dumb and The Blind'.

**Ulster Institution for the Blind and Deaf and Dumb
Lisburn Road, Belfast**
Photo: R. Bailey

Within five years, however, it was clear that the new building was totally inadequate to provide both education and boarding for deaf and blind pupils. A public subscription list was therefore opened, and in a short time nearly £2,000 was subscribed; a parcel of land comprising 5 acres was purchased on the Lisburn Road, and building work commenced.

The new school was ready for use in 1845, and the College Street premises vacated. By the end of the following year, 1846, the school had 77 pupils, of whom 52 were classified as deaf and dumb boarders, 2 as deaf and dumb Day scholars,

21 as blind boarders, 1 as a deaf and dumb Sabbath scholar, and 1 as a blind Day scholar.

In 1849, the whole of Ireland was ravaged by one of the greatest national disasters of all times, the Irish Potato Famine. Subscriptions to the Society plunged, and the School found itself with a considerable bank overdraft. Out of 71 applications for admission in 1850, funds could be found for only 13 new pupils. An austerity diet was also adopted by the school to save money, consisting of breakfast: meal pottage 6 oz, 2/3rd pint of buttermilk; dinner: household bread 6 oz, beef 5 oz, and its broth; supper: rice 5 oz, sweet milk half a naggan and treacle.

From thence onwards, however, the Ulster Society enjoyed good fortunes largely due to the appointment of the Rev. John Kinghan as Principal. In 1858 and again in 1907, additions and alterations were made to the school buildings until, in 1953, it was decided that new premises had to be found. Twenty-two acres of land at Jordanstown, Co. Antrim, 5 miles outside the Belfast city boundaries, were purchased, and the new school opened in 1961.

Today the school is known as the Jordanstown Schools for Children with Auditory and Visual Handicaps.

England: 1838 - 1842
Nine long years were to elapse between the founding of the Yorkshire Institution, and the next institution to be founded. Four were then to be founded in rapid succession - at Newcastle, Brighton, Bristol and Bath.

The Northern Counties Asylum for the Blind and Deaf and Dumb, Newcastle-upon-Tyne
A meeting was called in the city of Newcastle-upon-Tyne in June 1838 for the purpose of establishing an asylum for the education of the blind. However, the actual result of the meeting was the formation of an institution to be called the Northern Counties Asylum for the Blind and Deaf and Dumb, and the first school premises were secured in Wel-

lington Place, near Pilgrim Street, Newcastle (which has since disappeared from the map).

There were 19 pupils both blind, and deaf and dumb, and this number grew to 44 the following year (18 blind and 26 deaf children).

The Dining Room, Northern Counties Institution for the Deaf and Dumb 1890s
Photo: School Archives

Over the next few years, the number of blind pupils fell, until, in 1848, it was discontinued altogether, and the school transferred to rented premises at Westgate, becoming known as the Northern Counties Institution for the Deaf and Dumb.

Within 4 years, it was obvious that the rented premises were inadequate, numbers having doubled to 50 pupils, and that there was an urgent need to secure an owned property. After some search, a 4½ acre site on the Great North Road was secured on a 99-year lease from the Master and Brethren of St. Mary Magdalene Hospital, and building commenced.

The new school premises were occupied in October 1861, and the school has remained on the same site ever since. At its peak, it had over 200 pupils, and is now known as the Northern Counties School for the Deaf.

Brighton: Deaf and Dumb Institution.

The Brighton Deaf and Dumb Institution was started in 1840 by a Mr. W. Sleight, a former teacher at the Yorkshire Institution for the Deaf and Dumb, who was to remain as Headmaster for an astonishing 70 years.

Gymnastics Class: 1890s
Brighton Institution for the Deaf and Dumb
Photo: School Archives

In its heyday, in the 1880s, the school had 84 pupils.

Education for the deaf in Brighton is now undertaken by two schools - Ovingdean Hall School for the Partially Hearing, which replaced the old institution, and Hamilton Lodge School for the Deaf which was created to cater for profoundly deaf children.

Matthew Robert Burns (1798 - 1880)

No writing on the history of deaf education of this era would be complete without the mention of Matthew Robert Burns as the first born-deaf person ever to be a school Principal, and to found a number of schools.

Matthew Robert Burns was born on 10th November 1798 in Dundee to a Major in the 84th Regiment of Foot and his wife, the daughter of a Lombard Street banker.

The first schooling he received came from his mother, and from attendance at a day school for the hearing in Dundee, but at the age of 10, his family moved to London and enrolled him at the Asylum for the Deaf and Dumb in Old Kent Road, which provided him with useful mental training as he had learnt nothing more than writing or sports in Scotland.

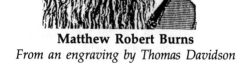

Matthew Robert Burns
From an engraving by Thomas Davidson

The next we learn of Matthew Burns is in 1830 when he appeared in Edinburgh and helped to form the deaf church in that city. In 1832, he opened a day school for deaf children in Carruber's Close Chapel, but left after a short while to go to Dundee in 1833 to try and establish a Sabbath School.

In 1834, Matthew Burns was appointed the Headmaster of the Aberdeen Institution for the Deaf and Dumb where he remained for seven years.

In 1841, Matthew Burns went to Bristol where he helped to found the Bristol Institution for the Deaf and Dumb at Tyndall's Park, Bristol, as Principal.

He did not stay long at the school in Tyndall's Park - a mere two years. The cause of his leaving is a mystery; Matthew Burns would only say that the 'heathen Bristol' did not contribute much to the institution of the deaf children.

He never taught again except in bible classes, for he was a fervent religious man and spent much of his remaining years preaching and acting as secretary to the committee of the then 'Adult Institution for providing Employment, &c. for the Deaf and Dumb' (forerunner of the Royal Association for the Deaf).

He died of bronchitis in Barnsbury on 21st January 1880.

Bristol: Institution for the Deaf and Dumb

As stated earlier, it was founded with the help of Matthew Robert Burns in 1840 and was managed by the Tyndall's Park Trustees.

It never enjoyed a very good reputation for the quality of its education - the minutes of meetings of the Adult Deaf and Dumb Mission of Bristol between 1884 and 1886 frequently expressed concern that no reading was taught to the children at the school aged between 7 and 12, and that no trades were taught to enable them to seek employment.

The school was finally closed in 1908, and a new state school, Elmfield School for the Deaf, came into being, and education was vastly improved.

Bath: Institution for the Blind, the Deaf and the Dumb.

This school was opened in 1842 at Walcott Parade, and by 1884 had a total of 30 blind and deaf children, with a staff of 4.

It closed soon afterwards.

Dundee: Institution for the Deaf and Dumb

Dundee's school for the deaf was unique in this country as it

was the only school for the deaf which had two successive deaf people as Headmasters, and their combined reign
spanned a period of nearly fifty years. It was also unique in
that for over 70 years, the school and the adult mission for
the deaf shared the same building.

First attempts to educate the deaf children of Dundee were
made by Matthew Robert Burns as early as 1833, but these
were more on the lines of a Sabbath School, and such
intentions did not last very long as Burns accepted the
Principal's position at Aberdeen.

In 1845 Alexander Drysdale, a deaf man, opened a private
school, which became so successful that it was turned into an
institution supported by charity.

Alexander Drysdale continued as Headmaster and also as
missioner to the local adult deaf (from 1853) until his death in
1880, when another deaf man, James Barland, was appointed
in his place.

Only when James Barland retired in 1893 did the school get
its first hearing Headmaster.

In the late 1890s, the school (and the adult mission) moved
to Dudhope Castle under the auspices of the local school
board.

Dundee School for the Deaf closed its doors for the last
time in 1984, and currently education for the deaf is either
mainstreamed or housed in a hearing-impaired unit.

Swansea: The Cambrian Institution for the Deaf

The education of deaf children in Wales followed the line of
development common to all social activity in our islands. In
1846 an agent of the Cambrian Educational Society was
perturbed to find considerable numbers of deaf people apparently without education and with little prospect of getting
any.

Conscience became aroused, and at a public meeting called
by the Mayor of Aberystwyth on 1st February 1847, it was
unanimously agreed that an institution for the education of
the deaf children of Wales be established in Aberystwyth.

Temporary premises were taken, this being a house in Pier Street, and a Mr. Charles Rhind was appointed Principal.

The school opened with 2 day boy scholars on 24th July 1847, and by the end of the year 8 children - 3 of whom were sisters - had been admitted, all aged between 9 and 13 years old.

Staff and Pupils of The Royal Cambrian Institution for the Deaf and Dumb, Swansea, 1915
Photo: Church of the Holy Name Mission to the Deaf, Swansea

In 1850 it was decided that Aberystwyth was difficult of access for many pupils and that the school should be moved to Swansea - *'a place more easy of access than Aberystwyth, of growing importance and blessed by having so many gentlemen of wealth and influence.'* The school was removed to Picton Place, Swansea on 7th April 1850.

In 1851 the 'Graig Field' was leased from Swansea Corporation, and building work commenced on premises capable of accommodating 50 children and staff. The work was completed in May 1857, and the school vacated Picton Place.

In 1898 Queen Victoria granted the title prefix 'Royal' and the school became the Royal Cambrian Institution for the Deaf and Dumb.

During the 1940s it became apparent that the school needed to be enlarged, and the Trustees of the Royal Cambrian purchased a mansion together with 30 acres of land at St. Mellons. Unfortunately an extensive fire destroyed the property before it could be occupied as a school, and the Trustees found themselves in severe financial difficulties, and ceased to operate. The Welsh Joint Education Authority, with the support of all Local Education Authorities in Wales, took over responsibility for the education of deaf children in 1950, and established the school in magnificent premises in Llandrindod Wells. Thus the title 'Royal Cambrian' ceased to exist.

Llandrindod Wells School itself closed in 1973, and education for deaf children in South Wales is now located at the Ashgrove School for the Deaf, Penarth, operated by the South Glamorgan Education Authority, with another new school for the north at Mold.

Edinburgh: Donaldson's Hospital

Edinburgh is a city of many fine buildings. This was so even in Victorian times, and one of these magnificient buildings was Donaldson's Hospital: even Queen Victoria once reputedly said she would like to live in it. It looks like a palace, with its terraces, its sweeping towers and its sense of size and grace, occupying such a prominent position.

Donaldson's Hospital has an interesting history, and is unique in that it was the ONLY boarding school in Britain where hearing and deaf children were educated together. Many of the hearing children became fluent in the use of sign language, and there were no communication barriers within the school. In its heyday, it had about 300 children, of whom around 120 were deaf.

The story starts with the death of a Mr. James Donaldson, a wealthy Edinburgh bookseller, in 1830. In his will, he bequeathed the whole of his estate, amounting to nearly £240,000, to build and found a hospital for poor boys and girls, and to be called after him. In his will no mention was made of the deaf, but upon representations being made to the Trustees of the Hospital, they decided to admit a proportion of deaf children to the benefits of the institution. Thus, when the Hospital was opened in 1850, deaf children were being educated with the hearing and gaining considerably.

Deaf children continued to be educated alongside hearing children for nearly one hundred years, but after merging with the Royal Edinburgh Institution for the Education of Deaf and Dumb Children in 1938, the Hospital specialized in the education of deaf children, with the new title of the school being Donaldson's School for the Deaf.

The building stands to this day, still serving deaf education.

Classroom at Donaldson's Hospital, Edinburgh: 1890s
In the above picture, the teacher on the right by the fireplace is Ernest Aycliffe, later the secretary of the B.D.A. and editor of the Deaf Quarterly News.
Photo: Courtsey of the Governors of Donaldson's School:

Chapter 4
1800 - 1850

The Drunk Man *by Walter Geikie, R.S.A.*
Reproduced by the courtsey of the Talbot Rice Gallery,
University of Edinburgh:

CHAPTER 4

1800 - 1850
People and The Origins of the Adult Deaf Community.

The first half of the nineteenth century saw a notable development in deaf history aside from the growth of educational facilities. It was in this period that the first organised adult meetings began to be held, first in Glasgow then in Edinburgh, London, Manchester and Leeds.

It was also during this age that Scotland provided two notable genre painters in James Howe and Walter Geikie, whilst Thomas Arrowsmith flourished in Liverpool.

Scotland also produced the first ever court case in which a sign language interpreter was used, as well as a remarkable heroine in Charlotte Bain. Deaf Sport provided a world heavyweight boxing champion in James Burke.

Academically, there was the first ever born deaf person to become a barrister, and the deaf world also produced one of the best-known and famous biblical scholars ever.

The Formation of Missions (later clubs) for the Deaf.
The origin of the present-day adult deaf organisational network was sowed one Sunday evening in 1822 in St. Andrew's Square, Glasgow where John Anderson, former Headmaster of the Glasgow Institution for the deaf who was now teaching privately from his house in St. Andrew's Square, held a prayer meeting for a number of pupils and adults.

When Mr. Anderson left Glasgow in 1824 to go to Liverpool to take the post of Headmaster at the new institution there, a short time elapsed without any Sunday Meeting until it was revived by a J. Ferguson who was an assistant teacher at the Glasgow Institution. It took the form of a Sunday afternoon prayer-meeting in a private medical lecture room in North Portland Street during the latter part of 1825.

Mr. Ferguson conducted these meetings regularly until early 1827 when he became an ordained minister of the Church of England and left the city. The regular number of persons attending these meeting varied between 15 and 20.

After Mr. Ferguson's departure, there was an interval of many years without any regular meetings. Only a rare occasional meeting was held, usually conducted by a deaf person.

Glasgow Deaf Mutual Improvement Society 1864
Photo: Glasgow & West of Scotland Society for the Deaf

In 1844, there was now an ever-increasing number of adults who had received education from the Glasgow, and in some cases Edinburgh, Institutions who felt cut off and in need of a regular meeting place for worship and social contact. A meeting of deaf adults was called, and they appointed a deaf man called William Ure as their delegate. He approached Duncan Anderson, then Headmaster of the Glasgow Institution, for assistance to procure premises and to place the Society on a firmer basis.

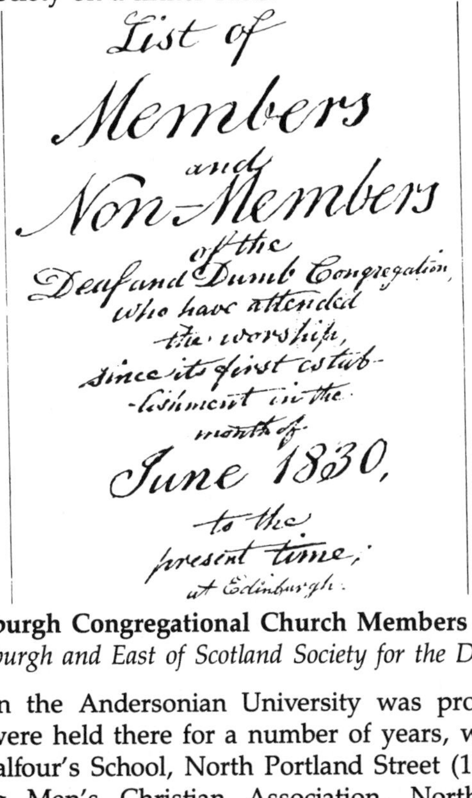

List of

Members

and Non-Members

of the
Deaf and Dumb Congregation,
who have attended
the worship,
since its first estab-
-lishment in the
month of

June 1830,

to the
present time;
at Edinburgh.

Edinburgh Congregational Church Members Book
From: Edinburgh and East of Scotland Society for the Deaf Archives

A hall in the Andersonian University was procured, and meetings were held there for a number of years, with periods spent in Balfour's School, North Portland Street (1848 - 1850), the Young Men's Christian Association, North Frederick Street (1857-8). With regard to the latter, it should be noted that many Glasgow deaf church members around that time were very religious and so strongly disapproved of drinking that they formed their own temperance Society, the Glasgow Mutual Improvement Society.

In the 1870s, the Society was established in premises at

Renfield Street where it remained until the splendid new building in West Regent Street was erected through the efforts of William Agnew in 1894.

Meanwhile, in Edinburgh, there were also a number of deaf adults, former pupils of the Edinburgh Institution, who desired a meeting place for prayers and social contact. A number of them, including Matthew Robert Burns, *q.v.*, and Walter Geikie *q.v.*, got together and established the Congregational Church for the Deaf and Dumb, Edinburgh, in June 1830. The first meeting place was in a small room with only one window in Lady Stair's Close, Lawnmarket. As the congregation gradually increased between 1831 and 1838, constant moves were made, always into larger premises, and accommodation was obtained in Rose Street, Frederick Street, George Street, Leith Street and at St. Stephen's Church.

It was at the Leith Street premises that the Edinburgh Deaf and Dumb Benevolent Society, the first properly constituted adult deaf organisation in the world, was instituted in 1835.

In 1838 the congregation (and the Society) moved to premises in South Bridge Street where they remained until 1852 when they returned to St. Stephen's Church, this time in the school buildings. In 1881 the next move was made to 11 York Buildings, where the congregation remained until 1890.

In 1890 the Edinburgh Deaf and Dumb Benevolent Society acquired its present premises at 49 Albany Street, where the Congregational Church was also erected the same year next door.

So while Glasgow can lay claim to having had the earliest adult deaf organisation, Edinburgh's Deaf Society has the longest continuous existence.

In London the situation was very similiar to those of Glasgow and Edinburgh, particularly in that many deaf adults had been educated at the Old Kent Road Asylum where they received religious instruction from two earnest ministers, the Rev. Henry Mason, Rector of Bermondsey, and the Rev. John Townsend.

In any case a number of these old pupils found that neither the church nor the State made any provision for them, and agreed among themselves to meet together for prayer and worship. The first meeting place was a small room in Fetter Lane in 1840 which became known to some interested people who took a house in Red Lion Square where some destitute deaf men and women were lodged and taught trades.

From these small beginnings, the Association for the Deaf and Dumb (later to become the Royal Association for the Deaf) took its roots. It reorganised itself in 1854, and took an office in Regent Street, and a year later took the important step of appointing as lay-missioner a Samuel Smith, a teacher at the Yorkshire Institution for the Deaf and Dumb.

Samuel Smith took the view that the spiritual needs of deaf people could only be properly provided for if they had their own church and an ordained minister. The Committee agreed: Samuel Smith got busy raising funds for the new Church, and studied for Holy Orders.

He was ordained in 1861, and finally in 1870, after much fund raising, the foundation stone of St. Saviour's Church for the Deaf and Dumb was laid by H.R.H. the Prince of Wales.

St. Saviour's Church, London

St. Saviour's Church was formally opened in 1873 by the Lord Bishop of Carlisle with several members of the Royal Family in the congregation.

The church premises at Oxford Street had to be given up in 1922, and All Saints Church, Paddington, was purchased. The name, St. Saviour's, however continued with the building of a new church and Institute at Acton in 1925.

The founding of the Manchester and Salford Adult Deaf and Dumb Benevolent Association (now the Manchester Centre for the Deaf) in 1846 is a little obscure as its first reports do not commence until 1873. However, popular legend has it that Andrew Patterson, then Headmaster at the Manchester Schools for the Deaf at Old Trafford, was perturbed to counter on several occasions a group of ex-pupils gathered around a certain gas-lamp in the city - the gas-lamp being a popular meeting place of local deaf people (this was the subject of a Victorian drama as well.)

Deaf and Dumb Institute Manchester

Upon learning that these deaf people had no place to go

to, or even to worship, Mr. Patterson held a meeting at which the above Association was formed, and enough money was raised to purchase a plot of land at Grosvenor Street where a social meeting place incorporating a small chapel was built.

This building was opened in 1878 and known as the Manchester Adult Institute for the Deaf and Dumb. This was the first ever building specifically erected as a social meeting place, as opposed to a church, in this country - or for that matter, anywhere else in the world.

In Leeds, a clergyman, the Rev. Edward Jackson, had found a similiar situation. Youths who had left the Yorkshire Institution for the Deaf and Dumb at Doncaster roamed the streets at a loose end, causing mischief.

Through his own efforts, he got together a group of people interested in the spiritual care of the blind as well as the deaf and formed the Leeds United Institution for the Blind, the Deaf and the Dumb in 1850 although it was not until 1875 that the foundation stone of their first centre was laid.

This association of societies for the Blind and the Deaf continues to this day in the present building at Centenary House, North Street, Leeds.

Artists in the 1800 - 1850's

James Howe (1780 - 1836)
James Howe was Scotland's first - and is arguably its greatest - animal painter. His drawings and paintings offer a richly detailed, often humorous, view of Scotland in the early ninteenth-century - of social custom, of transport, of life and town and country. He was fascinated by horses - so fascinated that he came to be called 'The Man who Loved to Draw Horses,' although he could and did draw a wide range of other domestic animals.

James Howe was born on 31st Angust 1780 in the village of Skirling in Peebleshire, the second of four children, all boys, of his father's second marriage. William Howe, his father, had been minister of the parish for fifteen years.

James Howe
Self Portrait reproduced by permission of
Scottish National Portrait Gallery

James Howe attended the village school in Skirling but left still young and incompletely educated on account of his deafness. It has been suggested that despite his lack of education, James was considerably influenced by the schoolmaster Robert Davidson who had such neat handwriting that he was often asked to write people's names in their bibles and would do so, adorning them with little drawings of flowers and animals. James was always making drawings on every piece of paper he could lay hands on - even his father's sermons were not safe. He would sometimes open his notes in the pulpit when ready to preach and find that they had been decorated with James' latest drawings of animals.

When 14 he was apprenticed to the Edinburgh firm of Norie, who were house painters - hardly an ideal apprenticeship for what he wanted to be. When this ended, he set himself up first as a portrait painter. He did paint a number of portraits, but a painting of a piebald pony in the window of his studio was so lifelike that people started to ask him to paint animals.

Howe's reputation as an animal painter was made when Sir John Sinclair of the Board of Agriculture commissioned him to draw details of various breeds of cattle, and he went on to paint hundreds more pictures, mostly of horses.

After the Battle of Waterloo Howe visited the battlefield and on his return produced a panorama covering many feet of canvas which depicted incidents in the fight. This was exhibited in various places with great financial success.

However, Howe was turning into an alcoholic owing to his frequenting many alehouses around Edinburgh and this, coupled with his deafness, meant he was preyed upon by unscrupulous acquaintances so that when he died in 1836 at Newhaven, near Edinburgh, he was almost a pauper.

Walter Geikie, R.S.A. (1795 - 1837)

One of Scotland's most famous artists was the 'deaf and dumb Geikie,' as he was commonly known and so quoted in a publication in 1837 called *Bibliographical, Antiquarian and Picturesque Tour in the Northern Counties of England and Scotland* by Charles Frognall Dibdin. He was a genre painter in the tradition of Wilkie.

Walter Geikie was born on 9th November 1795 in Edinburgh, the eldest son of Archibald Geikie, a pharmacist by occupation but a philosopher by inclination, and when still only two years old, contracted a 'brain fever' (probably meningitis) which left him deaf for life.

Archibald Geikie somehow learnt the manual alphabet, and there being no school for the deaf in Edinburgh at that time (Braidwood's Academy had moved to Hackney in 1783), undertook the teaching of his son himself. He was so successful that Walter was able to read, and write, and he did read many books.

When the new Institution for the Deaf and Dumb was opened in Edinburgh in 1810 with John Braidwood, grandson of Thomas Braidwood, as Principal, Walter Geikie was enrolled as one of the first students. He was then fourteen years old, a rather late age at which to start a formal education.

Walter Geikie
From the frontspiece of Geikie's Etchings held by
Edinburgh & East of Scotland Society for the Deaf

Braidwood, however, found that Geikie was so well educated and so far in advance of the other students that he began to use him more as an assistant teacher rather than as a pupil.

When Braidwood left the Institution in 1812 to go to the United States, Archibald Geikie was asked to assume direction of the school with his son as an assistant teacher, but he would not assume the responsibility, and resumed teaching Walter at home.

Later that year, he was admitted to the Academy run by the Board of Trustees of Edinburgh after proving his skill in competition with other artists. In the Academy, he was a pupil of John Graham who had been the famous artist David Wilkie's teacher. (Wilkie had left the Academy only eight years previously, so his reputation there was still high).

Geikie's drawings first appeared in the art markets in 1815 and during his lifetime he turned out an immense number of sketches, many of which were sold after his death when his fame had spread widely.

Geikie developed a talent for paying particular attention to individual traits of feature and form and character that appeared in the men and women he met. He could retain their features in his mind and produce a lifelike sketch from memory. He also developed the ability to sketch as he walked with his pad and pencil.

His friend Sir Thomas Lauder of Grange and Fountainhall tells of one humorous incident where Geikie once followed a particularly pompous, pot-bellied and self-assertive porter through the marketplace sketching as he went until the victim got angry and chased him into a house from whose attic window Geikie completed the sketch with some extra touches to show features of indignation to perfect the picture.

He maintained his strong links with the world of the deaf formed during his two years at the Institution by getting together with Matthew Burns, *q.v.*, and Alexander Blackwood to start Sunday services for the deaf of Edinburgh in June 1830. Out of these humble beginnings grew the Edinburgh Adult Deaf and Dumb Benevolent Society and the present-day Edinburgh Centre for the Deaf. He sometimes took his turn to conduct services in sign language, for the Bible was one of his favourite books for reading.

His friend Lauder once attended such a service and was moved to comment that this assembling of the deaf was an affecting spectacle :

'not for the purpose of repining that they had been deprived of the important blessings of hearing and speech, but to manifest their love and gratitude to God for all those other things He permitted them to enjoy.'

In 1834, Geikie was made a Fellow of the Scottish Academy.

Deaf Art 1800 - 1850

William Durning
*by Thomas Arrowsmith. Reproduced by the kind permission of the
Walker Art Gallery, Liverpool*

All Hallows Fair
*by James Howe: In a Private Collection. Reproduced by the kind
permission of the National Gallery of Scotland*

The Fruitseller
by Walter Geikie
Reproduced by the kind permission of
the National Gallery of Scotland

Girl Scouring a Pot Lid
by Walter Geikie
Reproduced by the kind permission of the
Talbot Rice Gallery, University of Edinburgh

He never married, and had led a very healthy life which caused him to have over-confidence in his constitution and thus neglected to go to a physican at the onset of a serious illness, until it was too late. Five days before his death, he took to his bed and soon sank into a coma from which he never recovered and died on 1st August 1837 at the age of 41.

He was buried in Greyfriars Churchyard.

After his death, a volume of his etchings was published in 1841 with comments and a biographical introduction by his friend, Sir. T. Lauder. Thus much of his work is preserved in print. This particular book *Etchings Illustrative of Scottish Character and Scenery*represents the first appearance of a deaf artist in pictorial literature.

Thomas Arrowsmith (1772- about 1830)
Thomas Arrowsmith was born on Christmas Day in 1772 to a wealthy London merchant in Westminister.

Thomas Arrowsmith Self Portrait
Reproduced from John Paunceforth Arrowsmith's
The Art of Instructing the Infant Deaf & Dumb by the permission
of the British Library, London

He was educated at home by his family, particularly by his elder brother John Pauncefort Arrowsmith who later published an account *The Art of Instructing the Infant Deaf and*

Dumb in 1819. This education enabled Thomas to attend an ordinary school for hearing children where he learnt to read and write, though not to speak. In J.P. Arrowsmith's published account, he advocates the deaf being educated in ordinary schools as opposed to special institutions, citing his brother as an example - this is the first occasion anyone has advocated an *integrated* educational system for the deaf.

Arrowsmith entered the Royal Academy Schools in 1789, and began to exhibit there from 1792 onwards.

He married an illiterate woman named Elizabeth Carpenter at St. Marylebone on 17th September 1812, but left London afterwards to work in Liverpool around 1822. A number of his paintings are in the Walker Art Gallery, Liverpool.

In 1827 to 1830, he is mentioned by a number of deaf people as living and working in Manchester, where he died sometime in 1830, exact date unknown.

Sign Language In Court

The case of the *Crown* vs. *Jean Campbell*, alias *Bruce*, which came before the High Court in Glasgow on 17th July 1817 is of considerable interest for two reasons. One - in the important legal sense - raised the question of whether the untaught deaf and dumb could be held responsible for their crimes.

The second point of considerable interest is that this court case provided the first occasion anywhere in the world where a sign language interpreter was appointed by a court to assist in the questioning of, and providing answers from, a deaf person.

Jean Campbell, in 1817, was an uneducated deaf person without any speech who could only write the initials of her name in reverse order, eg. C.J. She was an unmarried woman who had three children by different men, one of whom at the time of her arrest in April 1817 had been living with her as a common law husband but who had a few days earlier taken off the ring that he had given to her and which she wore on her finger in the fashion of a married woman, and had left home.

The crime for which Jean Campbell was charged was one of wilful murder of her own three-year old child by throwing it over the Old Bridge in Glasgow into the River Clyde where it drowned.

The question raised by the Law Lords on the Circuit who referred it to the High Court was whether despite being deaf and dumb and uneducated, did the defendant know the difference between right and wrong, did she know that a consequence of guilt was punishment, and did she have the power of communicating her thoughts?

The prosecution decided that Jean Campbell knew the difference between right and wrong and the consequence of punishment for any wrongful deed, and that she had the power of communicating her thoughts, albeit by signs, and put her on trial at the next sessions, which took place on 24th September 1817.

In the meantime however, Robert Kinniburgh, the Head-master of the Edinburgh Institution for the Deaf and Dumb, was engaged for his sign language skills as interpreter for the Court.

At her trial, Jean Campbell pleaded not guilty by signs and gestures interpreted by Robert Kinniburgh, and went on to show that she knew the difference between right and wrong, was indignant at the imputation of having murdered her child, and that she had a notion of what marriage was by signing the ring on her finger and removing it, and going away. By this means, she therefore gave her version of the events.

Her common-law husband (who was never traced) having left her with the ring from her finger, she went to several alehouses carrying her child and drank 8 glasses of spirits in a fit of depression. While crossing the Old Bridge, she suddenly wondered if she still had her money in her breast purse. She rested the child she was carrying on the parapet, the child being asleep, and held it with one hand as she used the other to search at her breast purse for her money. While she was doing this, the child slipped from her grasp, and fell into the river where it was drowned.

She was found not guilty.

This important legal ruling that the untaught deaf and dumb could be held responsible for the crimes they committed helped to ensure that another uneducated deaf woman was punished for the infanticide of her child.

Sheffield Murder

In 1828, in a village called Ecclesfield on the road from Leeds to Sheffield, the body of a newly-born child was discovered without its head.

Esther Dyson, a pretty deaf woman aged 23 without any speech, who worked at a thread-mill in Ecclesfield and lived with her brother, who was also deaf without speech, was accused of the murder. She had been seen carrying something under her apron in the area where the body was found.

Her next door neighbour, a Mrs. Ellen Greaves, gave evidence that she had constantly challenged Esther Dyson in sign language (which she had learnt through daily contact with the deaf brother and sister) over the preceding few months about her being in the family way. Esther Dyson had consistently denied being pregnant, but two days prior to the discovery of the child, she had appeared very big in the family way, then the next morning, Mrs. Greaves noticed that Esther Dyson was pale, languid, weak and thinner, as if she had delivered a child.

Other witnesses corroborated this evidence, and mentioned that the bedroom where Esther Dyson slept in the house she shared with her brother was splattered with blood.

In her first defence, Esther Dyson admitted by signs she had borne a child, but had pulled its head off when delivering it herself.

This story did not impress the court who took the view that she had used a knife to cut off the head soon after its birth, and eventually she had to admit the truth.

She was found guilty.

Deaf Witnesses and Plaintiffs in Court

Prosecuting uneducated deaf people with no speech, and accepting what they said in their defence in those days was however a different matter altogether from allowing the same people to go into the witness box and testify against other people.

In 1829 in Cork (it must be remembered that Ireland was still part of the United Kingdom then) a sergeant in the 21st Fusiliers was charged with the brutal assault and rape of a deaf girl without speech, Mary Brien, who was uneducated.

Mary Brien was ordered to be sent to the Dublin Institution for the Deaf and Dumb for evaluation and to have her story checked, but the defendant was acquitted because the court ruled that the plaintiff could not utter the oath. This happened on a number of occasions in the nineteenth century.

Deaf Heavyweight Boxing Champion of the World
James Burke (1809 - 1845)

The days of the Prize Ring were such a brutal business, fought under rules which enabled men to inflict terrible

A Prize Fight in the 1800s

injuries on each other, and fights were fought to a finish when a man was downed and had been battered into insensibility. It might therefore be expected that many contests would provide fatalities, but this was not the case.

All the more tragic therefore that one of the earliest deaths in boxing, and perhaps the most controversial, resulted from a fight in which a deaf boxer took part.

James 'Deaf' Burke, or the 'Deaf 'Un' as he was generally known was born in Westminster, London on 8th December 1809, and became orphaned in early childhood. He thus became a gutter urchin who haunted the London waterfront.

One day, to escape heavy rain he wandered into a tavern called the 'Spotted Dog' which was kept by Joe Parrish, a veteran fighter, who became impressed with the young lad - then aged 16 - and began to teach him the science of the ring. Although he could not read or write, Burke learnt fast, but it was not until he was 18, nearly 19, that Parrish gave him his first fight.

This was againt an Irishman named Ned Murphy. They fought 50 rounds, only to have the fight stopped because of darkness. However, Burke's outstanding performance had boxing enthusiasts agog with excitement and wanting more. After this, Burke went on to win 3 out of 4 fights in less than a year, and in 1828 was matched with William Fitzmaurice at Harpenden which went 106 rounds and lasted 3 hours.

Before his fight with Fitzmaurice took place, Burke achieved fame in entirely different circumstances. He became a hero when he rescued a number of people from a blazing house fire. A newspaper described his feat as follows:

'He (Burke) dashed into the blazing furnace with reckless abandon, making trip after trip until he had rescued many persons. He carried out a child, then went back and brought out another, and a third time carried a woman to safety. Again and again, he returned amongst the debris and succeeded in bringing out two more children, one of whom died in his arms.'

Next, he lost to Bill Cousens after 111 rounds, but instead of being discouraged went on to beat all foes in the next ten years.

When Jem Ward, the champion, announced his retirement in 1833, James Burke claimed the title and this angered an Irishman called Simon Byrne who had fought, and lost, to Ward in 1831.

James 'Deaf Burke'
World Heavyweight Champion

Byrne was not a particularly big man, standing only 5 feet 9 inches and weighing 13 stone, but Deaf Burke was even smaller at 5 feet 8½ inches, and 12 stone 7 lbs, so the Irishman felt he was onto a good thing.

It was a hard, bloody fight lasting 3 hours and 16 minutes (this time still stands as a world record for a championship fight) before Burke knocked out Byrne with a tremendous punch, thus becoming recognised champion.

Byrne was carried away from the ring unconscious and died three days later without coming out of his coma. The deaf boxer and all those connected with the fight were arrested and charged with manslaughter. However, conflicting opinions of several doctors gained their acquittal.

However, the tragedy upset Burke and he became convinced people regarded him as a murderer, so he sailed across to the United States. He was the first person to bring Prize Ring fighting to America.

He had a fight with a man called Connell, and demolished him in ten minutes. News spread like wildfire, but it brought Burke unexpected trouble in that a man called Samuel O'Rourke claimed to be a friend of the dead Byrne and challenged Burke to a fight which Burke did not want.

Unable to avoid it, however, he faced O'Rourke in New Orleans where it became apparent that the Irishman had no idea of fighting; Burke was able to hit him at will.

This made the local mob angry. Knives were drawn, and Burke's life was threatened as he punched O'Rourke into helplessness. Suddenly the ropes were cut, and the ring was invaded and Burke had to fight for his life. Somehow, he got hold of a bowie knife, and managed to escape. Someone grabbed his arm, and led him to a waiting horse on which he galloped away leaving behind his winnings.

From New Orleans, Burke went to New York where he had several fights before returning to England in 1837 to face William 'Bold Bendigo' Thompson. Burke was not in the best of condition and had lost his fighting spirit because of his troubles with Byrne and O'Rourke. In the 10th round, he was ruled out for a foul, and lost his world championship.

He reclaimed it when Bold Bendigo retired, but lost it again to Mick Ward when the crowd broke into the ring to save Ward from further punishment. That was on 22nd September 1840 at Lillingstone Level, Oxfordshire.

Burke never fought again, becoming a stage actor advertising his magnificent physique, but excessive drinking, long fasts and many women took their toll and he died penniless of tuberculosis in a lane off Waterloo Road in 1845.

The Stotfield Fishing Disaster
Charlotte Bain (1785 - 1846)

On Christmas Day in 1806, three boats comprising of the entire fishing fleet of Stotfield, a fishing village near Lossiemouth in Scotland, prepared to put to sea for a day's fishing.

As the 22 men in the three boats had just taken their respective stations, a young girl came running down from the village to the shore in breathless haste.

It was Charlotte Bain, a 21-year-old uneducated deaf girl without speech.

She instantly jumped into the boat in which her father was seated, and seizing him by the breasts of his coat, motioned him to return to the shore. The father, thinking it was some foolish notion she had taken to have him out of the boat, took no notice of her frantic signs, but she would not let him go, and dragged him with almost superhuman effort out of the boat. Her father feared for her reason, and left the boat telling to his fellow fishermen he would remain at home that day.

Stotfield village in the 1880's viewed from the seashore
Photo: Moray District Libraries

Charlotte then employed every sign that she knew to tell the other fishermen that none of them should put to sea on that day, to no avail. She then took her father's hat from his head, laid it upside down on the sand, rocked it backwards and forwards a few times, then upset it. The fishermen understood what she meant, that there could be a capsize if they put to sea, but they laughed at her, thinking she had mental hallucinations and put out to sea - at that time in calm conditions.

They cast their lines not far off-shore, and appeared to take excellent catches of fish. It was when they decided to return to shore that a terrible storm unleashed itself in the Moray Firth. The seas swamped their boats, and all three boatcrews perished in the waters, their lifeless bodies being washed ashore the next morning.

Stotfield was not the only village to suffer tragedy this day. Further up the coast, in Burghead harbour, a boat was upset and three men perished; two boats each with a crew of seven were also lost at Portessie and Avoch, but Stotfield was the only village to lose its entire fishing fleet, and the storm left 17 widows and 47 orphaned children.

When the extraordinary circumstances were known, Dummie Bain, as she was called, passed through the rest of her life as a seer. Young girls would come to her to have their fortunes read, to see what sort of husbands they would get, the number of children they would have and so forth, all of which circumstance she would signify by movements of her hands and fingers. With the general spread of schooling becoming available, her occupation as a seer waned and Charlotte used her second sight in later years sparingly.

She died on 5th August 1846, unmarried.

The Fetlar Islander
Before the stories of Helen Keller and Laura Bridgman, two educated deaf and blind ladies in America, became known, deaf and blind people were regarded as a great curiosity.

So in 1818 when a doctor called Herbert was told of a

young man living on the island of Fetlar in the Shetland Islands off the north of Scotland who had been deaf and blind from birth, he hastened to see this object of curiosity for himself.

David Graham Tate was twenty years old when he was seen by Dr. Herbert and the sight appalled him.

The young man was living with his parents and his blind sister in a pitiful hovel, one of the worst on the island.

David was warming himself by a fire in the centre of the hut; he was almost nude and had never worn anything other than a coarse blanket which was slightly tied round him to cover his back.

From an original engraving British Deaf Times

He could not walk erect, and invariably crouched on his heels with his knees drawn up to his chin, and he existed on meal pottage fed to him by a spoon by his mother.

It is not known when he died but one hopes that he did not have to endure such a miserable existence for many years.

Deaf Barrister
John William Lowe (1804-1876)

The law as a profession is regarded as a difficult one for *hearing* people, and not many manage to become solicitors; still fewer get called before the Bar to become barristers. For people deprived of hearing, the law is regarded as a forbidden or impossible profession. All the more remarkable then that in 1829, a born-deaf person with no speech was called to the Bar and became a barrister.

John William Lowe was born in London on 24th September 1804 to a solicitor, William Lowe.

James William Lowe:
Source of engraving unknown

When he was six years old, he became a private pupil of Dr. Joseph Watson, Principal of the Asylum for the Deaf and Dumb Poor. His father being a man of means, he remained under Dr. Watson's care for twelve years receiving the best of attention because of his undoubted abilities and studious industry.

By the time he left the Old Kent Road school, he had absorbed the classics, learnt French, and was proficient in mathematics and in the sciences which were attainable only by university students.

Although Lowe under Dr. Watson had also learnt enough speech to make himself understood by members of his family, he was to say that his usual method of communicating with his family was by his fingers, and with strangers, by writing.

There is no doubt that Lowe used sign language - during sometime in his career, he must have spent a period or periods in Edinburgh because the Member's List of Edinburgh's Congregational Deaf Church lists a John William Lowe of London as Member no. 125, married to a hearing wife, for the period 1836 to 1838. As seen earlier in this Chapter, services in this church were conducted by deaf people themselves in sign language.

The phrase 'married to a hearing wife' is written in a different hand and must have been entered after 1839 which was the year Lowe married a Francis Charlotte Jellicoe in London.

John Lowe's mental attainments at the age of 18 were so great that his father saw nothing incongruous in advising him to take up the law as a profession. Through influential friends, he was made a member of the Society of the Middle Temple in 1820, and placed in the office of two eminent solicitors, a Mr. Justice Patterson, and a Sir Nicholas Tindal who later became the Lord Chief Justice of England and Wales.

Lowe was quick to learn the various practices of the law profession, and decided upon conveyancing - transferring property from one person to another by purchase, lease or deed - as that branch of the law where his deafness was less of a handicap, and did so well that in the Michaelmas Term of 1829, he took the prescribed oaths publicly in the Temple Hall and emerged as a Barrister of the Middle Temple - a most unprecedented event which created a sensation in the profession. Soon afterwards, he commenced practice as a conveyancer, one of his clients being his old teacher, Dr. Watson.

By Frances Jellicoe, he had four children and the three who survived infancy quickly learnt sign language in order to communicate with their father.

In his leisure hours, Lowe was a linguist and by the time he was 34 years old, he could read and write in French (modern and Old Norman), Latin, Greek (ancient and modern), German, Italian, Spanish, Portugese, Dutch and Danish. His chief means of learning a vocabulary was to read a foreign-language translation of the New Testament side by side with the English version. In his 35th year, he commenced the study of Hebrew and the Psalms became his favourite reading in that language.

Lowe continued his career until 1871 when he fell victim to a pulmonary disease which prevented him from joining the services for the deaf at the new St. Saviour's Church. He died on 3rd February 1876.

The Biblical Scholar
John Kitto (1804-1854)

Born in Plymouth, Devon, to a poor stonemason, also called John and his wife Elizabeth, John Kitto was a sickly lad who cared for nothing but books.

Between his eighth and twelfth years, he was at four Plymouth schools, and then, not even on a regular basis; he only attended when his grandmother could get together the few pence required to pay his fee. This was all the education that he had.

Dr. Kitto
From an engraving

At the age of 12, Kitto was taken on by his father to assist him in his trade, and it was shortly afterwards when he was working for his father slating a new roof that he lost his footing in the act of stepping off a ladder and fell thirty-five feet to the ground.

In his book *Lost Senses* Kitto relates his feelings and impressions when awakening from the coma caused by his fall, and how when he demanded that people around his bed speak to him, someone wrote on a slate, 'YOU ARE DEAF'. Kitto never heard sound again.

Being now unfit to work, he was left to spend his time as he pleased, and he devoted himself to reading, selling scraps of old iron and painting childrens' books and shop labels to raise the few pence needed to buy the books.

In November 1819 the poverty of Kitto's family finally forced them to send him to the workhouse, where he was set to learn shoe making. After two years, he was judged to have learnt sufficient skills, and was apprenticed to a Plymouth shoe maker who treated him so harshly and badly that he was re-admitted to the workhouse where he stayed until he was 19 years old.

He was then placed in a situation where he could get as many books to read as he wished. The position was that as a sub-librarian in Plymouth. After a year of this, he was then taken on by an Exeter dentist, a Mr. Groves, as a dental technican. Mr.Groves had aspirations to become a missionary and was instrumental in getting Kitto a place in the Missionary College in Islington, London where he learnt printing with a view to being of some service in some foreign missionary institution. In 1827 he was sent to Malta but because of his declining health, he returned to England in 1829.

Shortly afterwards, his former employer Mr. Groves desired a tutor for his children when he went on a missionary tour of the Middle East, and selected Kitto for the position. This tour of Europe and Asia gave the opportunity for Kitto to acquire the knowledge of customs and scenery which he put to good use on his return to England in 1833 by writing articles in the *Penny Magazine* under the title, 'The Deaf Traveller.'

This led Charles Knight, Editor of the *Penny Magazine*, to suggest to Kitto that he prepare an illustrated bible. Kitto embraced this cause with such enthusiasm that the *Pictorial*

This book established Kitto as a writer, and in the following years, he wrote a number of books - many of them based on the Scripture, including the work which is still regarded as the best of its kind, *Cyclopaedia of Biblical Literature.*

John Kitto was honoured with the Doctorate of Divinity by the University of Giessen in 1844, and in 1845 was made a fellow of the Society of Antiquaries.

His health, never very good, began to fail in 1851, and in August 1854, he proceeded to Germany to try out the mineral waters there, but died on 25th November 1854 at Cannstadt, near Stuttgart.

He was survived by his wife whom he had married in 1833, and seven children.

Chapter 5
1850 - 1880

**Founders of Aberdeen Adult Deaf Mute Improvement
Association: 1879**
*J.T. Lyon (Deaf); C. McHardy (Deaf) J. McHardy (Deaf); A.
Pender (Missioner). Photo: R. Cormack*

CHAPTER 5

1850 - 1880
The Rise of Oralism, Missions and Sport.

In the period 1850 to 1880, eighteen more schools for the deaf were started, eleven of them in London alone - eight day schools of the London School Board Classes, and three private or charitable schools including one for children of the Jewish faith.

Of the seven other schools outside London, two were also day schools in Hull and in Sheffield.

Of these eighteen schools, only two are still in existence - St. John's, Boston Spa, and the Royal School for the Deaf, Derby.

St. John's, Boston Spa.
Before 1869, there was no Institution in England and Wales (nor for that matter, in Scotland) where deaf children of Roman Catholics could be educated in their own faith, and when a Belgian priest, Monsignore de Haerne, a deputy in the Belgian Senate, learnt of this, he came to Britain for the purpose of establishing one. He procured a cottage at Handsworth Woodhouse, near Sheffield, provided a teacher and entrusted the running of it to a management committee at his own expense. Monsignore de Haerne had previously already founded Catholic institutions for the deaf in Belgium, France and Portugal and was later to found one in India.

In 1874 the Bishop of Beverley adopted it as a public

institution and the Bishops of England passed a resolution to recognise St. John's Institution as a Catholic Institution for England and to assist in the cost of its foundation.

In 1875 Boston Spa College was purchased, and this became the nucleus of the present School.

The Royal School for the Deaf, Derby.
It was founded in 1873 by William Robert Roe in a modest house in the Mount Pleasant area of Derby before becoming established at Friargate where it grew into a fine school.

Original School for the Deaf, Derby
Photo: Royal School for the Deaf Derby

In the 1970s, the school moved into new modern premises on the Ashbourne Road where it has now also developed a Further Education department to cater for this increasing need among deaf students. The School also possesses the magnificient Duke's Barn Countryside Centre at Beeley, provided through the generosity of the 11th Duke of Devonshire.

Oral Schools

Of greater significance than the numbers of schools established in 1850 to 1860 is the fact that some of them were founded for the express purpose of teaching deaf children through the Oral System.

The teaching of deaf children by oral methods alone was not new; the earliest teachers of the deaf such as Dr. William Holder and Dr. John Wallis tried it in the 1660s with (as evidence shows) far less success than they wrote about in the publications which earned them fame. In the eighteenth century, British teachers such as Henry Baker and Thomas Braidwood used oralism as part of a combined system which is nowadays known as Total Communication.

It was Samuel Heinicke who pioneered the pure oral system of teaching the deaf in Germany with the foundation of his school in 1760, a method of teaching which has persisted in that country ever since and which in the nineteenth century came to be known as the 'German System'. Its introduction into British schools for the deaf, first by the Rev. Thomas Arnold at Northampton in 1868 then by Mr. William Van Praagh at 11, Fitzroy Square, London in 1872, rapidly spread, especially after 1880, until it came to be both detested and feared by leading deaf people everywhere who saw that it could - and indeed as it did - seriously damage the systems of education that had served so well since the growth of deaf education.

The Rev. Thomas Arnold, founder of the Oral School for the Deaf at Northampton in 1868 after trying out the system with only a limited success with a special class at the Yorkshire Institution where that great advocate of sign language, Charles Baker, was Principal, did probably more than any other person to establish the oral system in Britain with the fine academic record of his school.

The Oral School for the Deaf's fine academic record is not disputed - the school produced the first deaf Fellow of the Geological Society, and the first deaf Ph.D. as well as a host of other academic successes - but neither Arnold or his successor, Dixon, ever took more than eight boys a time and most of them carefully selected - few were born deaf. This is not always appreciated by those who point to this success compared to the systems in use at the larger institutions.

Be that as it may, Arnold's and Van Praagh's schools laid the foundations for over a century of controversy and the beginning of the end of sign-language-dominated educational systems.

The First Unit.

Today, most of our deaf chidren are being educated in units attached to ordinary schools, under various names such as 'deaf units', 'partially hearing/partially deaf units', 'units for the hearing-impaired'. It is not, however, generally known that the first-ever 'unit' was established in 1873, well over a hundred years ago!

At the instigation of the Greenock Deaf and Dumb Christian Society, the authorities in Greenock, Scotland, approved the use of a room in Greenock Academy (opened 1855) for the teaching of the few deaf children in the town. The first method used was sign language.

However, in 1878, deaf education in Greenock faced a crisis because there was no-one able to continue to teach the children, and one parent was not happy about his child being taught in sign language. The person that this parent approached for advice was Alexander Graham Bell, the inventor of the telephone.

Bell was a supporter of the oral system, and upon learning of the difficulties faced by the Academy, he took over the teaching of the deaf children in the school for two months until the arrival of a Mr. Jones all the way from the U.S.A. to take over from him.

Bell, therefore, not only saved the deaf class in the school from closure, but also introduced the oral method of teaching and laid the foundations for the present day Garvel Centre for the Deaf (as the unit is called). It was the experience he gained in Greenock which enabled him to go to the United

States and feature so prominently in American deaf education.

First Deaf Unit in an Ordinary School, Greenock, 1873
Greenock Telegraph

Intermarriages.

One of the issues about which Alexander Graham Bell was so forthright in the States in the 1880's was the subject of intermarriages between deaf persons. He had noted the recurrence of surnames among deaf people and deduced it was highly probable that a considerable proportion of deaf people in the country belonged to families which had more than one deaf member, and suspected that the reasons for this were hereditary. He believed that if intermarriages of deaf people continued, there would be a 'deaf variety' of the human race.

Twenty-five years earlier, in England, Dr. David Buxton, the Principal of the Liverpool School for the Deaf and Dumb, had published a pamphlet *On the Marriage and Intermarriage of the Deaf and Dumb* in 1857, in which he produced statistics to back up his belief that while it should not be forbidden for deaf people to marry, it was highly objectionable that they should intermarry.

That deaf people marry other deaf people was not, as could be supposed at that time, a new phenomenon - it will be recalled from Chapter I that John Dyott married a deaf girl after the Civil War in 1645. It is probable, however, that this was an exception rather than the rule - most deaf people before the start of deaf education did not marry, and those that did, like Sir John Gawdy, Sir Edward Gostwicke and Alexander Popham, all came from wealthly families where there was a desire to continue the family line and marriages were made with daughters of families that were of the landed gentry. There is no record that these mens' wives were deaf.

Since the start of deaf education, however, marriage of deaf people had increased, and out of 63 married males 53 married females in London, 50 males and 50 females were married to each other; in Manchester, out of 22 married males and 18 married females, 14 males and 14 females were married to each other; in Liverpool, 14 out of 18 married males were married to 14 females - there were no females in Liverpool married to hearing persons. So in these three cities, a total of 78 males and 78 females had intermarried. While only 25 males and 7 females were married to hearing persons.

In addition, there were over ten deaf children resulting from deaf intermarriages, and only two or three from a marriage of a deaf person to a hearing person - this being a deaf mother married to a hearing man, and the deaf mother's father was also deaf.

The statistics given of one in seven offspring of deaf parents being deaf themselves, as opposed to one in 135 offspring of deaf-hearing parents being influenced Dr. Buxton to argue against the desire of deaf people to intermarry. These statistics were probably available to Dr. Alexander Graham Bell when he raised the spectre of a 'deaf variety of the human race'.

The Growth of Deaf Missions and Associations.

The founding, and the success, of the first five adult organisations for the deaf in Britain at Glasgow, Edinburgh, London (St. Saviours), Manchester and Leeds prompted many deaf people in other parts of the country to seek the same sort of opportunities for themselves.

In the case of the first one to be founded after 1850 - Dundee in 1853 - a deaf person, Alexander Drysdale who was then headmaster of the Dundee School for the Deaf took the lead to establish an adult mission. This was quickly followed by deaf people in Liverpool (George Healey - 1864), Birmingham (W.A. Griffiths - 1867), Stoke-on-Trent (J. Davis - 1868), Cardiff (J. Rowlands - 1869), Kilmarnock (James Paul - 1874) and Aberdeen (1879).

St. Barnabas Church, Deptford, 1873

Many of these deaf men served the needs of their fellow-men for years - in George Healey's case until his death in 1927!

Other missions and adult societies for the deaf were formed by local interested persons, mainly clergymen. Often, this interest was aroused by the tireless efforts of the Rev.

Samuel Smith of St. Saviour's Church, London, in visiting numerous locations. This was the case in places such as Leicester, Nottingham, and Southampton.

In London it was found that deaf people in East and South London had difficulty in getting to St. Saviour's Church, so in the same year, 1873, two new branches were opened - one at St. Barnabas Church, Deptford (forerunner of Lewisham Deaf Club) and at West Ham.

Some societies, such as the Bolton and District Society, and others at Halifax (1860), Sheffield (1861), and Bradford (1864) were offshoots of the original societies at Manchester and Leeds. The same was true of Greenock (1870) and Paisley (1874) in Scotland (from Glasgow).

In Northern Ireland, the Kinghan Mission was founded in 1857 in Belfast due to the interests of the Rev. Kinghan who was then Headmaster of the Ulster Institution.

The National Deaf and Dumb Society

The rapid growth of adult missions and societies prompted a few determined men led by James Paul to found the National Deaf and Dumb Society in 1879, with James Paul as the first secretary.

Unfortunately, this was short-lived and it folded in 1884 having been torn asunder by internal dissensions, but before its collapse it inaugurated two important undertakings, the Stockton-on-Tees Mission and the Ayrshire Mission to the Deaf and Dumb.

The formation of the National Deaf and Dumb Society, however, laid the ground for the foundation of the British Deaf and Dumb Association eleven years later.

Deaf Sports Clubs

Hitherto, provision of adult deaf organisations had largely been confined to church services and other pastoral services, but in 1871, a most important step was taken with the founding of Glasgow Deaf and Dumb Football Club, the first sports club for the deaf in this country.

Liverpool Deaf Cricket & Football Teams in the Late 1800s
Photos: Merseyside Centre for the Deaf:

Matches were played against local hearing teams, and after a promising start, the club almost folded in 1879 following a disastrous season but was re-organised, and has since gone from strength to strength, with various changes in name.

The first adult sports clubs to be formed in England were Derby Deaf and Dumb Cricket and Football Club and Manchester Deaf and Dumb Sports Club, both in 1876 (Manchester's first sport was rugby union). They were followed by the Liverpool Deaf and Dumb Cricket and Football Club (1878), Armstead Deaf and Dumb F.C. (Dundee) and Doncaster Rovers F.C., both in 1879, although this was not strictly speaking an adult deaf sports club.

Glasgow Deaf and Dumb F.C. 25th Anniversary 1896
Photo: Glasgow and West of Scotland Society for the Deaf

Doncaster Rovers Football Club
Now a professional football club playing in the 4th Division of the English football league, it owes its origins to a team formed by the pupils and staff of the Yorkshire Institution for the Deaf and Dumb.

**Ceremony to mark 100th Anniversary of Founding of
Doncaster Rovers Football Club: Manager Billy Bremner
Receives Plaque from School**
Photo: Doncaster School for the Deaf Archives

Alex Noble
First and only known Deaf Freemason   *Photo: R.Cormack*

Freemason

On 20th April 1874, a deaf man with no speech was apprenticed to Solomon Lodge as a Freemason. He passed Fellow Craft and was raised to the sublime degree of Master Mason in the same month.

This was Alexander Noble of Fraserburgh, Scotland, a

asailmaker by trade who also had two deaf-without-speech sisters.

So far as it is known, Noble has been the only born-deaf person ever to be a Freemason in Britain.

Alexander Strathern (1844-1890)

One of the giants of the fledgling deaf community in the 1870s was Alexander Strathern of Glasgow.

The son of one of the Sheriffs of Glasgow, he lost his hearing at an early age and after first attending an ordinary day school, became one of the private pupils of the Headmaster of the Glasgow Institution.

Alexander Strathern

After a spell as a woodcarver, he became a printer by trade and had his own printing works in Glasgow.

In 1872, the Glasgow Mission for the Deaf was properly reorganised, and Strathern was secretary for them then acted as treasurer for many years until he resigned due to differences with the then committee.

He was married in 1873 to a hearing lady who bore him five children, one of whom died in infancy, and died in December 1890 after a lingering, incurable illness.

Harriet Martineau (1802-1876)

One of the literary giants of the period 1850- 1880 was the authoress, Harriet Martineau - referred to by Charles Dickens in one of his books as 'the little deaf woman ofNorwich'.

Her deafness became evident at the age of 12 while she was attending a school run by a Reverend Perry, when she found that she could not hear very well if she sat too far from the teacher, and by the time she was 16, it had worsened as to become very noticeable and inconvenient to herself.

Harriet Martineau - Authoress
Reproduced by the kind permission of the
National Portrait Gallery, London

In the solitude resulting from her deafness, Miss Martineau turned to journalism and literary writing. She became a profilic contributor to magazines and newspapers, and began to have books and novels published.

Her reputation was established with the nine-volume *Illustrations of Political Economy,* and she received a good income from her magazine contributions which enabled her to go to America in 1834.

In America, she showed that her sympathies lay with those who favoured abolition of slavery. Always a forthright woman, she incurred the wrath of the anti-abolitionists and her life was threatened.

On her return to England in 1837, she published an account of her travels followed by two best-selling novels, *Deerbrook* and *Life in a Sick Room*. Earlier, she had written *Letter to the Deaf* in which she gave advice to deaf people based on her experiences.

Always a sickly woman, she expected to die in 1855 after a doctor had pronounced a disease of the heart to be fatal, and quickly wrote her autobiography.

However, she lingered until June 1876, preserving her mental powers to the last, before dying in Birmingham.

Railway Accident, 1875

The first recorded death of a deaf person in a railway accident occurred in Cardiff in June 1875 when a 60 years old Irish visitor, John Thomas Morris, was struck by a train whilst walking along the tracks. He had failed to notice the approach of the goods train, which was being pushed backwards, and was hit by the leading wagon after stepping onto the track. He was run over by at least twelve wagons before the train was brought to an halt.

Taken to hospital, he managed to communicate by writing that he was deaf and dumb, that he lived in Dublin, and that he was temporarily resident in Cardiff. He then had his right hand, left foot, and right leg below the knee amputated, but lost consciousness afterwards and died from his injuries.

The Coroner's Court jury at the inquest donated all their fees to the Llandaff School for the Deaf and Dumb.

Chapter 6
The 1880s

Scene from a Period Play: 1930s
Photo: Northern Counties School for Deaf, Newcastle

The 1880s: The Beginning of the Decline

In 1880 Queen Victoria had been on the throne for forty-three years; Gladstone began the second of his four terms as Prime Minister; Great Britain was at the zenith of its powers.

In 1880, the industrial revolution was at its height, and the Forth railway bridge was opened in Scotland.

Unfortunately, in the year 1880, what came to be viewed as the greatest injustice ever to be perpetrated against deaf people occurred in September when the highly-misleading International Congress of Teachers of Deaf-Mutes was convened in Milan, Italy.

The International Congress of Teachers of Deaf-Mutes, Milan: September 6th - 11th 1880.

This Congress had its roots planted in Paris in 1878 at the French Universal Exhibition when a hastily-assembled meeting of twenty-seven teachers of the deaf was arranged. Of this number, twenty-three were French, and the other four came from Belgium, Switzerland, Sweden and Austria. It was no coincidence that the majority of the French delegates were members of the little-known Le Societe Pereire, which sought to recognise Pereire as the first teacher of the deaf in that country - Pereire being a man who practised teaching by the oral method. The objective of this association was to promote the adoption of the instruction of deaf children not through the use of sign language or any method that used it as then prevailed in many countries including the U.S.A. and Britain, but through oral methods to the total exclusion of sign language altogether.

The Paris meeting appointed a committee of twelve from those present to make arrangements for a second international conference. Of these twelve, eleven were from France (and naturally Le Societe Pereire.)

They chose Milan as the venue because of the presence of two schools which for the previous ten years had pursued the Pure Oral System, or the German System as it was more commonly known, and to help to give the Congress credibility, they chose as the President one of the schools' headmasters, while the other school's headmaster was Secretary. In addition, they appointed four Vice-Presidents and four Vice-Secretaries of whom seven were staunch supporters of the German System.

It is therefore not surprising that once assembled, the Congress exuded a strong oralist flavour. Out of 164 participants, eighty-seven were Italians and fifty-three were French. The only truly representative delegation was that of the United States whose five delegates had been chosen earlier that year at a convention in Cincinnati.

The British delegation of eight comprised of two Principals of Oral Schools for the Deaf which had a combined total of less than 25 students! (Rev. Thomas Arnold and a Miss Hull). One (A.A. Kinsey) was the Principal of the Ealing College for Training of Oral Teachers of the Deaf. He was accompanied by his Secretary, Dr. David Buxton, formerly headmaster at the Liverpool Institution for the Deaf and Dumb, who had become a convert to oral methods.

Two others, a Mr. and Mrs. Ackers, were parents of a deaf girl who had been orally-educated by them at home. They had no experience whatsoever of any deaf school.

Only Richard Elliott, Headmaster of the Asylum for the Deaf and Dumb at Margate, and the Reverend William Stainer, chairman of the London Schools Board Classes for the Deaf, could be said to be representative of the dominant system of education then prevailing in British schools.

Many of the great institutions in Edinburgh, Glasgow, Manchester, Birmingham or Yorkshire - which had in their employ a considerable number of deaf teachers of the deaf - were not even present. (In reality, none had even been invited.) The only deaf person at the Congress was one of the American delegation.

Eight resolutions were put before the Congress, the most crucial being the first two which proposed that since education of deaf children by the *proven* Oral Method was far superior, the use of sign language in education should no longer be used.

These resolutions were carried by a massive 160 votes to 4 - these four being three Americans along with Richard Elliott. For reasons of his own, the Rev. Stainer voted for the introduction of the Oral Method.

The consequences arising from the resolutions passed at this *unrepresentative* international congress had serious repercussions on deaf education, not to mention the status of deaf adults.

The Milan Congress not only severely retarded the development of generations of deaf children for whom the Oral Method was totally inappropriate but also caused the loss of hundreds of teaching jobs held by deaf people throughout the world in schools for the deaf. Apart from the appointment of Edward Kirk to the post of Principal at Leeds in 1881 it was to be almost 100 years before deaf people once again became acceptable as teachers of deaf children.

Report of the Royal Commission on the Education of the Blind and the Deaf and Dumb.

The Milan Congress gave impetus to those who favoured the Pure Oral method to agitate for the inclusion of education of the deaf in the proposed Royal Commission that was to be formed to look at educational provision for the blind in Britain, on the grounds that the Education Acts of the 1870s had ignored educational provision for the deaf and dumb. While it was true that previous Education Acts had not looked at deaf education, the real motive was the need to provide a powerful argument to a Royal Commission for the establishment of the Pure Oral system throughout Britain.

As it turned out the final Report, published in 1889 after almost five years of investigation, did embody a number of recommendations regarding the education of deaf children in future Education Acts, thus setting out for the first time proper legislation with regard to compulsory entry, ages of admission, the length of education, the size of classes, and even that Principals/Headmasters of boarding institutions had to reside on the premises.

However, it also leant heavily on the opinions of people like Alexander Graham Bell who were fervent supporters of the Pure Oral Method, and even Dr. David Buxton who managed to get in a recommendation on his pet subject, that intermarrige of deaf people should be discouraged (see Chapter 5). Arguments presented by Dr. E.M. Gallaudet, a firm believer of the combined system, and by leading deaf people like George Healey of Liverpool, and by experienced teachers or missioners of the deaf in favour of the combined or sign system like Elliott, Welsh, Rhind were all largely dismissed or ignored in the Report's recommendations, which were in essence that the Pure Oral system should be used to educate the deaf and that teachers for the deaf should be properly qualified, experienced in teaching in ordinary schools, and be in possession of all their faculties.

When the Report was subsequently embodied into an Act of Parliament, many born-deaf people of undoubted ability found themselves debarred from taking up teaching as a profession unless they could first prove they were able to teach in ordinary schools. The situation still exists to-day in the 1980s but there is a more flexible and liberal attitude and deaf teachers of the deaf are once more gaining teaching appointments.

Day Classes

One significant consequence of the Milan Congress, and also recommended in the Royal Commission's report, was the rapid growth of day classes for deaf children in urban areas large enough to support such classes.

The trend was started with Hull and Sheffield, as well as in London, but the 1880s saw others established in Leeds, Nottingham, Leicester and in Airdrie in Scotland.

Leeds School and Home for Blind and Deaf Children

Of these classes, perhaps the most significant was the one established in April 1881 in Leeds with the local missioner Joseph Moreton as the first teacher. However, Moreton was unable to give sufficient time to the class, and within six months, he was replaced by Edward A. Kirk.

This appointment was unique, and was the only instance of its kind - it was also to be the last for over a century, because Edward A. Kirk was deaf.

Edward A. Kirk (1848-1917)

Born near Doncaster, Edward Kirk lost his hearing through a severe illness when aged 2, and was sent to be educated at the Yorkshire Institution for the Deaf and Dumb where his abilities so impressed the headmaster, the great Charles

Baker, that he was kept on first as a classroom assistant, thence from 1871 as a teacher.

When the pro-oralist John Howard succeeded Charles Baker at Doncaster upon the latter's death, Kirk felt he needed to move and waited for the opportunity to do so. In truth, he also wanted to get married and could not afford to do so on the salary he was receiving at the Yorkshire Institution - one of the worst paid in the country

When the vacancy created by the resignation of Joseph Moreton at the newly-created Leeds half-day classes arose, Edward Kirk applied for the position, ignoring the advice of John Howard.

Edward A. Kirk

Edward Kirk was to remain as Headmaster at Leeds until his death, and was to see his school grow from a small class of 6 pupils on a half-day basis into a fully-fledged school taking in boarders and day scholars with a roll of over 100 children, with a reputation second to none.

He remains the *only* deaf person in Britain ever to be appointed headmaster of a deaf school by a *local education authority*. The high esteem in which he was held was shown at his funeral where a tribute to his great accomplishments for deaf education in Leeds was paid by the Director of Education for the district.

More Deaf Clubs

While deaf education was being given a severe blow first by the Milan Congress and then by the Royal Commission, life for adult deaf people continued to improve with the establishment of recreational and spiritual services in Reading (1880); St. Barnabas, London (1882); Bristol, Dumfries and Jersey (all 1884); Warrington (1885); Chester (1889) and many others. All these clubs were opened through the influence of the clergy and philanthropists.

St. Barnabas Church for the Deaf

However, two institutes were opened through the efforts of the National Deaf and Dumb Society as well - mainly through James Paul. The Ayrshire Mission to the Deaf and Dumb was instituted in 1881 at Kilmarnock followed by the Stockton-on-Tees Mission in 1882.

Sport: Cricket and Football
This decade also saw the start of organised inter-club sport activities with the first cricket matches between two deaf institutes taking place in 1882. In the first match, played at Derby, the visiting team from Sheffield mustered 68 all out, and Derby won by one run. In the return match, however, Sheffield thrashed Derby by 34 runs to win handsomely.

In 1889, the first ever football competition was organised in Scotland by the newly-formed Scottish Deaf Football Association, and the final was played between Edinburgh and Glasgow in front of about 2000 spectactors at Falkirk. Edinburgh won 3-1.

Deaf and Dumb Institute, King Square, Bristol
From an engraving; Bristol Centre for the Deaf

Chapter 7
The 1890s

**Ceremony of Laying the Foundation Stone
Glasgow, February 1894**
Photo: Glasgow & West of Scotland Society for the Deaf

The 1890s

The 1890s were probably the most remarkable decade in British deaf history - no other decade with the possible exception of the 1980s saw the social status of deaf people held so high in public esteem. This was especially true in Scotland, and in particular, Glasgow, which may justly claim to be the deaf 'capital' during this era. In this decade, Glasgow held a Grand Bazaar and the first ever exhibition of deaf art; it also built its new deaf centre, had a flourishing soccer team and staged the first soccer international between Scotland and England.

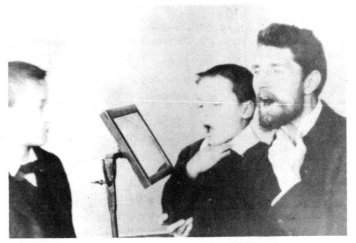

An Early Speech Training Lesson
Photo: Royal West of England School, Exeter

Glasgow also had a weekly deaf column in the Glasgow Evening Times, written by a variety of people. Through their own efforts, deaf people were in the forefront of Glasgow society.

Despite the reversing trend in deaf education from sign to oral methods, the social standing of deaf people who relied on fingerspelling and sign language was given a tremendous boost by the dignity and bearing of people like William Agnew (who was on 'fingerspelling terms' with Queen Victoria), the Docharty and Williamson brothers, James Paul, Alex McGregor and, in England, Sir Arthur Fairbairn, Thomas Davidson, S. Bright Lucas and the Reverend W. Pearce amongst others.

All these people were firm supporters of sign language - William Agnew in particular used to bombard the Glasgow Evening Times and the London Times with letters denouncing the spread of the 'German Method' in our schools.

The social standing of deaf people may also have in no small way been aided by the Princess of Wales (later Queen Alexandra) who was stone deaf and who used fingerspelling as well as lipreading to communicate.

The year 1890 was also a very significant year in deaf history for it saw the birth of the British Deaf and Dumb Association.

The British Deaf Association

The National Deaf and Dumb Society, the first ever national organisation for deaf people in Britain, had had a very short-lived existence - a mere 6 years - before it dissolved in internal strife in 1885.

The N.D.D.S. had, however, shown, albeit briefly, how a nationwide organisation for deaf people could be beneficial, and a number of determined people resolved to continue the fight to establish another body. With strong backing from George Healey of Liverpool, Francis Maginn of Belfast and William Agnew of Glasgow, a convention was held in Leeds, and from this meeting, the British Deaf and Dumb Associa-

and from this meeting, the British Deaf and Dumb Association was born. (The word Dumb was dropped from the title in the 1970s.)

The Association proved to be more resilient than the defunct N.D.D.S. although it led a precarious existence for a number of years before becoming established.

3rd Congress of The British Deaf & Dumb Association
Royal Cambrian Institution, Swansea. 1893
Photo:- Church of the Holy Name Mission to the Deaf, Swansea

New Schools in the 1890s

Two schools which opened their doors to deaf children in the 1890s were the Royal Cross School, Preston, and the Hugh Bell School, Middlesbrough.

The Royal Cross School in Preston was founded by Mary Cross and opened in 1894. It was one of the three schools which came about as a result of pressure from adult deaf societies. Derby and Greenock were the others in the 1870s. The Royal Cross School is due to close due to falling numbers in 1990.

There was almost a tragedy in 1905 when a major fire broke out one night in the early hours of the morning while 44 boys in the boys' dormitories were asleep. The fire was discovered at 3 a.m. by a master working late, and together with two boys - one of whom climbed a waterspout to get to the juniors' bedroom via the roof and the other operated a hand-pump in dense smoke - managed to raise the alarm.

The Royal Cross School at that time operated on the Pure Oral system, but the boys were all led to safety by using *sign language* to communicate amongst the glare of the flames and through dense smoke!

The two boys involved were awarded silver medals for bravery, and damage was kept to a minimum through their courageous actions.

The Hugh Bell School in Middlesbrough opened on 7th January 1895 with 7 scholars as a deaf class in a cold, cramped room near the magistrates' courts - who were wont to complain frequently about the noise from the alleyway between the classroom and the courts where the children played. In winter, the classroom frequently recorded temperatures of between 38F and 48F; no wonder so many children and staff were frequently absent ill.

The class remained in this room for 5 years before the proper Hugh Bell Schools were opened. This was a deaf unit attached to a Central High School. The numbers attending remained very small for a number of years - three children were once expelled because it was found they could hear.

School Activities in the 1890s

Above and Right:
Physical Exercises being
performed by pupils of the
Royal Institution for the Deaf
& Dumb, Derby.
All-England Challenge Shield
Winners 1896-1900 and 1902-07,
11 years out of 12.
Photo: School Archives

The heating system in the new schools was no better than that in the old classroom; for 8 months in 1919, the boiler was out of commission, and the logbook shows frequent temperatures in the 40o's. From 1895 to 1926, the children - never more than 17 at any one time - were taught largely by one person, a Miss F. Bodily.

Cookery Class
Royal West of England School for the Deaf and Dumb, Exeter
Photo: School Archives

The Hugh Bell School closed on 1948, and the deaf classes were transferred to Homewood in Orchard Road, in enlarged premises ready to receive pupils from the Stockton School for the Deaf which was also to close. The two schools later relocated to Saltersgill and are now known as the Beverley Schools for the Deaf, Middlesbrough.

A third school which was opened in 1894 was in Birmingham when a day class using oral methods was established. This grew into what is now Braidwood Schools for the Deaf. This early class endured a miserable existence in damp, cramped circumstances and when it outgrew these premises, it moved into a building in Gem Street which although much larger was equally gloomy, dark and ugly.

Maypole Activities
Top: Royal School for Deaf Children, Birmingham
Photo: School Archives
Bottom: Institution for the Deaf & Dumb, Brighton
Photo: Herbert Colville:

When the old Gem Street school moved out to Perry Common in the suburbs of Birmingham, and was renamed Braidwood, things were much better - the architecture was more modern, and classrooms light and airy.

Elementary Education (Blind and Deaf Children) Act, 1893

The recommendations of the Royal Commission's report of 1889 (Chapter 6) were embodied in a Bill which was presented to Parliament, and needed to be introduced four times before it was finally accepted onto the Statute book.

The main reason for the first three failures to carry the Bill through Parliament was that the then Secretary of State for Education, George Kekewich, objected to the clauses in the Bill whereby it was not compulsory for local authorities to make any provision for the education of deaf children in their area.

Only when the Bill was amended to make it compulsory for local authorities to provide and maintain facilities for deaf children did the Liberal Government of the day allow the Bill to become law.

This was an important provision; the Act of 1893 now gave every deaf child the right to have an education. Previously, under the Poor Law Act of 1834, a clause empowered boards of guardians to use local rates to pay for deaf (and blind) children's education in asylums. In both 1845 and 1862 they were encouraged to assist their education by the same means, and the 1870 Act created school boards and the London Schools Board. The latter did lead to the establishment of classes for deaf children, but because the provision of this education was not compulsory, many local school boards evaded their responsibilities and pleaded poverty.

Conversely, conditions in deaf institutions and asylums were often grim and unhygenic. At Boston Spa, for example, there were no adequate washing facilities for 16 years; at Exeter, it was 1887 before the school got hot water facilities; at Old Kent Road, the installation of gas pipes which could have provided better lighting was rejected in 1833 on the grounds the cost was exhorbitant and that the children could make do with candles. And so it went on: poor or non-existent sanitation, overcrowded dormitories, dull and unappetising food, workhouse conditions.

The 1893 Act allowed institutions a Parliamentary grant per pupil, but only if the institution/asylum met the standards set by the periodic visits of Her Majesty's Inspector, so in order to meet these standards and obtain their grants, schools had to improve on the conditions in which the pupils were taught. While this was a good thing, such improvements were at first only superficial, and it was a long time before everyday living conditions in deaf boarding institutions and day classes were of acceptable standard.

Criticism in the 1893 Act regarding the poor status and qualifications of teachers of the deaf led - in 1895 - to the formation of the National Association of Teachers of the Deaf.

National Association of Teachers of the Deaf, 1895

Prior to the formation of this body, three entirely independent examining bodies, each giving its own certificate to successful students, existed for persons wishing to become teachers of the deaf.

These were (1) 'Association for the Oral Institution of the Deaf and Dumb' based at Fitzroy Square, London, founded in 1872 (2) 'Society for Training Teachers of the Deaf and for the Diffusion of the German System', based at the training college at Ealing, founded in 1877 (3) 'College of Teachers of the Deaf and Dumb', founded in 1885.

The first two training colleges also had schools for deaf children attached to them, and teachers' certificates were awarded to students who taught on the oral system to the exclusion of any other method. The third, the C.T.D.D., awarded certificates to students using any mode of communication.

Needless to say, the Board of Education did not recognise any of these diplomas until 1909 when all three joined together to produce one diploma, at the insistence of the

N.A.T.D. Even then, the Scottish Department of Education still refused to recognise the diplomas.

In 1918, the C.T.D.D. and N.C.T.D. merged to form the National College of Teachers of the Deaf (N.C.T.D.) which took over examinations for the diploma in the teaching of deaf children. In 1976, the N.C.T.D. re-formed itself to become the British Association of Teachers of the Deaf (B.A.T.O.D.)

The Mount School for the Blind, Deaf and Dumb, Stoke-on-Trent

While the 1893 Act encouraged local authorities to provide day classes, wherever possible, the five local authorities that encompassed the Potteries area around Stoke-on-Trent decided that it would suit their needs better to combine their resources and establish one residential school. With the support of the Wedgwood family the Mount School was founded in 1897.

Deaf Clubs in the 1890s

The only new Mission for the deaf that seems to have opened for the first time in the 1890s was that at Oxford, although the deaf people of Bradford almost lost their own when a fire was discovered in the coal cellar under the offices by one of the deaf members who ran to summon the fire brigade from its nearby station. They arrived within minutes to save the building from being burnt down.

It was in Glasgow, however, that many momentous events were taking place.

Glasgow in the 1890s

For a number of years, it had been obvious that the Glasgow Mission premises in Renfield Street had become inadequate to cater for the social, pastoral and spiritual activities of the deaf citizens of Glasgow, and that a better and bigger building was needed.

The deaf of Glasgow were at that time extremely fortunate

to have in William Agnew a most intelligent and capable man, an artist in his leisure time, who through his hobby had come into contact with Queen Victoria and who enjoyed a friendship with Lord and Lady Blythswood (Glasgow Deaf and Dumb F.C. in the 1890's were renamed Blythswood Athletic). William Agnew, although he could not speak and relied entirely on sign language, was a forceful personality and moved about amongst the rich merchants of Glasgow.

He took it upon himself to promote the idea of having a noble building for an Institute in Glasgow, and in this he was ably supported by brothers James and Edwin Docharty, sons of a famous Scottish painter, and a number of other deaf people of exceptional ability. An added advantage that the deaf people of Glasgow had over any other deaf community in the country was that they had a regular 'Deaf and Dumb Notes' column every week in the *Glasgow Evening Times,* the largest selling Scottish evening paper. This meant that fund-raising news and any other news about the deaf was in the forefront of everyone's attention.

In a short period of time, they had raised the cost of the building, including contributions from Queen Victoria herself, but now needed money to purchase a prime site in the centre of Glasgow. In order to raise this sum required (£5000), they organised a Grand Bazaar which was held in St. Andrew's Hall and formally opened by the Duchess of Montrose. Thanks to the connections made by William Agnew amongst Glasgow's high society, the Bazaar was extremely successful and raised more than enough to purchase a prime site on the corner of West Regent Street and West Campbell Street.

Never a person to let anything grow under his feet, Agnew arranged for ceremonies for every possible occasion; the laying of the foundation stone was greeted with great fanfare and a sense of occasion, and the official opening of the institute was a most elaborate affair in which beautifully designed invitations were sent out to many dignitaries.

This was followed by an exhibition of paintings and works

of art by deaf artists in Britain - so far the only kind ever held. All artists presently living in Scotland, and many of the better known artists from England like Thomas Davidson, Rupert Dent and William Trood all sent paintings. Many were sold to raise further funds to furnish the new institute.

Events in Glasgow in the 1890s

The Glasgow Deaf Grand Bazaar

This was held at St. Andrew's Hall on the 19th, 20th and 21st of November 1891, and opened by the Duchess of Montrose whose son was ironically soon to become totally deaf. The Bazaar totally exceeded all expectations, and was a rousing success, raising in excess of £6,000 when the Building Committee had only dared to hope to raise at the most optimistic a sum of £5,000.

The monies raised by this Bazaar enabled the Glasgow deaf people to purchase a very prime and desirable site in the centre of the city.

The Laying of the Foundation Stone

The ceremony of the laying of the foundation stone of the new Institute building was a very elaborate affair, and attracted many civic dignitaries.

Glasgow Deaf Members at the Ceremony
Photo: Glasgow and West of Scotland Society for the Deaf

In the picture shown above, William Agnew is in the centre, with the Rev. John Henderson, the missioner. Other deaf people identified in the picture include Edwin Docharty lounging indolently on the left, his brother James L.C. Docharty to the right of the Rev. Henderson, and Alex McGregor, the regular columnist of the deaf column on the *Glasgow Evening Times* standing behind him.

Opening of the New Deaf Adult Institute

On the next page is an exact copy of the elaborately-designed Invitation that went out to many civic dignitaries and wealthy merchants in Glasgow to commemorate the opening of the new institute. Also illustrated is the front cover of the programme of the exhibition of paintings and works of art by British deaf artists held in conjunction with the opening.

Football in Scotland - 1890s

In the previous chapter, we saw that the start of organised football in Scotland amongst the deaf commenced in 1889 with the formation of the Scottish Deaf and Dumb Football Association which launched a knock-out cup competition. For years before that, however, football enthusiasts in Glasgow had long been agitating for an international match against the deaf footballers of England, without success. The established deaf football clubs in England were based in Midlands and Northern cities and towns where work was hard and money was scarce. London at this time did not even have any sports teams outside of schools.

**Footballers of Leeds Deaf F.C. and Glasgow Deaf F.C.
Before Their Match in 1895**
Photo: Glasgow & West of Scotland Society for the Deaf

At long last in 1891 the secretaries of the Scottish Deaf and Dumb F.A and Leeds Deaf and Dumb F.C. came to a mutual arrangement to play a match between England and Scotland in Glasgow on the Easter Saturday. An English team drawn from deaf football clubs in Newcastle, Leeds, Sheffield, Nottingham, Stoke and Manchester, accompanied by hundreds of supporters, made the trip to Glasgow (eleven hours by train from Manchester), and the match was played in excellent weather conditions at Ibrox Park before about 3,000 spectactors and resulted in a 3-3 draw.

THE DEAF AND DUMB TIMES

GRAND INTERNATIONAL

DEAF & DUMB FOOTBALL MATCH

(UNDER ASSOCIATION RULES)

ENGLAND
v.
SCOTLAND

To be played at Glasgow (ground not yet selected),

ON SATURDAY, MARCH 28th, 1891

(Under the auspices of the Scottish Deaf and Dumb Football Association).

Special two or four days Cheap Easter Excursion Trains will leave Leeds, Manchester, Nottingham, Sheffield, and all other large towns, for Glasgow, on Thursday night, the 26th March.

For further particulars as to ground, time of kick off, &c., &c., apply to Mr. J. Macpherson, Hon. Secretary, S.D. & D.F.A., Gayfield Street, Glasgow; or Mr. R. Hawcroft, Hon. Sec. of the English Team, 70, Prince Street, Ashton Old Road, Manchester.

Publicity Poster: 1st England v Scotland Football Match 1891

In 1895, Leeds Deaf and Dumb F.C. travelled to Glasgow to take part in the celebrations of the opening of the new institute and came away severely thrashed 6-0.

Events in the North-West

Momentous things were also happening socially in the North-West of England following the highly successful venture by the local society in the opening of the first social club for the deaf in the country in 1878 at Manchester. Members began to go out into the country on day trips, and the first cricket match between two deaf clubs in the country, which later led to the formation of inter-institute sports activities of billiards, darts, and other sports, took place on 23rd July 1892 at Manchester between Manchester Deaf and Dumb Institute and the Bolton and Bury Institutes. The match resulted in a win for Manchester who having batted first & scored 72 dismissed Bolton for a mere 14 runs.

Manchester Deaf Members' Day Out: 1890s
Photo: Manchester Centre for the Deaf

Joseph Barnes, the Bolton captain, was the main motivator of this match, and latterly organised events in the North-West for other sports.

Titbits from the *Glasgow Evening Times* 'Deaf and Dumb Notes'

A William Churcher of Surrey was sentenced to three months hard labour in 1890 for wilfully driving a horse and cart against a deaf lady, Victoria E. Brown, who had spurned his advances.

The tallest deaf mute in 1890 was a Hugh McIntyre, a Scotsman living in Buenos Aires, Argentina, who was 7 feet 1 inches tall, and the smallest deaf mute was a man named West living on the Isle of Wight who was barely 3 feet tall.

Chapter 8
Notable Deaf Persons 1875 - 1899

**The Silver-Gilded and Jewelled Damascus Sword Presented
to the Deaf Artist William H.H. Trood by the Sultan of
Morocco for Services Rendered**
Photo: R. Cormack

CHAPTER 8

Notable Deaf Persons
1875-1899

The last quarter of the nineteenth century was a tremendous time in British deaf history, not just because of the events that took place and the deeds that were done, but also because of the men of remarkable ability and calibre who were to be giants amongst deaf, and hearing, people.

It is thanks to these men of ability and vision that the deaf communities in Britain became so well established and repected, and that the deaf communities were drawn together into a national movement which after a false start exists to this day in the British Deaf Association.

James Paul (1848-1918)

If any one man could lay claim to the title of 'Father' of the national British deaf movement as embodied by the British Deaf Association, it was James Paul of Kilmarnock, Scotland.

Born at Cardross, Dumbartonshire, he lost his hearing in infancy through illness and was admitted at the age of 8 into the Glasgow Institution for the Deaf and Dumb where he remained for seven years.

The then headmaster, Duncan Anderson, remarked that James Paul was 'one of the brightest of a clever band of scholars'.

Upon leaving the Institution, he was apprenticed to a bookbinder but this did not satisfy his ambitions, and he began to take a leading part in the affairs of the deaf. His forcefulness, intelligence and personality soon established him as a national leader.

As early as 1872, he was proposing the formation of a national body for deaf people, but it took long and persistent efforts on his part before the National Deaf and Dumb Society was founded in 1879.

James Paul
Photo: British Deaf Times

James Paul saw the National Deaf and Dumb Society as the principal backers of establishing a network of missions for the deaf throughout the country, and the Society did indeed succeed in establishing the Ayrshire Mission to the Deaf at Kilmarnock in 1881, with Paul himself as missioner, and the Stockton-on-Tees Mission in 1882.

Others, however, saw the N.D.D.S. in a different light and role, and soon there was internal strife within the Society which tore it asunder in 1885 after a general meeting had been held in London without Paul's knowledge.

James Paul was terribly hurt by the collapse of the N.D.D.S. and although he helped to establish the British Deaf and Dumb Association in 1890, accepting the position of Treasurer in the first year, he preferred to devote himself to developing the social status and services for the deaf people of Ayrshire. Through his efforts a fine property was obtained in Kilmarnock where the headquarters of the Mission became established, and a home for deaf women was founded in Ayr.

Paul married a Jane M'Caig in June 1879, and by her had a son and daughter. He remained as Missioner to the Ayrshire Mission until his death in 1918.

George Frederick Healey (1843-1927)

George Healey was a remarkable man who devoted his whole adult life to the cause of deaf people, both in Liverpool and nationally first through the N.D.D.S. and thence the B.D.D.A. He was born in Gateacre, Liverpool and lost his hearing at the age of three months as a result of brain fever following a fall from the arms of his nurse, although his deafness was not discovered until he was two years old.

George Frederick Healey
Photo: Merseyside Centre for the Deaf

At the age of 8 he was sent to the private school for the deaf at Rugby run by Mr. Bingham, formerly headmaster of the West of England Institution at Exeter. When this school closed, he was educated privately at home.

After his education, he was apprenticed to his father's coach-building premises, graduating after three years to an office position which he retained until his father retired in 1890.

George Healey, as a young man in the early 1860s, paid a visit to London where he learnt of church services for the deaf conducted by the Revs. Samuel Smith and Charles Rhind. Impressed by what he saw, he resolved to do the same for Liverpool.

Through his efforts, the Liverpool Society for the Deaf was formed on 23rd April 1864, with simple services held in the school buildings in Oxford Street. These, however, could not be held regularly, and it was not until 1874 that regular services were held in St. Mary's Cemetery Chapel, Cambridge Street, but these were still not satisfactory. What the deaf people of Liverpool needed was their own building, so in 1876, Healey started a building fund for a new institute.

Contributions were slow in coming, and it was not until 1887 that the new institute was opened by H.R.H. Princess Louise on 16th May.

From its inception in April 1864, George Healey was Honorary Secretary of the Liverpool Society for over 50 years, and still found the energy to back James Paul in his efforts to establish a national society.

Whereas James Paul was deeply wounded by the failure of the N.D.D.S., Healey was made of sterner stuff. Indeed, he was extremely furious and led the fight to establish a new body and was present at the first meeting of the British Deaf and Dumb Association in Leeds in 1890. He was later elected honorary treasurer - a position he was to retain for an incredible quarter of a century, earning himself the title of 'Grand Old Man'.

He was active in deaf work right up to his death in 1927.

Francis Maginn (1862-1917)

Francis Maginn was born in Johnsgrove, Co. Cork, Ireland, the son of the Rector and Rural Dean of Castletown Roche, and lost his hearing through scarlet fever at the age of five.

At the age of 9, he was sent to the London Institution where he excelled himself so much that when the school's Margate branch was opened in 1875, the headmaster, Dr. Elliott, appointed him one of the first pupil-teachers, promoting him three years later to a junior teachership.

Francis Maginn
Photo: British Deaf Times

In 1883, Maginn quitted teaching and spent a year studying at home before going to Gallaudet College, Washington, U.S.A. (the first British deaf student to do so) in 1884.

However, the death of his father in 1887 intervened and Maginn returned home before he could complete his course. It so happened that the Missions to the Adult Deaf and Dumb of Ireland were seeking a missionary, and Maginn applied for the position. It was largely due to his powers as an organiser that the Belfast mission achieved the success that it did.

Maginn was also a firm believer in the national deaf movement, and was one of the first vice-presidents of the B.D.D.A.

Intervening in a dispute between two deaf people. Francis Maginn was stuck a severe blow on his chest, from which he never fully recovered and this ultimately led to his early death in 1917.

Joseph Hepworth (1865-1921)
Born in Wakefield, Yorkshire, he lost hearing at the age of 8 but to his death retained his speech.

He was educated privately at home, and never knew there were other deaf people in the world until he came across the manual alphabet in one of the publications he was reading, and out of curiosity mastered it.

Joseph Hepworth
Photo: British Deaf Times

He needed this knowledge on the day a deaf house-painter called to decorate his house, and asked him in sign language which school he went to (a conversational gambit which remains unchanged to this day.)

From this house-painter, he learnt there were other deaf people, and that there was a society in Leeds, so he went along to see for himself. He never looked back.

For some years, Hepworth was assistant missioner at Leeds before securing the post as Missioner to the Glamorgan and Monmouth Mission to the Deaf and Dumb at Cardiff in 1896.

However, Joseph Hepworth was better known as the editor of the British Deaf Times, which he was for some years up to his death.

Reverend Richard Aslett Pearce (1854-1928)

Born in Southampton, he was educated as a private pupil at the Brighton Institution for the Deaf and Dumb by the sign and manual system. (The Rev. Pearce could never talk right up to his death).

On leaving the Institution at the age of 18, he became interested in church work through the influence of a Rev. Mansfield Owen whose cousin was Pearce's boyhood deaf friend. The Rev. Owen could therefore use sign language, and together with another clergyman, encouraged the young man to seek out as many local deaf people as possible and bring them to church services.

Rev. R. A. Pearce
Photo: British Deaf Times

In 1879 Pearce, the Owen cousins, and the Rev. Samuel Smith of St. Saviour's Church for the Deaf in London got together and established the Winchester Diocesan Adult Deaf and Dumb Mission. This interested the Bishop of Winchester in work amongst the deaf, and soon afterwards Pearce commenced studying for Holy Orders.

He passed the Bishop's examination and was ordained a

Deacon in the Church of England in an interesting ceremony at the Parish Church of Farnham, Surrey, in 1885. The ordination was conferred upon him by the special approval of the Archbishop of Canterbury.

Richard Aslett Pearce was the first born-deaf man to be ordained in Britain, and he continued to do pastoral work throughout Hampshire until his death in 1928. As his diocese included the Isle of Wright, The Rev. Pearce would often have occasion to hold signed conversations with Queen Victoria who was acquainted with some deaf people near her favourite retreat at Osborne.

Samuel Bright Lucas (1840-1919)

Born in London, he was educated partly privately and partly at the Tyndall Park School for the Deaf and Dumb, Bristol.

Though he was to achieve some distinction as a water-colour artist, exhibiting at several galleries, he was to become better known through his voluntary work for the Royal Association for the Deaf and Dumb (R.A.D.D.) for which he was honorary secretary for many years.

S. Bright Lucas
Photo: Ephphatha

Although he helped to form the National Deaf and Dumb Society, he was also to be the main reason for its demise. A typical Londoner through and through, he believed that the aims of the N.D.D.S. were in conflict with those of the R.A.D.D. Following the demise of the N.D.D.S., he played no part in the formation of the British Deaf and Dumb Association, concentrating instead on improving the services and influence of the R.A.D.D. throughout London and nearby towns. To this day, the Royal Association for the Deaf (R.A.D.- as it is now known) retains a considerable influence in the affairs of deaf people in London and surrounding counties whilst the B.D.A. has poor support in the region.

In spite of his opposition to the aims and ideals of the N.D.D.S. and the B.D.D.A., S. Bright Lucas did sterling work for the deaf and dumb poor of London and was a considerable influence in the founding of the National Deaf Club of which he was President.

William Agnew (1846-1914)

William Agnew was born deaf in Glasgow, and at an early age was sent to be educated at the Glasgow Institution for the Deaf and Dumb, where he proved to be a remarkable scholar.

William Agnew
Photo: Glasgow & West of Scotland Society for the Deaf

Throughout his life, Agnew could not speak and relied entirely on sign language and fingerspelling, but was a highly articulate man - he penned a great number of articles in Scottish and national newspapers giving his views on the introduction of oralism into British schools.

A man of immense dignity and bearing who would converse (in fingerspelling) with royalty and aristocracy on equal terms, he was also a talented amateur artist in his leisure time outside his employment as a writer with the Glasgow law firm of Moncrief, Barr, Paterson and Company.

His artistic fame rested primarily on the series of paintings he did of Queen Victoria and Elizabeth Tuffield, nee Groves - 'The Royal Condescension' paintings of 1883, 1889 and 1900, 'True Nobility' (1897) and 'Post Office, Whippingham I.O.W.' (1899). No trace exists of any of these five paintings, which are now much sought-after by deaf people.

Royal Condescension: 1889 Version
by William Agnew
Photo: Glasgow & West of Scotland Society for the Deaf

'The Royal Condescension' paintings of 1883 and 1889 are very similar except that the 1883 shows a dog on the hearth and the 1889 picture has a baby on the hearth; the 1900 picture shows Mrs. Tuffield and Queen Victoria differently positioned and no dog or baby on the hearth. The 1889 picture was exhibited at the Edinburgh Exhibition in 1890 and won an award; it was also specially exhibited to Queen Victoria at Lord and Lady Blythswood's house in Glasgow in 1891, at which time the Queen agreed to become patron of the proposed new Glasgow Institute's building fund. She also made a handsome donation although she had not been asked for money.

Through William Agnew's painting, and the notice it received, the Building Fund (Agnew's brainchild) got off to a splendid start, and Agnew's energy and his business contacts throughout Glasgow soon saw the Fund grow quickly. The Grand Bazaar on 19th-21st November 1891 realised over £6,000 - much more than Agnew had hoped for, and by the end of 1892, Agnew had met his target for the Building Fund, and work commenced on the new Institute.

The new building was opened with great fanfare in January 1895, and the grateful deaf members appointed William Agnew a director, a position he retained until his death after a long illness in 1914.

James L.C. Docharty (1868-1928)
and Edwin Docharty (1869-1931)
William Agnew's splendid efforts on behalf of the deaf of Glasgow could not have been entirely successful without the support he received from a number of other deaf individuals. Two such were James and Edwin Docharty, talented artist brothers, sons of Scottish painter James L. Docharty, who were a tremendous help to Agnew in the organisation of the Grand Bazaar, and in providing numerous paintings for sale in aid of the Building Fund.

Both brothers were educated in the Glasgow Institution, and both were employed as artists on the *Glasgow Weekly Mail*.

Edwin Docharty was later to became missioner for the East Lancashire Deaf and Dumb Society, Blackburn.

James L.C. Docharty **Edwin Docharty**
Photos: Glasgow & West of Scotland Society for the Deaf

Deaf Artists in the 1890s

The 1890s were also a period in which deaf art flourished. Many deaf people painted in their leisure time, and had their pictures exhibited, like William Agnew, S. Bright Lucas and James L.C. Docharty. Others painted professionally and relied on the sale of works of art to earn a living - these included Thomas Davidson, William Trood, Rupert Dent and John T. Rennie Reid.

This era was the age of many illustrated newspapers and magazines such as the *Graphic* and *Punch* magazine - Trood and Dent sold much of their work to these publications, as did Davidson on occasion.

Thomas Davidson (1842-1910)

Thomas Davidson became deaf at the age of four due to illness and was educated as a private pupil of Dr. Thomas Watson of the Old Kent Road Asylum. Upon the latter's death, he was educated at a hearing school in Clapham and thence at the Marlborough School of Art.

Thomas Davidson
Photo: British Deaf Times

From the very first, he painted professionally for a living and achieved fame primarily for his paintings of Nelsonian and Roman events. Most of his paintings were elaborate, detailed, large-scale affairs, some of which found their way to city municipalities in Canada and Australia

He was a regular attendant at services for the deaf held at St. Saviour's Church, and was on the committee of the Royal Association for the Deaf and Dumb. He was also one of the first members of the British Deaf Association when that was formed in 1890.

He died on 15th November 1910 whilst living in retirement at Walberswick, Suffolk, and is buried in St. Andrew's Church in the same plot of ground as his hearing wife

wife Charlotte, and painter son Allan Douglas Davidson (1873-1932).

Deaf Art in the 1890s

Battle of St. Vincent   by Thomas Davidson
Reproduced from the British Deaf Times

My Family   by William H.H. Trood
Reproduced by courtesy of Lawrence Fine Art, Crewkerne, Somerset

Ephphatha
by Thomas Davidson
*Reproduced by the permission
of the Royal School for Deaf
Children, Margate*

England's Glory
by Thomas Davidson
*Reproduced by the permission of the
National Maritime Museum, Greenwich*

William Henry Hamilton Trood (1859-1899)
Born in Taunton, Somerset to a wealthy coal merchant, he became deaf at the age of 5 due to illness.

Of his education little is known but it seems likely that his family engaged a private tutor for him - he may have also have been a private fee-paying pupil at the West of England School for the Deaf at Exeter.

William H. H. Trood
Photo: R. Cormack

He started painting professionally from an early age, and was soon contributing regularly to publications such as *Punch*, *Illustrated London News* and the *Graphic* newspaper. Many of his paintings were of dogs, generally in humorous and sentimental situations. He also contributed drawings of political satire, where politicians' faces were imposed on dogs.

William Trood was also an intrepid traveller, and once made a trip to Morocco, where he was presented with a silver-inlaid Damascus sword by the Sultan of Morocco.

He died, unexpectedly, after a short illness aged only 39 whilst staying at the Phoenix Hotel in Taunton.

William Frederick Mitchell (1854-1914)

Fred Mitchell was born deaf without speech at Calshot Castle, Hampshire, in 1845 and was educated at the Old Kent Road Institution in London.

He made his living as a lithographer and by painting pictures of ships for naval officers, and had an arrangement with Griffin's Bookshop in Portsmouth to take orders for his work, and the firm printed two volumes of *The Royal Navy in a Series of Illustrations*. The same firm framed and sold a lot of Mitchell's paintings.

Fred Mitchell, although he led a reclusive life at Ryde on the Isle of Wight, nonetheless took an active part in deaf community life. He was one of the first deaf people to join the British Deaf Association.

He died in Ryde in 1914, but in 1987, Ashford Press printed a book by Conrad Dixon titled *Ships of the Victorian Navy*. All 48 colour plates in this book were by Fred Mitchell, but the artist was barely mentioned in the credits. Many of his paintings are held by the National Maritime Museum, Greenwich.

Adventurers

It may be of interest to readers to detail two stories of born-deaf people who led an adventurous life during this period, for their experiences are unique.

Alexander Ferguson (1841-1889)

Alexander Ferguson was born deaf in Dundee, and was sent to the Edinburgh Institution for the Deaf and Dumb. Upon leaving the institution, he obtained employment as a mason in Dundee Docks.

What distinguished Alexander Ferguson from the rest of his fellow men was his exceptional ability as a swimmer. Starting as a boy of 10, he rescued a large number of people from drowning in various parts of Scotland and also in England. For some of these rescues, he was awarded medals, including one from the Royal Humane Society.

Alexander Ferguson
Photo: Deaf & Dumb Magazine

However, some of his more publicised swimming feats were done for cash, and include swims that the majority of exceptional swimmers would baulk at. For example, he swam across the Firth of Clyde on four occasions, and across the Firth of Forth on one occasion - perhaps his greatest and most dangerous feat was to swim across part of the often stormy Pentland Firth at the top of Scotland from John O'Groats to the island of Stroma.

Alexander Ferguson died in 1889 of pneumonia after making one swim too many.

Murdoch Macleod (1872-1951)

Murdoch Macleod was born in Edinburgh and educated at Donaldson's Hospital after which he was apprenticed to an Edinburgh tailoring firm, but this existence did not meet with his taste for adventure, so at the age of 19 he embarked on a steamer from Southampton to South Africa in 1892.

After working for a while in Capetown and Orange Free State to acquire funds, Macleod bought a wagon and eighteen oxen, and set out with his elder brother to trade with the tribesmen around Kimberley. Trading was carried out under a barter system - two blankets for a cow, and so on.

While in Matabeleland, Macleod was one of the 634 men

under Jamieson who declared war on the Zulu Chief Lobengula and defeated him. After a bad attack of malaria, Macleod worked in the Kimberley diamond mines, then took part in the Zulu War against Cetaweyo.

He was also one of those who formed the force that took part in the famous Dr. Jamieson's Raid that led to the outbreak of the Boer War, and after the war, was a farmer in Rhodesia for ten years before returning to Scotland, where he died in 1951.

Murdoch MacLeod with his brother in Matabeleland
Photo: The Deaf News

Chapter 9
Royalty and the Aristocracy

Tomb of Princess Katherine Plantagenet: Westminster Abbey
Photo: By courtesy of the Dean and Chapter of Westminster

CHAPTER 9

Royalty and the Aristocracy

There has never been a British monarch, or before the union of England and Scotland, an English or Scottish monarch, who was deaf.

There have, however, been several deaf Princes and Princesses, and a number of Dukes and Earls, and a Queen Consort (wife of a British King). Through these people, we find that links between deaf people and Royalty and the Aristocracy were quite strong.

The earliest known deaf royal was Princess Katherine Plantagenet, one of the daughters of King Henry III of England. She was born in 1253, and at the feast held on her christening on 5th January 1254, those assembled consumed 14 wild boars, 24 swans, 135 rabbits, 250 partridges, 50 hares, 250 wild duck, 1650 fowls, 36 female geese and 61,000 eggs.

By the age of two, which was when Princess Katherine next saw her father, the King, who had been away fighting wars in France, it was quite apparent that the Princess was deaf. She was also subject to frequent spells of illness, and she died at Windsor Castle on 3rd May 1257, only 3 years and 5 months old. Princess Katherine was buried in Westminster Abbey.

The next known deaf royal was Princess Jean, one of the daughters of King James I of Scotland. She was born in 1426, and Scottish records indicate that she was fragile but beautiful. She was never given any form of education, and spent much of her time secluded with her two sisters and her aunt, the Duchess of Rothesay. She was gifted at embroidery, and could communicate with her younger sister, Princess Eleanor, by signs. She died, aged 19, in 1445 before she could be married to James Douglas, third Earl of Angus.

The nearest Britain came to having a deaf monarch was in the case of Prince Albert Victor, eldest son of the Prince and Princess of Wales, later King Edward VII and Queen Alexandra. Prince Albert had inherited the hereditary disease, otosclerosis, from his mother who had herself inherited it from her own mother, Queen Louise of Denmark. However, Prince Albert Victor died of thyroid even before his father became King.

Queen Alexandra is probably the best-known deaf royal. She was already deaf when she married the Prince of Wales on 10th March 1863. Then aged 19, she looked every inch the fairy princess - incredibly beautiful. Her stunning good looks were to overwhelm her mother-in-law, Queen Victoria who was, however, heard to lament, 'Alas! She (the Princess): is deaf and everyone observes it, which is a sad misfortune.'

Queen Victoria had been overjoyed at her son the Prince of Wales's marriage to Alexandra, because of the increasing scandal of the Prince's bed-hopping and association with women of loose morals. However, the marriage did not stop the Prince's favourite pastime of bedding as many women as he could, though he became more discreet. Alexandra learnt to live with it, and her unfailing courtesy and thoughtfulness brought her closer to the elderly Queen, in spite of whatever misgivings they both shared about the erring Prince

Alexandra's deafness had also one unfortunate aspect in that, because she was not given any formal education, she frequently appeared unsophisticated. The Prince, and later also as the king, was often embarrassed in her presence and sometimes poked fun at her. On occasion, however, Alexandra would sometimes get her way and drag the Prince to services at the church she favoured, St. Saviour's Church for the Deaf in Oxford Street, where she could enjoy being in the company of other deaf people, and be able to follow the services, as she was a fluent fingerspeller.

Alexandra of Denmark (Queen of Edward VII)
Artist: L. Fildes
Reproduced by the courtesy of
The National Portrait Gallery, London

Indeed it was probably Queen Victoria herself who taught the Danish Princess the British fingerspelling method, as the Queen had become fluent in her younger days. (In 1874, whilst at her favourite residence at Osborne in the Isle of Wight, Queen Victoria made a number of trips to the post office at nearby Whippingham where she would stay for some hours comforting a dying deaf woman, Mrs. Elizabeth

Tuffield, nee Groves. Elizabeth Groves, as a young girl, had been befriended by the Queen who met the cost of her education at the London Asylum for the Deaf and Dumb. Latterly, Elizabeth had married but had been the victim of a cruel and brutal husband, and had retreated to her parents' home at the post office where she fell ill and later died. The Queen communicated with Mrs. Tuffield until the day she died. This association with Mrs. Tuffield explains Queen Victoria's ready acceptance of Princess Alexandra, and also explains her willingness to grant the prefix 'Royal' to a number of deaf schools throughout the country.

During her period as Queen Consort, and after the King's death as the Queen Dowager, Queen Alexandra would frequently purchase a number of works of deaf art and sculpture, especially if the work of art was of herself. A number of deaf artists and sculptors therefore enjoyed her patronage.

Queen Alexandra died in 1925 at the age of 81.

The Dukes and the Earls
Lesser known than Royalty's connection with deafness, but still of considerable interest are those deaf people who were born into the aristocracy. However, very little is known of any deaf aristocrats prior to 1750, but there were some in the nineteenth and twentieth centuries, a number of whom achieved political renown.

Amongst these was Lord Lytton (Sir Edward Bulwer-Lytton: 1803-1873) the novelist, who was a minister in Disraeli's Government. His deafness was a severe handicap in an assembly where quickness of hearing and readiness of speech were essential. On the other hand, his political opponents suffered too: Lord Lytton's speech was so bad that many people had great difficulty in understanding him, and because his deafness did not allow him to take part in debates, everyone was often forced to wait until the next day for any reply from Lord Lytton because he would insist on reading what had been said in Hansard, the Parliamentary publication, before making his own speech.

The Earl of Wemyss was another hearing-impaired states-man who made his mark in Parliament. He was especially noted for his hostility to the scheme to form a territorial army.

However, the deaf politican who did more for deaf people than any other politician apart from Jack Ashley was the 6th Duke of Montrose.

Sir James Graham, 6th Duke of Montrose (1878-1954)

Eldest son of the 5th Duke of Montrose, he was educated at Eton where he caught diptheria during the great floods of 1894. This was the cause of his deafness, which put paid to a planned career in the army and in politics. Deafness, how-ever, did not prevent him from going off to South Africa and taking part in the Boer War.

6th Duke of Montrose
Photo: By kind permission of the National Portrait Gallery, London

It was while he was travelling to South Africa in 1899 via India that he became the first man ever to take a cine-film of a total eclipse of the sun. After the South African War, he tried unsuccessfully to stand for the South African parliament before returning home to marry Lady Mary Douglas Hamilton.

In the 1914-1918 War, he was largely responsible for re-activating the Royal Naval Volunteer Reserve, and was appointed Commander of the Clyde Division, rising to Commodore in 1921 before retiring in 1927. While a naval officer, he invented and designed the first-ever aircraft carrier, the *Angus*.

On the death of his father, the 5th Duke, he succeeded to the Dukedom of Montrose, and took his seat in the House of Lords. It was in that House that he scored his greatest triumph for the cause of deaf people by persuading the Labour Government of Attlee that to provide free spectacles to the partially-sighted, free dentures to those whose teeth had rotted, free artificial limbs to the disabled, but to *actually charge* the sum of £10 to deaf people for National Health hearing-aids was blatant discrimination! By his speeches, he shamed Attlee's government into changing this policy so that free hearing-aids and batteries were available under the National Health Service. For many years, he served as President of the Royal National Institute for the Deaf, up to his death in 1954.

Incidently, the 2nd Duke of Montrose (1712-1790) was also deaf, unable to speak, and for the last thirty years of his life from 1760 onwards, totally blind as well and needed an interpreter for even everyday communication with his wife.

Other Dukes and Aristocrats (Non-political)
There have been a number of other dukes, earls and barons who were deaf but who have not aspired to political life. Perhaps the saddest instance was that of Philip Joseph Mary Fitzalan-Howard, (1879-1902) Earl of Surrey and Arundel and the eldest son of the then Duke of Norfolk, the premier British dukedom. He was born deaf, dumb and blind and was also mentally-deficient, and died in 1902 before he could

accede to the bewildering duties and titles that went with the Dukedom of Norfolk, Earl Marshal of England.

Another rather sad deaf aristocrat was the 2nd Duke of Sutherland (1786-1861) who was deaf all his life. He developed a hopeless love for the Queen of Prussia, which was not returned. On her death, he became dangerously ill with grief but recovered sufficiently to marry the granddaughter of the 5th Duke of Devonshire. At least, she could understand him for her uncle, later to be the 6th Duke, was deaf as well.

William Spencer Cavendish, 6th Duke of Devonshire (1790-1858)

'Hart', as he was known to his friends, became severely deaf in early childhood, which caused him to become reserved and studious.

Sixth Duke of Devonshire
Artist: Sir George Hayter
Devonshire Collection, Chatsworth
Reproduced by permission of The Chatsworth Settlement Trustees

He was never at ease in large company but preferred the few friends he made through his education at Eton and Cambridge.

His undoubted talents never blossomed in public life, and he devoted himself to an immense rebuilding and renovation programme at Chatsworth House, Derbyshire, where he loved to spend many hours in the library.

It was he, the 6th Duke, that turned Chatsworth into one of the biggest tourist attractions in the country today. His chief fame rests not on any achievement of his own, but on that of his protege, Sir Joseph Paxton. Paxton was a young gardener at Chatsworth when, encouraged by the 6th Duke, he built a giant conservatory 300 feet long, 145 feet wide by 60 feet high which soon attracted the world's attention and led to Paxton being commissioned to build the Crystal Palace for the Exhibition of 1851. (The conservatory at Chatsworth was sadly demolished after World War I but many of Paxton's improvements still remain to be seen).

The 6th Duke never married, and died in 1858 a rather disappointed and unhappy man.

The connection of deafness with the Dukes of Devonshire persists to this day: the 11th Duke is Patron of the National Deaf Children's Society, and also of the Royal School for the Deaf, Derby. It is through the generosity of the 11th Duke that the Duke's Barn Countryside Centre, a marvellous study and conference centre on the Chatsworth estate, was presented to the school in 1986.

Note: Reports that the 10th Duke of Devonshire was also deaf are incorrect.

George Percy Patrick, Baron Carbery (1810-1890)

Perhaps the one aristocrat that felt the greatest affinity with his fellow deaf was Lord Carbery, who was born deaf and never spoke in his life.

Lord Carbery was born in Co. Wexford, Ireland, and was sent to the Institution for the Deaf and Dumb at Paris after no expense had been spared educating him at home.

He lived for most of the time at his family seat at Laxton Hall, Northamptonshire, with his wife and only daughter, and frequented St. Saviour's Church for the Deaf in London. He contributed heavily from his family wealth to this Church, and also to many other organisations for deaf children and adults both in Britain and on the continent of Europe; he had a special interest in the deaf people of Ireland, and was the first President of the National Deaf and Dumb Society, forerunner of the British Deaf Association.

Lord Carbery
Photo: The British Deaf Times

Chapter 10
The 1900s

**Members of the Committee of
Winchester Diocesan Deaf Mission**
*Photo: Hampshire, Isle of Wight and Channel Islands Association
for the Deaf*

The 1900s

Around the turn of the century, oralism was at its most fervent in British schools for the deaf while at the same time many deaf people were extremely worried by the lack of education being given. Time which might have been devoted to instructing deaf children in the acquisition of English grammar, arithmetic and other school subjects was, in the view of many leading deaf people including deaf businessmen like A.J.Wilson and George Edward, being curtailed in order to try and give deaf children speech training.

Even Abraham Farrar, pointed out by oralists as the most exalted example of their method of teaching, showed concern that oralism was being carried to too great an extreme at the expense of education but this concern fell on 'deaf' ears of those in teaching establishments though perhaps not that of Dr. Eichholz the Government inspector for the overseeing of deaf education, as the two extracts opposite taken from the logbook of the Hugh Bell School, Middlesbrough, show.

Two schools for the deaf which were opened in the 1900s were both from the start to establish a pure oralist tradition. These were the Anerley Deaf School in London, founded in 1902, and the Thomasson Memorial School for the Deaf, Bolton, founded in 1907. Of these two, only the Thomasson Memorial School survives to this day, and now includes a further education department where sign language is used in the curriculum.

Also opened, in 1905, was the Sir James E. Jones Industrial Training School attached to the Royal Residential Schools for the Deaf at Old Trafford which sought to teach school-leavers the bootmaking, tailoring, carpentry and bakery trades.

June 27th Dr Eichholtz examined the class this morning, & expressed himself satisfied with the progress made. Suggested that all the Manual lessons should be made Language ones as well. That the present manual work be continued, but suggested rug-making for the boys, & paper flower making for the girls as pleasant work. Strictly Prohibited signing & finger spelling, & advised

Extract from the log book of the Hugh Bell School. Middlesbrough - June 1899

31st of October.

9.11.10 A. Eichholz

Dr Eichholz recommended that finger-spelling should be used instead of Speech. especially in memorizing facts. and more attention should be given to the writing of Series Actions.

9.11.10 Half holiday given by the Mayor.

Extract from the log book of the Hugh Bell School, eleven years later in Nov. 1910 - fingerspelling and signs to be used to give language

(Note: The use of the term 'manual' here does not refer to the use of sign language and/or fingerspelling but to the learning of trades such as carpentry etc.)

Meanwhile many intelligent deaf people who might have gone into education, but now finding these opportunities non-existent because of the Education Act of 1893 which had implemented the Royal Commission for the Education of the Blind and the Deaf and Dumb's recommendations, were now turning to missioner positions in deaf societies and institutes for a living.

Although many were appointed to established societies and institutes some were to found their own missions - such was the case of George Annand Mackenzie, the first born-deaf man in Britain to get a M.A. degree.

George Annand Mackenzie
Photo: British Deaf Times

George Annand Mackenzie, M.A. (1871-1951)

George Annand Mackenzie was born in Liverpool, one of three deaf brothers. Up to the age of 13, he was privately educated by his mother by means of signing and fingerspelling as she did not agree with the oralist method used by the Liverpool School for the Deaf. In this, she was ably assisted by Robert Armour, the deaf missioner for Liverpool.

When 13, Mackenzie was sent to be educated at a hearing school where the teachers did not know what to do with him, and left him to his own devices a lot of the time. Even so, he came top of the class in many subjects. After two years at this school, he left to study at the School of Art in South Kensington, where he won many prizes.

In 1901, he accepted the post of Missioner to the Deaf and Dumb in Oxford; it was here that an undergraduate suggested he should try for a University degree at Oxford, but permission was refused.

In 1906, he went to Cambridge to found the Mission for the Deaf and Dumb, and it was here that he entered University.

His deafness debarred him from lectures, and he was unable to avail himself of the help of tutors, but he persevered and he graduated in 1911, overnight becoming front-page news as the only deaf man (then) to achieve the academic distinction of Master of Arts of Cambridge University.

George Annand Mackenzie was active in the work of the British Deaf Association and was to be Missioner at Cardiff after leaving Cambridge in 1922, retiring in 1931. He was unique amongst deaf men of the early twentieth century.

Deaf Clubs and Missions: The National Deaf Club

The 1900s saw the opening of a number of new centres and missions for the deaf, among them Bury, West Ham, Plymouth and Chester (although the latter had first been meeting at Stockport from 1889 onwards).

However, probably the most important organisation formed in this decade was the National Deaf Club, formed in the autumn of 1906.

The title was then, as it still is now, largely a misnomer borne out of optimism for a nationwide club membership of deaf people. It is true that the National Deaf Club attracted a few members from the provinces, but by and large, its membership has been confined mostly to London and its environs.

It was originally founded as the Deaf Friends' Club for the oral deaf who desired to have the opportunity of meeting together for social intercourse and mutual improvement. The first meeting place was above a cafe in Newgate Street in the City of London, but this did not prove satisfactory and they then met on a weekly basis at another cafe near Marble Arch.

It was in September 1908 that the club moved to rented premises in Store Street and changed its name to the National Deaf Club and opened its membership to deaf people of whatever school, not just oralist. It was the first deaf club in the country to levy an annual subscription charge.

Membership of the National Deaf Club tended to attract those deaf people of a certain social standing, and included S. Bright Lucas (who was the first President), wealthy businessman A.J. Wilson, the artist Thomas Davidson, the editor of the *British Deaf Times*, Joseph Hepworth, explorer and photographer Henry Newton-Lowry, and the type of activities pursued tended to reflect the membership: chess, table-cricket, tennis, badminton.

Notwithstanding the type of membership, the formation of the National Deaf Club was an important development for deaf people, for through it there grew the camaraderie that we see today in the deaf community - a sense of belonging to a body that was quite acceptable in social terms.

One of their most distinguished members was a C.J. Bromhead who was unique amongst deaf people in that he was a Fellow of the Royal Meteorological Society with responsibility for weather observation in Lincoln. Bromhead had been educated at the private school for the deaf in Rugby and was a fluent writer and reader of German, French and Latin.

However, perhaps the National Deaf Club's most distinguished member was Arthur James Wilson, who succeeded S. Bright Lucas to the presidency and held it for the rest of his life.

Arthur James Wilson (1858- 1945)

Cyclist, Racing Driver; Businessman

Born with normal hearing, he became deaf from scarlet fever when 12 years old. His education following the onset of deafness was self-acquired due to reading and writing.

Arthur Wilson was better known to thousands, perhaps millions, of his countrymen in Britain and Ireland as 'Faed', the pen-name by which he contributed hundreds of articles on cycling to cycling magazines, including his own, and published books on the sport.

Arthur James Wilson
Photo: British Deaf Times

A keen cyclist, having ridden one of the original boneshakers in 1869, he once cycled 3200 miles in a year competing in races. He founded two cycling associations - the North Road Cycling Club and Cyclists' Road Records Association, of which he was President for nearly 30 years - an unique achievement for a deaf man in a mainly hearing organisation.

Arthur Wilson was also the first deaf Briton to own a car, (in 1896) and competed in races not only in cars or on cycles, but also on motor bikes. He was probably the first deaf man in the world to do so.

A keen all-round sportsman, he graduated from cycle and motor-car racing when he began to feel his age and then to speedboat racing. He owned a motor launch named *Splash* which he lost to the Navy in the war.

This was the man who became President of the National

Deaf Club in 1909 and held the position for over thirty years. He was also the founder of Coventry Institute for the Deaf. During the war he used his wealth to establish the Sir Frederick Milner Hostels for Deafened Soldiers, and served as Chairman.

The Motor Launch Splash
Photo: British Deaf Times

After the war, he was made a Freeman of London, again a unique achievement for a deaf man.

He died in Leamington in 1945 at the age of 87.

George Edward (1867-1929)
Another successful deaf businessman and sportsman of the 1900s was George Edward of Glasgow, a partner in the manufacturing jewellery firm of G. Edward and Sons.

George Edward
Photo: British Deaf Times

Born deaf, and educated partly at the Langside Institution, Glasgow and partly at William Van Praagh's Oral School in London, George Edward was a fine designer of silver cups, challenge shields and the like, and also a fine yachtsman who won many trophies in his racing yachts *Osprey* and *Majel*. He was also associated with the Glasgow Institute for the Deaf as a director.

Abraham Farrar, F.G.S. (1861-1936)
Third in this trilogy of deaf men of remarkable achievements of this era who were mainly oralist but who respected those that used sign language was Abraham Farrar, born at Leeds, who became deaf at the age of 3 due to scarlet fever. His father had an estate near Leeds which yielded a considerable income, and which later helped Farrar to pursue his academic quest.

Abraham Farrar
Photo: British Deaf Times

Farrar was educated at the Rev. Thomas Arnold's private oral school at Northampton and was a child prodigy who passed both the London University and Cambridge University examinations by the time he was 17, and could no doubt have gone on towards a degree had he been inclined to do so . His father, however, preferred that Farrar went in for a professional career, and Farrar was articled to a firm of architects and surveyors in Northampton, becoming a Fellow of the Geographical Society.

On his father's death, Farrar abandoned his professional career content to live off the income from his father's estate which he managed admirably, and instead concentrated on what was to be his lifetime's consuming interest - the compilation of literature on deafness.

'Farrar was the first real researcher into the history of teaching the deaf, and unearthed many previously unknown items of literature about the deaf and was largely responsible for building up Oxley's Library of the Deaf (this Library was largely fragmentated after Oxley's death, and many rare articles and books disappeared).

Although scrupulously fair in his writings on deaf history, neither favouring use of sign language or oralism, constantly giving credit where this was due to either method, Abraham Farrar was always regarded by oralists as the greatest triumph for the oral method of teaching the deaf, though Francis Maginn once told a B.D.D.A Congress that 'Oral' pupils could not be kept from signing. Even Mr. Farrar spelt on his fingers very well.'

> *Author's Note* :- The compilation of earlier chapters of this book could not have been possible without Abraham Farrar's researches to point the way.

The Rise of Deaf Women

The 1900s were also to see for the first time deaf women beginning to acquire their own identity through achievement by their own talent although not one as yet played any prominent part in deaf organisations which remained the preserve of the deaf male. Three women were to achieve national renown in this decade, two of them as sculptors, and one as Christmas-card Laureate.

Helen Marion Burnside (1844 - 1920)

Born at Bromley Hall, Middlesex, Helen Burnside became totally deaf at the age of 12 and learnt sign language so that she could communicate - she never mastered the art of lipreading.

Helen Marion Burnside
Photo: Glasgow Evening Times

Up to the time of her deafness, she had ambitions to be a music composer but her deafness put paid to that. Instead, she turned to writing and discovered a talent for writing verses, particularly Christmas verses.

From 1864 onwards, Miss Burnside wrote about 200 Christmas verses a year which were used in Christmas cards. Many of the verses were in fact small poems, and some were set to music.

Her greatest compliment came in 1900 when she was accorded the title of Christmas-card Laureate which earned her national fame.

Kathleen Trousdell Shaw, R.H.A. (1870-1958)

Born in Middlesex of an Irish doctor, she grew up in a pleasant and comfortable home in Ireland and was 5 years old when she noticed that her hearing was failing, and by the age of 17, she was almost totally deaf.

Her gift for sculpture was first observed when she was nine years old, still uneducated, and watching a stonemason at work in the local churchyard. She stood there for hours watching the stonemason so that when he returned the next day, he gave her a piece of stone and two chisels. At once, she set to work and made such a remarkable copy of a Michelangelo that she was sent, when ten years old, to the Dublin School of Art where she learnt drawing and sculpture.

She gained medals and prizes which enabled her, at age 15, to go to Paris where she was accepted into the free Ecole des Beaux Arts and studied under the most eminent French artists and sculptors.

Silver and Bronze War Memorial Font of Mother and Baby in Cadmore End Parish Church
Photo: Author's collection

Returning briefly to Dublin, she next went to Rome and Athens to do more studying before coming to work in the British Museum, and going to live in Knutsford, Cheshire, where she did her greatest work, the bust of Archbishop Alexander, Primate of All Ireland, which stands today in Armagh Cathedral.

For this, and other sculptures in Ireland, she was made a Member of the Royal Hiberian Academy in 1907. She was the first woman sculptor, and only deaf woman, to be made a member of any Royal Academy in the British Isles.

Miss Shaw retired to the little village of Cadmore End, near High Wycombe after the 1914-18 war. She designed and made a gift to the village of a beautiful war memorial - a font cover in bronze and silver of a mother and baby.

She stayed in Cadmore End until her death in 1958.

Dorothy Stanton Wise (c1880-1918?)

Dorothy Stanton Wise was born deaf at Dover where she was educated at home by her mother who had taken her to see the Rev. Thomas Arnold at Northampton for advice.

Dorothy Stanton Wise
Photo: British Deaf Times

She also attended a kindergarten school where she first

demonstrated her talent for modelling with clay. When her kindergarten time was up, her parents engaged a modelling tutor to come in twice a week, and she was so good that at the age of 7 she was admitted to the Dover School of Art where she stayed until she was eighteen. Her parents then moved to London and admitted her as a free scholar to the sculpture studio in the Royal College of Art, where she stayed for four years and graduated an A.R.C.A.

'Demester' by D.S. Wise
Photo: British Deaf Times

Then she started to earn her living by designing and sculpting many items of distinction and merit, earning gold medals at exhibitions at the Royal Academy, Manchester Art Gallery and Liverpool's Walker Art Gallery. A number of her sculptures were also sold to Queen Alexandra.

One of her best-known works is a marble memorial to Bishop Prideaux which is in Worcester cathedral. Miss Wise was a strong supporter of the B.D.D.A. and wrote a number of articles for the British Deaf Times, mostly about travel in France.

No works of art were produced by Miss Wise, nor was she

heard of again after 1918; she is believed to have been one of the victims of the influenza epidemic of that time.

Gallaudet College Student's Courage

John W. McCandless was born in 1884 in Londonderry, the son of a Justice of the Peace, and became deaf at the age of 10 months through scarlet fever, and was sent to the Langside Institution at Glasgow, Scotland.

Following a desire for further education, he was admitted into Gallaudet College, Washington D.C., USA., in 1903.

In April 1905, the wife of a lock-keeper in the canal near the Potomac River at Great Falls made a trip in her rowing boat across the river to the Virginia shore accompanied by her two dogs.

Unknown to Mrs. O'Connor, for that was the woman's name, the river was rising and the current becoming stronger. When she returned to her boat, she did not notice this, and proceeded to row back to her lock-house.

However, the strong current carried her away, sweeping her over a weir where the boat overturned. A strong swimmer, she managed to reach a rock jutting above the water, and there she stuck; it would have been suicidal to attempt to swim through the rapids to either shore.

McCandless, accompanied by a Canadian student named Arthur Jaffray, spotted Mrs. O'Connor about an hour later and whilst Jaffray ran for a boat and some ropes, McCandless with complete disregard for the dangers, fought his way through the strong current to reach Mrs. O'Connor and supported her until Jaffray arrived in a boat with the woman's father. The boat was wedged across a rock where the current was not as bad as that elsewhere, and they threw a rope across to McCandless who tied it around himself and the near-unconscious woman. They were both then hauled through the treacherous water to the boat, but while paddling for the shore, the current seized the boat and it capsized throwing everyone into the water.

McCandless kept the woman with him and reached

183

another rock, to which he clung totally exhausted. The woman's father and Jaffray also reached the same rock. Jaffray left them there, and battled across to the shore on his own where he summoned other help. A rope was thrown across to the three marooned on the rock, and they were hauled to safety, McCandless still carrying Mrs. O'Connor.

The whole rescue took four hours, and Dr. E.M. Gallaudet, Principal of the College, recommended McCandless and Jaffray to the British authorities for the Albert Medal (the highest civilian award in Britain and the British Empire at that time, since superseded by the George Cross). However, this award was not given.

McCandless stayed on in the U.S.A. as a teacher of the deaf (deaf teachers not being permitted in Britain) at the Mississippi School for the Deaf. He died in 1965.

Two Successful Football teams

An excellent achievement was made by the boys of the Royal Institution for the Deaf and Dumb, Derby in 1902-3.

Derby Elementary Schools F.A. Champions 1902-3
Photo: Royal School for the Deaf, Derby

In an open competition involving the elementary schools throughout Derbyshire, the deaf schoolboys won the championship.

Manchester Deaf F.C. League Champions 1905-6
Photo: British Deaf Times

Amongst adult clubs, there was some success as well when Manchester Deaf F.C. won their local hearing league championship.

The same young men celebrated their success by taking a holiday in the Isle of Man later that summer.

Manchester Young Men's Camp on the Isle of Man
Photo: Manchester Centre for the Deaf

Teacher of the Deaf Journal

In 1903, the first issue of the journal *Teacher of the Deaf* was published.

It is still being published, and is the longest continuous magazine about or of the deaf in Britain which still bears the same title.

Chapter 11
The 1910s

Fire Drill Practice, Royal School for the Deaf, Derby - 1910s
Photo: School Archives

Chapter 11

The 1910s

The beginning of the decade saw storm clouds gathering over Europe with displays of militarism and aggressiveness which were ultimately to lead to the Great War of 1914-18 when millions of soldiers died in the mud-filled trenches of Flanders and experienced other horrors such as Gallipoli.

British deaf men and women were spared much of this horror, and went on with their lives, but they were having a grim time of it too. The introduction of the National Insurance and Workmen's Compensation Acts meant that many employers were becoming reluctant to employ deaf people in case they had to pay higher premiums just to employ them. The result was that many deaf men were unable to obtain work.

The decade also saw the passing away of many of the old stalwart deaf missioners, such as James Paul, and they were being replaced by hearing missioners. The Milan Congress of 1880, having successfully removed deaf people from teaching positions in deaf schools, was now seeing the process being carried a little further by quite unintentionally closing the doors on employment of deaf people as missioners. Here and there, deaf people were still being appointed, like Edwin Docharty at Blackburn, but already, they were a dying breed.

The welfare of deaf people was thus becoming a grave concern to many people, and this led in 1911 to an important milestone being reached through the efforts of a wealthy merchant banker, a Mr. Leo Bonn, who was himself deaf.

The Founding of the Royal National Institute for the Deaf
On 9th June 1911, Leo Bonn founded the National Bureau for Promoting the General Welfare of the Deaf, a cumbersome title which was quite sensibly reconstructed as the National Institute for the Deaf in 1924.

Leo Bonn
Photo: Royal National Institute for the Deaf

The Bonn family financed the Bureau for a number of years and enabled it to recruit a small staff which laid the foundations for the development of the organisation into what it is to-day.

The Institute moved into its present premises at 105 Gower Street, London, in 1936 and was granted the prefix 'Royal' in its Jubilee Year in 1961.

The Growth of Institutes and Centres for the Deaf
The general concern over the welfare of deaf people led to the formation of more institutes and to centres for the deaf being opened in towns and cities where previously none had

existed. This included important towns and cities such as Coventry and Brighton, but others were also opened in Pontypridd, Salisbury, Cambridge, and Exeter - the last being one of the last cities where a deaf school had been long established to found an adult institute.

The Cardiff Institute for the Deaf
Photo: British Deaf Times

In London, the St. John of Beverley Institute, Green Lanes, was opened by H.R.H. Princess Christian for the R.A.D.D.

In other areas, the name 'Mission to the Deaf' was beginning to be dropped as new buildings replaced older ones. This happened in Cardiff when the new institute was opened - the institute was a gift from a local philanthropist, John Cory, who paid for its erection.

In other long-established deaf centres, members began to arrange day outings now that omnibuses were more readily available, and these were to be a feature of deaf life in the next few decades.

In Liverpool, the Jubilee of the Society was celebrated by a special service in the Institute's church at Princes Street where a tribute was paid to George Healey for his 50 years of service to the deaf people of Liverpool.

Merseyside Centre for the Deaf
(now vacated)
Photo: Author's collection

In London, the National Deaf Club boasted as a member a Henry John Jacobs, who was a barrister of the Inner Temple. He was not the only deaf person connected with the legal profession for Wakefield, Yorkshire, had a fully practising solicitor, Gerald Smith, of the firm Beaumont, Smith and Beaumont, who had been educated at the Yorkshire Institution for the Deaf and Dumb, Doncaster.

The President of the National Deaf Club, A.J. Wilson, donated the first national trophies to be played for at golf and at billiards. The first golf tournament took place on 27th October 1914 at the North Middlesex Golf Club, and was won by Eric Withers of Liverpool, with George Healey (also Liverpool) and Maxwell S. Fry (Coventry) as runners-up.

Three Scenes from the Margate School, 1910s
Photos supplied by J Hammond

Scenes of Outdoor Gymnastics, Margate School, 1910s
Photo supplied by Mrs A. Humphrey

Southampton Deaf Members
Photo: Hampshire, I.O.W. & Channel Islands Assoc. for the Deaf

Charabancs & Picnics

Cambridge Deaf Members
Photo: Ely Diocesan Association for the Deaf

Members of Clapham, St. Bede's
Photo: W. Hallett

Members of the Leeds Centre for the Deaf
Photo: Leeds Centre for the Deaf

Members of Oxford and Reading Deaf Clubs en route to Radley College   *Photo: Ronald Lee*

Bristol Deaf Members
Photo: Bristol Centre for the Deaf

**Oxford and Reading Deaf Members
at Lunch in Radley College**
Photo: Ronald Lee

Cambridge Members at a Christmas Gathering, 1913
Photo: Ely Diocesian Association for the Deaf

Air Travel

In July 1914 air travel was still a novelty to many people and during an outing by employees of an Accrington firm of billiard table makers to Blackpool, a deaf employee named Jack Hargreaves became possibly the first deaf man ever to go up in an aeroplane when he went up as a passenger in a two-seater Fokkers biplane piloted by a Mr. H. Blackburn.

The flight lasted over an hour as the plane was flown out to sea, returning over Fleetwood, then back to Blackpool.

Bomb Plot Foiled!

It was also during this decade that women first became entitled to vote in elections in Britain, but not before they led a very militant, suffragette campaign to get the right.

Women would chain themselves to railings, throw themselves under horses and do a dozen other crazy things in the cause of suffragettism.

Dunhope Castle where a bomb failed to go off

In 1914 they launched what was one of their crazier attacks, and on 4th June, the deaf community of Dundee was very nearly the victim when a massive bomb was placed against the doorway of Dunhope Castle, the home of Dundee School for the Deaf and the Dundee Mission to the Deaf and Dumb.

The bomb had a lengthy fuse attached to it, and when it was discovered by one of the schoolboys, the fuse was burnt almost up to the bomb. But for this timely find, Dundee School for the Deaf would have been blown to pieces, along with the Deaf Centre.

Sir Arthur Henderson Fairburn, Bart. (1852-1915)

The decade saw the death in 1915 of one of the greatest supporters of the British deaf community in Sir Arthur Henderson Fairbairn, who rejoiced in the title of 'the only deaf and dumb baronet in the world'. The British landed gentry can look back on a past filled with special glories due to the responsibilities of their rank.

Sir Arthur H. Fairbairn, Bart.
Photo: British Deaf Times

Sir Arthur Fairbairn was a man great enough to shoulder these responsibilities gracefully, tirelessly and successfully, leaving behind him some concrete examples of generosity and philanthropy as well as the memory of a genial heart and a simple soul doing good in an aristocratic manner.

Sir Arthur Fairbairn was born deaf to Sir Thomas Fairbairn, and was the grandson of Sir William Fairbairn who was a great inventor and builder of bridges and dockyards which earned him a fortune. His sister, Constance, was also born deaf but the youngest child, James, was not.

He was educated at the private school for the deaf at Rugby, and then by private tutors - all entirely by sign language and fingerspelling, as was his sister. Neither Sir Arthur or Constance Fairbairn could speak or lipread throughout their lives.

Sir Arthur married a Florence Long in 1882, a marriage that was useful to him in social circles as his brother-in-law was a powerful Member of Parliament, but Sir Arthur's true love was reserved for British deaf people. He was never ashamed of being deaf without speech when he moved in society, and mingled with deaf people on every possible occasion.

He was a tireless worker for the cause of deafness, opening many missions and institutes, attending many bazaars and functions to which he always managed to bring influential friends who would spend money freely. He was a President or Vice President of many deaf organisations, including the Royal School for Deaf Children, Margate; the Charitable and Provident Society for Granting Pensions to the Aged and Infirm Deaf; London Deaf Cricket Club; the London branch of the B.D.D.A. He was also a committee member of the Brighton Institution for the Deaf and Dumb, and of the Winchester Deaf Diocesan Mission. As treasurer of the R.A.D.D., he once balanced the books, which had a serious deficit, with a handsome donation.

St. Saviour's Church for the Deaf owed its new electric lighting and heating system to his generosity, and he contributed to many deaf charities.

He was President of the Reception Committee of the 8th Biennial Congress of the British Deaf and Dumb Association in 1903 when he received his guests with magnificent and lavish hospitality.

Although in poor health in 1912, he accepted an offer to be chairman of the delegates to the Congress of the Deaf in Paris 1912 on their visit to London and entertained them lavishly.

His name lives on in the Fairbairn Centre for the Deaf, Southampton, where he was a committee member for many years.

Dr. Francis Maylett Smith (1877-1945)

Francis (Frank) Maylett Smith became totally deaf at the age of 20 after receiving an education at St. Paul's School in London. When he was in his teens, his father moved to South Africa taking the family with him. Having secretly decided during his childhood to be a doctor, he had to give the idea up due to his deafness and decided to take up a farming career, enrolling at the Elsenberg Agricultural College, 30 miles from Cape Town.

Dr. F. M. Smith
Photo: D. H. Crofton

Whilst studying at the College, Frank was instrumental in bringing an unconscious man round, and was henceforth known to his fellow-students as 'the doctor', and every day thereafter had some 'visits' to make. Although Frank obtained a first-class diploma from the College, he did not find an opening in farming and his thoughts turned once more to medicine for which his experiences at College led him to think he had an aptitude.

Frank returned to England, and after years of study at Steevens' Hospital, Dublin, qualified as a doctor.

To be totally deaf was bound to be a professional handicap, and after some difficulty, Frank managed to secure the post of assistant doctor in the South Wales coalfield of Aberffrwd, where he served his apprenticeship as a general practitioner from 1908 until 1915.

In 1915 he learnt of a doctor's practice going for sale at Collier's Forge, near Stourbridge in the Midlands. The retiring doctor had advertised the practice as covering a small town of 8000 people, and that there was no other doctor in the locality. It sounded promising to a young man seeking his first practice, and he bought it.

Dr. Francis Maylett Smith remained the General Practitioner at Collier's Forge until his retirement in 1933.

Although there have been other doctors in Britain who became deaf, Dr. Francis Maylett Smith remains only one of two deaf persons known to have successfully qualified as a doctor.

The Great War 1914-18

When the First World War broke out in 1914 schools were on holiday, which proved to be an advantage to the military authorities who promptly requisitioned the Yorkshire Institution for the Deaf at Doncaster and the Dundee School for the Deaf. Although the military authorities soon vacated the school to move into Doncaster Racecourse across the road, the re-opening of the school had been delayed and the Christmas holidays had to be cut to make up for the loss of time. Dundee was not so lucky, and had to seek alternative premises to continue the school.

In addition, the Non-Oral department at the Royal Residential Schools in Manchester was requisitioned as a military hospital for the duration of the war, and there was overcrowding in the Main School as a result.

The War drained men from many schools which then experienced great difficulty in maintaining staffing levels. A number of deaf men attempted to enlist for the Army, but many were rejected on grounds of deafness, including four who tried to enlist in one day at an enlisting station in Wales.

Clyne House - The Non-Oral Department of The Royal Residential Schools for the Deaf, Manchester
Requisitioned as a Military Hospital, 1914-1918
Photo: Royal Schools for the Deaf (Manchester)

Two men, however, both of whom came from Cardiff, succeeded in enlisting for different regiments.

Harry Ward, a 27-year-old born-deaf man orally educated at the Llandaff School in Cardiff and possessing excellent lipreading skills, managed to follow his three brothers into the Munster Regiment and undergo training at the Curragh Camp in Ireland.

Gower Jones, who was also educated at the Llandaff School, managed to enlist in the Monmouthshire Regiment despite being blind in one eye.

Another deaf man, a David Bedwell who had partial hearing, enlisted in the Army Service Corps as a driver, and his deafness cost him his life when he failed to hear three challenges as he was approaching the gates of a barracks. The sentry on duty shot him through the head.

Harry Ward   **Gower Jones**

In contrast, the nearest most deaf people got to the War was to receive training in rifle practice and to learn how to dig trenches in case the Germans managed to invade.

A number were unfortunate enough to be mistaken for spies after 'failing to heed warning challenges', and got shot at, although there was only one reported death: a James Waddell of Grangemouth, near Edinburgh, was shot through the hand and heart as he was examining flood damage in the course of his employment duties.

Francis Maginn, the Belfast Missioner and B.D.D.A. Vice-President, suffered the indignity of being arrested as a suspected spy while visiting Glasgow.

It was in fact some of the deaf schoolchildren who came

closest to experiencing the horrors of the 1914-18 War. On the night of 2nd April 1916, air-raid warnings sounded throughout Edinburgh, but it was not till five minutes past midnight when a huge explosion shook the city. A German Zeppelin had flown over the Scottish coast at Leith, and dropped a bomb which by pure luck hit a bonded warehouse full of whisky, which went up in large flames, thus lighting up the darkened city. Donaldson's Hospital and the nearby George Watson Hospital School, both impressive buildings, provided tempting targets, and received some bombs. Donaldson's took a near miss, but George Watson's was not so lucky, its top two floors being destroyed. The Zeppelin moved up towards the Castle, dropping large numbers of bombs but many fell short of the Castle. However, another whisky warehouse went up, illuminating beautifully the imposing building that is Donaldson's. It was too tempting a target, and the Zeppelin aimed for it with the last of its deadly cargo, but this time, they overshot the mark. The Zeppelin attack left ten people dead in the city, and scores wounded: if the Germans' bomb-aiming had not been so lousy, the toll could have included many of the sleeping deaf children in Donaldson's.

As it was, George Scott - who was later to captain the victorious Great Britain soccer team at the World Games for the Deaf at Amsterdam in 1928 (see photograph on page 310) - but then a small schoolboy at Donaldson's remembers:

'..a German Zeppelin flew over but I felt nothing. I was fast asleep. Next morning I awoke to chaos - everything overturned, furniture all over, beds moved, tables tipped over..'

Many windows were shattered all over Edinburgh, including many at Donaldson's - its most grievous loss was perhaps the oriel window in the chapel famed in Scotland as one of its earliest figure-stained windows. It was never replaced.

There was one positive side for deaf people arising from

the War: with so many men volunteering or going into the Armed Services, there was a desperate shortage of labour in the workplace, especially in munitions factories. Whereas before the War so many deaf men were out of work due to the reluctance of employers following the implementation of the National Insurance and Workmens' Compensation Acts, they were now able to pick and choose their employment as employers clamoured for their services.

Chapter 12
Scouts, Girl Guides and Cadets

Deaf Cadets
Photo: Northern Counties School for the Deaf, Newcastle

Chapter 12

Scouts, Girl Guides and Cadets

Deaf schools in Britain have traditionally had a long involvement in the Scout and Girl Guide movement, but Scouting has not been confined simply to schoolboys and schoolgirls. Between the wars, many deaf centres also had their Senior Scout and Rover troops.

The Boy Scout movement was formed by General Baden-Powell, the hero of Mafeking, in 1908 with the object of training boys how to become real men and to learn the lessons of loyalty, courage, obedience, cheerfulness and kindness of heart, and its ideals soon spread throughout the world.

The British Deaf Scout movement was born in 1910 when the Headmaster of the Royal Cross School, Preston, Mr. J.G. Shaw, was on a motor tour of Yorkshire during his July holiday, and got into severe difficulties at Skipton when his car ran off the road and broke down. Luckily for him, there was a troop of Boy Scouts camped nearby and they were able to get his car back on the road and Mr. Shaw on his way to York.

Impressed by the Boy Scouts he had encountered, Mr. Shaw resolved to start a troop at his school, and when the pupils returned to school after the summer holidays in August 1910, the Royal Cross School Troop was formed, followed shortly afterwards by the Royal Cross School Guides Troop.

The movement in Preston was so successful that in 1911

the school organised a jamboree for the Scouts and Guides of the district, and a total of 420 Scouts and Guides from all parts of Preston and district took part. The rally was attended by the Chief Scout, General Baden-Powell. It was the biggest event the school ever organised.

Royal Cross School Boy Scout Troop
Britain's first Deaf Scout Troop
Photo: Royal Cross School Preston

The first adult Scout troop formed was the 1st Duke of Grafton's Own (Clapham St. Bede's) which was formed in 1913, and within a few years there were also Scouters and Guiders established in London at West Ham, Green Lanes (St. John of Beverley's), North Clapham and Stoke Newington. Other Scout and Guide movements were established at Leicester, Newcastle-upon-Tyne, Liverpool, Coventry and in Glasgow which produced the first deaf Senior Scout in George Scott who took part in a Grand Rally of Senior Scouts at Ibrox Park which was inspected by the Duke of Windsor in 1931.

Most Scout and Guide troops did not survive the Second World War. Those that did disbanded in the late 1940s or early 1950s and only the schools continued to have Scout troops; the 8th Exeter (Royal Deaf School) troop was, for example, formed in 1949 and from this troop came a Queen's Scout, Andrew Ford, who attended the St. George's Day Parade at Windsor Castle in 1955 before the Queen and the Duke of Edinburgh.

Another Scout who was presented before the Queen at Windsor Castle was Glen Harris of Coventry.

Several schools also had a Wolf Cub pack, many of which excelled in sports meetings against other Wolf Cub packs. Manchester's Royal Residential Schools Wolf Cub pack were victorious in three successive years sports competitions against other Wolf Cubs in the area from 1954 to 1956.

Some schools, like the Northern Counties School for the Deaf in Newcastle, had a Cadet Corps movement before they changed to scouting. This school's Cadet Corps scored an unique achievement when they participated in the Royal Tournament at Olympia in 1927, and carried off the Lady West Trophy against fierce competition from other, *hearing*, Cadet Corps troops.

Today, in the 1980s, the Scout and Guide movement is almost non-existent throughout British deaf schools and clubs for the deaf, perhaps due to competition from other leisure interests, but in its heyday, the movement was responsible for giving hundreds of young men and girls great fulfilment and sense of purpose.

1st Duke of Grafton's Own, 1919   *Photo: W. Hallett*

Stoke's Scout Troop, 1910s   *Photo: British Deaf Times*

1st Duke of Grafton's Own   *Photo: W. Hallett*

4th Preston   *Photo: Royal Cross School*

8th Exeter   *Photos: Andrew Ford*

4th Preston
Photo: Royal Cross School

1st Duke of Grafton's Own
Photo: W. Hallett

**Royal Residential Schools for the Deaf,
Manchester's Victorious Wolf Cub Troop Winning the Sports
Trophy for the Third Year**
Photo: Royal Schools for the Deaf, Manchester

212

Victorious Cadets
Top and Bottom: Winners of the Lady West Trophy in the
Royal Tournament at the Olympia, 1927: Northern Counties
School for the Deaf, Newcastle
Photos: School Archives

Senior Scouts and Queen's Scouts

**Glen Harris meeting the
Queen at Windsor Castle**
Photo: G. Harris

Andrew Ford
Photo: Andrew Ford

**George Scott of Glasgow (extreme right of picture
on parade before inspection by Prince of Wales, Ibrox Park,
1931**
Photo: Glasgow & West of Scotland Society for the Deaf.

Chapter 13
The 1920s

A Cycle Ride by Deaf Ladies in the 1920s
Photo: Royal Cross School, Preston

The 1920s

The 1920s was the decade of the General Strike, the stock market collapse, Prohibition in the USA, the first crossing of the Atlantic by an aeroplane (Charles Lindbergh), the decade during which the optimism of a 'Land fit for Heroes to Live in' turned sour with rising unemployment and widespread poverty. And the deaf suffered along with the rest.

In many ways their lot became much worse due to the effects of poor education and little prospect of work. Very few deaf men and women of ability came through to lead the rest: the clergy retained a powerful grip on the affairs of deaf people, and the age of paternalism was at a high.

One deaf person who did come through to play a leading role in deaf affairs was David Fyfe.

David Fyfe (1883-1967)
Born in Kilmarnock and educated at the Langside School for the Deaf, Glasgow, he began his adult career as an apprentice brass-finisher, but this vocation was never enough for him. Membership of the local deaf club developed his talent and ability to a point where he was drawn towards working full-time as a welfare worker with deaf people.

When the post of Missioner at Warrington became vacant, he applied for it at the age of 38, and he remained at Warrington until his retirement thirty years later.

He was an active member of the British Deaf and Dumb Association and one of the select band that received its Medal of Honour for services to the deaf.

David Fyfe
Photo: Warrington Society for the Deaf

The appointment of Fyfe to Warrington in 1921 was, however, the exception rather than the rule in the 1920s when the majority of missioners appointed or holding the posts were clergymen or hearing persons. Only three other deaf men became missioners for the first time in the 1920s, although some moved from one place to another like George Mackenzie. These three were Alex McDonald at Stockport, Algernon Barnett at Northampton and Harry Rowland at Cambridge. Like Fyfe, all three were to remain at these places until the end of their working lives.

Concern for Deaf Children's Health
There was so much poverty during the 1920s that there was grave concern for the general health of children in residential schools for the deaf. Tuberculosis and malnutrition were prevalent, as was rickets.

217

A number of residential schools therefore converted part of their buildings to, or constructed new, hospital wards or sick bays to combat the poor health of their pupils.

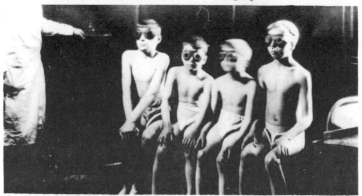

Children having Ultra-Violet Light Treatment
Photo: Royal School for the Deaf, Derby

Children in Sick Bay
Photo: Royal Schools for the Deaf, Manchester

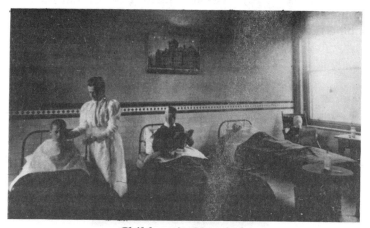

Children in Hospital
Photo: Royal School for the Deaf, Derby

A Deaf School Goes Overseas
In the 1920s, generally all state schools - whether for the deaf or for those with normal hearing - had conditions which were grim. This was especially true of those schools which were situated in poverty-stricken areas following the aftermath of the General Strike of 1926 and mass unemployment. There was little money available for luxuries, yet in 1928 a group of children from the Royal Cross School for the Deaf, Preston, made what may have been the first ever educational overseas school trip when they went to France and Belgium.

They travelled by ferry, and among the places that they visited were Paris, Lille and Bruges.

First Deaf Motorist Fined
A.J. Wilson, the President of the National Deaf Club, and the first deaf person to drive a car back in 1896, got another 'first' that was most unwelcome when he became the first deaf driver to fall foul of the road traffic laws and be fined for speeding.

To his chagrin, A.J. Wilson, a lifelong oralist and successful businessman, got headlines in the national newspapers describing him as 'deaf and dumb'.

Notre Dame de Paris
One of the sights visited by the schoolboys

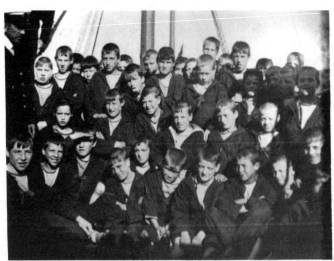

Group of Schoolboys on the Cross-Channel Ferry
Photos: Royal Cross School, Preston

Pupils and Staff
Photo: Yorkshire Residential School for the Deaf

A Classroom Activity
Photo: Royal Cross School, Preston

The Growth of Deaf Sports
One bright light in the depression of the 1920s was the tremendous growth of sports being played by deaf people. Regional competitions were held for most indoor sports like billiards, snooker and darts; many deaf institutes had their soccer teams with the B.D.D.A.'s annual Healey Cup being keenly fought for.

Some institutes did not ignore ladies sports - a number of hockey teams were formed and matches played. One of the keenly fought matches took place when Glasgow Ladies played Manchester Ladies in 1922.

The first International Games for the Deaf at Paris in 1924 created such interest that the B.D.D.A.'s Congress at Southampton included an international football match between England and Wales, which was won by England 3-0.

Swansea Deaf A.F.C. in the 1920s
Photo: Church of the Holy Name, Swansea

At cricket, Leicester Deaf Cricket Club became their local league Division I champions in 1927, and in 1929 the famous Lancashire and England batsman, Ernest Tydlesley, presented a cricket bat as a trophy for an annual Roses match between Lancashire Deaf and Yorkshire Deaf.

Club Outings and Charabancs

Adult deaf activities were not of course confined to sports. The advent of motor coaches enabled many deaf institutes to organise outings and charabanc trips.

Edinburgh Deaf F.C. in the 1920s
Photo: R. Cormack

The two captains toss at the start of the England v Wales match
Photo: British Deaf Times

Top: Glasgow Ladies   Bottom: Manchester Ladies
Hockey Teams 1922
Photos: Glasgow & West of Scotland Society for the Deaf
& Manchester Centre for the Deaf

**The English & Welsh Teams with the President of the
B.D.D.A.**
Photo: Church of the Holy Name Mission to the Deaf, Swansea

Leicester Deaf C.C. — Champions 1927
Photo: W. Gilbert

225

Lancashire and Yorkshire Deaf Cricket Teams 1929
Photo: Deaf Quarterly News

A Group of Cambridge Ladies enjoying a day out
Photo: Ely Diocesan Association for the Deaf

Members of Manchester Deaf Institute taking refreshments
Photo: Manchester Centre for the Deaf

Members of Stoke-on-Trent Institute on a coach outing
Photo: Staffordshire Society for the Deaf

Chapter 14
Deeds of Bravery

Medals of the Royal Humane Society

Deeds of Bravery

In common with any other community, the Deaf Community has had its share of people who have performed deeds of bravery that earned them recognition from the appropriate authorities.

In Britain, awards for bravery come in certain categories, eg. armed forces, civilian, police, societies for the protection of life. While no deaf person in Britain has been awarded any armed services medal - for the simple reason that no deaf person is permitted to serve in the armed services - or any government sponsored civilian award, or police award, deaf people have been given awards from such bodies as the Carnegie Fund, the Royal Humane Society, and the Society for Protection of Life from Fire.

The Carnegie Fund Awards

Before the Second World War, there were, apart from those from the Royal Humane Society and Society for the Protection of Life from Fire, no appropriate awards that could be given to civilians who had performed outstanding or exceptional deeds of bravery (the George Cross and George Medal were not instituted until World War II). The highest award that could be given in peacetime at that time, the Albert Medal, was confined largely to members of the armed forces.

Thus the Carnegie Medals were constituted. They were sparingly given, and the deed had to be exceptional for any award to be made; many of the Carnegie Medals were given posthumously.

The Royal Humane Society Awards

This Society was founded in 1774, and gives awards to people who have saved the lives of others from drowning. They have a three-tiered medals system, backed up by a number of Testimonial awards.

The highest possible award, the Stanhope Gold Medal, is only awarded once a year. The Silver and Bronze medals are awarded only in cases of exceptional bravery.

There were no Stanhope Gold Medals awarded in 1959-61, 1969 and 1973. In 1988, there was only one Silver Medal awarded, and 15 bronzes.

Society for the Protection of Life from Fire

They have a system similar to the Royal Humane Society, and make awards of gold, silver and bronze medals to people who have saved the lives of others from fire.

Carnegie Bronze Medal Award:
Incident at Dulverton Station

Just before five o'clock in the afternoon of Tuesday, January 8th 1935, in the gathering darkness, a Mrs. Ivy Thomas, wife of a farm worker from Dulverton, Somerset, and her four year-old son Robert John alighted from a train arriving at Dulverton Station from Tiverton on the Great Western Railway's Exe Valley line.

In common with most other passengers who disembark from Exe Valley line trains at Dulverton, Mrs. Thomas proceeded to the station exit across the railway tracks although a footbridge was provided for passengers. This footbridge was however at the other end of the platform, and most passengers got into the habit of going to the station exit across the tracks despite the standard railway warnings not to do so. This was a particularly dangerous practice at this station as trains approaching on the down line could not be seen until they were 40 yards from the station due to a bend and a road bridge.

She was the last passenger to set off across the tracks,

laden with parcels from her shopping trip, and the little boy tagging along behind.

Dulverton Station in the 1930s
Photo: Somerset County Council Local History Library

Most passengers had got across, and even out of the station altogether when the Barnstaple to Taunton train came around the bend under the bridge.

When the driver spotted the mother and the boy on the tracks, the mother had actually already reached the other side, but the little boy had fallen behind his mother and was still on the tracks.

Albert Tarr, a 54-year-old deaf tailor without speech, was standing in the place where he always stood to catch his train home to East Anstey after finishing work. He was the only one to spot the danger to the mother and child, and dashed onto the tracks in order to try and save their lives, waving his arms frantically.

At this moment, the driver who had already been braking

to come into the station, applied his brakes even more sharply and blasted out a warning on his whistle. This was the first time that everyone else on the station at that time became aware of the danger, and they could only watch helplessly as the child stood petrified with fright between the rails. They saw the mother drop her parcels and turn around to step back and try to reach her boy. They saw Albert Tarr reach the mother, and grab hold of her and also appear to try to push away the child, then the train hit them all.

When the train had stopped, it was found that the child's body was lying on one side of the rails but his head had been completely severed from the body. Albert Tarr was lying half on top of Mrs. Thomas between the rails. Both had terrible head injuries, and appeared to have been killed instantly.

Albert Tarr, who was unmarried and lived with his widowed mother at the tiny Devon village of East Anstey, was subsequently posthumuously awarded the Carnegie Bronze Medal - at that time before the introduction of the George Medal, one of the highest possible civilian awards that could be given for acts of heroism and bravery.

Just over a year later, in January 1936, a special dedication service was held at the little church at East Anstey when the Bishop of Exeter unveiled a memorial to Albert Tarr.

Sadly, this memorial has been neglected, and turned almost black with time and is difficult to read. It states:

'To the Glory of God and to perpetuate the Honoured Memory of Albert William Tarr of this parish who was accidently killed at Dulverton 8th January 1935 at the age of 54. Although deaf and dumb and so unable to raise an alarm, he threw himself in front of an approaching train in a valiant effort to save a mother and child. This record is made by many friends in recognition of his sacrifice. The bronze medallion incorporated is the highest award of the Carnegie Hero Trust Fund on whose illuminated roll the Heroic act is recorded.'

Albert Tarr's Memorial at East Anstey Church
Photo: Author's collection

ROYAL HUMANE SOCIETY AWARDS

Stanhope Gold Medal: The Sinking of the Venus Star
On the night of 22nd June 1957, the fishing vessel *Venus Star* from Portsoy, Banffshire, Scotland, was off Loch Ewe when a fire broke out in the engine-room.

It was spotted by William Robertson, then aged 20, a deaf man who had been educated at the Aberdeen School for the Deaf, and who had only been at sea for one year.

Robertson fought his way into the engine-room to try to confine the fire with blocks of ice taken from the hold, and was burned about the arms. However, the flames were near the petrol tank and the fishing vessel was in danger of being blown up so the skipper had to give the order to abandon ship.

In the confusion of fighting the fire, the dinghy had

gone overboard and was drifting away, trapping the crew. Robertson did not hesitate, and dived overboard and swam out to the dinghy which he succeeded in getting back to the fishing boat for the crew to get off.

William Robertson
Photo: Aberdeen & N. E. Scotland Society for the Deaf

By his quick thinking and brave action, Robertson saved the lives of five men, and the Stanhope Gold Medal for the Year 1957 was awarded to him.

Bronze Medal: Rescue at Porthtowan
On 25th July 1898, an Edwin Bailey was bathing on the beach at Porthtowan, Cornwall when he was caught by a strong current and swept out to sea.

One other man, a Henry W. Harris, a railway official, went to his rescue, and succeeded in reaching the drowning swimmer, but got into difficulties himself and could not bring the other to the shore.

It was then that James John Weeble, a deaf man from

Redruth, came upon the scene, and swam out fully-clothed, and succeeded in dragging both men back to the beach.

James J. Weeble
Photo: Ephphatha

James J. Weeble was awarded the Royal Humane Society's Bronze Medal on 15th August 1898 for this gallant rescue.

James J. Weeble died at Plymouth aged 87 on 4th April 1961.

Bronze Medal: Rescue from the River Avon

Thomas Albert Biggs, a born-deaf man employed as a coach-man at Bristol, was out on bail on 13 charges of bicycle theft on 3rd June 1905 when he came upon a drama in the River

Avon at a point where the river was over twenty feet deep and dangerous.

A man named Charles Lloyd had fallen into the river, and was in severe difficulties. Another man, Walter Latham, had gone in to try and save Lloyd but got into difficulty himself. Both men were in danger of being drowned when Thomas Biggs came upon the scene. Biggs immediately went to the rescue, and pulled both men to the shore, successfully saving their lives.

Biggs was awarded the Royal Humane Society's Bronze Medal the day before he was sentenced to nine months imprisonment on the charges of stealing bicycles, the judge saying that sentence would have been more severe but for his brave deed.

Testimonials on Vellum; Testimonials on Parchment; Certificates of Recommendation

The Royal Humane Society have a number of other awards where though the deed did not warrant a medal, some recognition was appropriate, and for this, they issue in descending order of importance, Testimonials on Vellum, Testimonials on Parchment and Certificates of Recommendation.

Testimonials on Vellum were awarded to James Roxburgh, aged 24, and Joseph Stephens, aged 26, for the rescue of a six-year-old from the River Thames at Blackfriars on 25th August 1923; John Connor, aged 60, and John Burton, aged 48, for the rescue of a man attempting suicide in the flooded River Aire at Leeds on 25th January 1925.

Testimonials on Parchment were awarded to John Hellier, a painter, for the rescue of a seven-year-old girl from the Union Canal at Edinburgh on 5th June 1914; Charles Harwood, aged 18, for rescuing a schoolboy of six from a canal at Leeds on 7th August 1924; Jack Kellett, aged 15, for the rescue of a schoolboy aged 4 from a canal at Leeds on 22nd July 1929; Derek Wylde for the rescue of a little girl from the River Ouse at Bedford on 10th August 1966.

Certificates of Recommendation were awarded to Thomas Mundy, aged 60, for the rescue of a boy aged 3 from a mill lode at Hull on 4th April 1906; Charles Pain in 1920 for saving a woman attempting suicide, and to Howard Swinbourne, aged 34, for saving a suicidal woman from the River Trent at Nottingham on 20th May 1985.

Howard Swinbourne
Photo: Nottingham & Nottinghamshire Society for the Deaf
Annual Report

Silver Medals: Royal Cross School Fire

In Chapter 7, it was mentioned that two schoolboys, John Jackson and Joseph Dalton of the Royal Cross School, Preston, were awarded silver medals for gallantry during the fire at this school in 1905. Those medals were from the Society for Protection of Life from Fire.

Jack Kellett receiving his Award
Photo: Deaf Quarterly News

Chapter 15
The 1930s

National Library of Scotland, Edinburgh
Photo: Iain MacFadyen

The 1930s

If the 1920s were a time of depression, the 1930s were not that much better, and morale amongst deaf people was still at an all-time low. Fifty years of oralism had by now so severely retarded the education of deaf people that those who became adults were largely judged incapable of managing their own affairs.

Social events for example were organised for the deaf rather than by deaf people themselves, mainly by hearing missioners; deaf magazines like the *Deaf Quarterly News* and the *British Deaf Times* were largely aimed at a readership far too sophisicated for the average ordinary deaf person, written and edited by missioners; the Guild of St. John of Beverley, an organisation of mainly clerical missioners interested in doing things for the deaf, flourished. It was not uncommon for these missioners to refer to their deaf clients as 'our poor deaf brethren'.

The whole of the decade may in fact be referred to as 'the era of the missioners'.

Formation of the Spurs Club

The growth of deaf missions and social clubs continued, although by now most large towns had their mission or institute for the deaf. Among those that were formed in the 1930s were Port Talbot and Bedford, while some long-established ones acquired new premises. Among the latter was Blackburn.

In such clubs and institutes sports matches and day outings were now commonplace. It was during this decade that the present deaf community's sports infrastructure was established, following the formation of the British Deaf Amateur Sports Association (later the British Deaf Sports Council) in 1930. In most regions of the country there were now inter-institute or inter-club sports matches played on a league basis.

It was in London, however, that the most significant new club was established.

For years, the choice in London for deaf people had been confined to church-based institutes under the umbrella of the Royal Association of the Deaf and Dumb, or to the more upper-class independent National Deaf Club, which still flourished and held regular meetings as well as badminton and tennis tournaments.

National Deaf Club Tennis Section, 1931
Photo: National Deaf Club

The National Deaf Club, as will be remembered, was

originally founded for the oral deaf, but by the 1930s had become so well-established aa a sports and social club for independent-minded deaf people who were mostly well-bred and upper-class, and so dominant in the Federation of London Deaf Clubs' sports tournaments, that oral deaf people were once more isolated from social activities.

In 1934 a Miss Kinzie was teaching lipreading in London and among her students was a Miss Cecilia Pollock, and her aunt, a Mrs Bagehot. These two ladies decided to form a social club, and organised a tea party which took place at the Ladies Park Club, where the Spurs Club was launched.

Cecilia Pollock
Photo: Volto Review

The Spurs Club was aimed at a deaf membership that did not use sign language.

In the beginning most of the members were elderly and the first meetings were ill-attended, but by the spring of 1935 more younger people had joined and, encouraged by the consent of the Duke of Montrose to be the President, it began to flourish, reaching a membership of about 150.

Meetings were usually held twice a month, and tended to

be of an intellectual nature, like art shows, plays, card games, outings and theatre parties.

The First Deaf Ph.D.
In deaf education, conditions throughout the country were still grim, with a lot of deprivation in poorer areas. In the words of one deaf man aged 70 interviewed in the course of a research project carried out by the author through a Durham University Fellowship in 1986,

> *'My education was neither good or bad. Of course, teaching was by oralist methods which was not helpful but what I remember more are the conditions in which we were educated. The food was unspeakable, most children wore threadbare clothes and badly worn shoes in need of repair. The hearing school next door was just as bad - we were in a poor area, and all children were victims of poverty. Most, if not all, of our parents were either out of work or poorly paid. There was no money available, and I suppose it showed in the quality of school life. The building was always damp, cold and we always suffered from chilblains in winter...'*

Not all schools, however, were that grim and bad. In Burgess Hill, a Miss Mary Hare had started a private school which was producing many academic successes, and the Rev. Thomas Arnold's school at Northampton, now being run by Frederick Ince-Jones, was still turning out large numbers of academic successes.

(These two schools, however, rarely had more than 25 pupils at any one time, so more individual attention was possible).

One of the pupils of Northampton High School to achieve distinction was Bernard L. Pitcher, who was born deaf and who received six years of private tuition before entering the school. He took the University of London Matriculation Examination in 1932, obtaining credits or better in every subject, while still at school, as a result of which he was admitted to the University, where despite enormous handicaps, he gained a Honours B.Sc., followed by the degree of Doctor of Philosophy in science and geology.

Dr. Bernard L. Pitcher was the first born-deaf man in Britain to gain a doctorate, and in 1988, was still alive living in retirement at Worthing, Sussex where he was the secretary of the local deaf club.

Dr. Bernard L. Pitcher
Photo: Northampton Independant

National Library of Scotland, Edinburgh

It was during this decade that the erection of the National Library of Scotland in Edinburgh was commenced. It is not generally known that among the sculptured panels at the top of the Library facade, there is one featuring two children fingerspelling at each other the first two letters of the alphabet.

Leeds visit Dublin

At Easter 1939, with Europe once more in the grip of events leading remorselessly up to the Second World War, Leeds Deaf F.C. made what was to be the last club trip out of Britain for many years when they travelled to Dublin, and played a football match on Easter Monday. The match ended in a 2-2 draw.

Panel at the top of the National Library of Scotland showing two children fingerspelling to each other
Photo: Iain MacFadyen

Deaf Clubs in the 1930s

Clapham St. Bede's
Photo: W. Hallett

Photofile:

Rose Street, Aberdeen
Photo: R. Cormack

Stoke-on-Trent
Photo: Staffordshire Society for the Deaf

Deaf Club Activities in the 1930s

Exeter Deaf Club at Exmouth, 1937
Photo: L. McGrath

Bury Deaf Club Coach Outing, 1936
Photo: Bury Deaf Welfare Society

Games at Swansea Deaf Centre
Photo: Church of the Holy Name, Swansea

Christmas Gathering, Manchester
Photo: Manchester Centre for the Deaf

Leeds visit Dublin

Leeds and Dublin Football Teams, Easter 1939
Photo: Leeds Centre for the Deaf

Chapter 16
The Second World War 1939-45

War-time Evacuees Clearing Snow at Camp, Winter 1939-40
Photo: Northern Counties School for the Deaf, Newcastle

The Second World War, 1939-45

The Second World War broke out the day before the majority of deaf schools were due to reassemble after the summer holidays. As a result, in some schools, half the children did not turn up.

Once the initial fright had subsided more and more of the children started to return and, apart from constant air-raid warnings which were more of a nuisance, schools were able to function normally.

Although some schools were quick off the mark to evacuate their children, it was not until May 1940 when the German Wehrmacht overran Holland, Belgium and struck deep into northern France that schools in danger areas began to take seriously the need for evacuation.

The Royal School for Deaf Children, Margate evacuated to Oxfordshire where three large houses were taken over in Goring-on-Thames and the school was able to carry on in a 'make-do' fashion.

The same 'make-do' fashion also had to be adopted by other schools. Donaldson's Hospital School for the Deaf was evacuated to Cockburnspath and North Berwick; the nursery department of the Royal Schools for the Deaf, Manchester, was evacuated to Middlewich in Cheshire; the Old Kent Road School for the Deaf to St. Alban, Glamorgan, temporarily before relocating at Banstead, Surrey, where they were joined by Anerley School for the Deaf who had originally evacuated to the Royal Cross School, Preston thence to the Royal West of England School at Exeter, hurriedly evacuating the latter following the Baedeker Raids on Exeter in 1942.

**Royal School for Deaf Children, Margate,
in their New War Time Home, Goring-on-Thames**
Photo: Royal School for Deaf Children, Margate

Anerley School were not at Banstead for long; they returned to their own school in November 1942 but had to move again, this time to Yorkshire when the flying-bomb blitz started.

At Middlesbrough, the Hugh Bell School was partially evacuated to Pickering, North Yorkshire, a number of parents refusing to let their children be evacuated.

Some schools, like Newcastle's Northern Counties School, were evacuated in early Sepember but soon returned to their proper premises. Others, like the Leeds School for the Deaf and Liverpool School for the Deaf, went to open-air schools on the city outskirts, although Liverpool later relocated at Birkdale, Southport. Some schools, like the one at Bristol, did not get evacuated until 1941 or 1942 because of the increasing likelihood of air-raids in their areas.

Evacuees undergoing Gas Mask Training, 1940
Photo: Northern Counties School for the Deaf, Newcastle

Trying to forget the War at Christmas
Photo: Northern Counties School for the Deaf, Newcastle

Some schools stayed put, and accepted evacuees, like the Royal West of England School at Exeter. Wherever they were at school, a number of deaf children were unfortunate enough to stay there the whole duration of the war, neither seeing their parents nor going home for any holiday. In some areas, notably the islands off the British mainland like the Outer Hebrides, the Orkneys and the Shetlands, some deaf children lost their opportunity of receiving an education.

The evacuation of many schools gave military and civil authorities the opportunity to requisition the buildings for their own use. Donaldson's for instance became a German prisoner-of-war camp; the Royal School for Deaf Children at Margate was taken over by the Corporation of Margate and used as the Civil Defence Headquarters, Food & Fuel Office, W.V.S. Headquarters, Emergency Police station, among a number of other wartime departments. Clyne House, the Royal Schools for the Deaf (Manchester)'s nursery department, was once again turned into a military hospital just as it was in the First World War.

The imposition of strict black-out regulations severely disrupted adult deaf club activities at the beginning of the war; many were forced to cancel long-arranged social events, and rearrange social club hours. One casualty of the war was the British Deaf & Dumb Association's plans to celebrate its Jubilee year in 1940.

There were moments of black humour as well regarding the safety of deaf people in wartime conditions. For example, a paragraph heading in the London Evening Standard reported as follows:-

HOW THE DEAF WILL BE WARNED OF AIR RAIDS...
WARDEN PULLS STRING - OFF COME BEDCLOTHES.

At Warrington, a deaf man decided to pay a visit to a relative he had not seen for some time, and set off to cycle there. Unfortunately, due to all road signposts being removed, he soon lost his way and had to ask someone for directions. Due to his speech-impediment, he was mistaken for a German spy and was arrested and spent some uncomfortable hours in custody before being released.

In Manchester, a deaf tramp who had roamed the country for 9 years was arrested as a spy because he had 55 Ordnance Survey maps in his possession, as well as two compasses and twenty crisp £1 notes.

How the Deaf Served in the War

As in World War I, deaf persons were not permitted to serve in the armed forces, yet there were thousands of able-bodied deaf men and women who could be used to serve their country in a civilian capacity.

This resource was fully realised by the Home Office who recommended that deaf men should be recruited as Air Raid Wardens (A.R.P.'s) and firewatchers, and many deaf men did in fact serve in these capacities, and also as stretcher-bearers in air-raid conditions.

Harry Macdonald of Truro, A.R.P. Warden
Photo: Melinda Napier

NATIONAL SERVICE (ARMED FORCES) ACT, 1939.

MINISTRY OF LABOUR AND NATIONAL SERVICE,
Employment Exchange,

39 DYKE ROAD, BRIGHTON

Date 10 JUL 1940

To Mr. *Herbert Colville*

Courtland Hotel. The Drive.

Hove. 3.

Registration No. *BKW. 9521.*

DEAR SIR,

I have to inform you that notification has been received that you have been medically examined and found to be permanently incapable of being placed in medical Grades I, II, IIa or III. You will, therefore, not be liable for service under the National Service (Armed Forces) Act, 1939.

Yours faithfully,

NATIONAL SERVICE (ARMED FORCES) ACT, 1939

After examination by all the members of the Medical Board assembled at _____

on ____ *8 July 1940* ____ it is unanimously agreed that the man stating himself to be _____ *Herbert Colville* _____

residing at _____ *Courtland Hotel* _____ *The Drive Hove* _____

and described on his Medical Examination Record as suffering from _____

is in consequence permanently incapable of being placed in Grades I, II, IIa or III.

Names of members of the Medical Board

Dr *Gillies*
Dr *Coes*
Dr *Bedow*
Dr *Snell*

Signature of Chairman.

Date *8 July 1940*

N.S. 66.

Exemption Certificate listing Deafness & Dumbness as not fit for service in the Armed Forces
From: Herbert Colville

They did immensely valuable work; in many localities, the largest body of able-bodied fully fit men were mainly deaf members of institutes. (At the end of the War, it was found that over 50 deaf men from Manchester Institute for the Deaf were entitled to the Defence Service Medal for their work with the Civil Defence, and this could be repeated throughout the country. (Many never got to receive their medals though.)

One deaf person who did much sterling work in the front-line city of Southampton was Herbert C. Street, an A.R.P Warden and sergeant in the Home Guard. He was later awarded the British Empire Medal for 'admirable services rendered to Civil Defence'. Another A.R.P. Warden was Harry Macdonald of Truro.

A desperate shortage of labour caused by so many workers in industry being called up enabled hundreds of deaf men and women to get employment. One deaf woman millworker, Mary Swain of Oldham was awarded the B.E.M. for her wartime work.

One of the B.D.D.A's Mobile Units given to the Red Cross
Photo: Deaf Quarterly News

In deaf clubs and institutes throughout the country, there was also much fund-raising and knitting for the armed services. One deaf centre contributed over 700 knitted pairs of woollen socks; Wakefield, Birmingham and Belfast some hundreds of knitted pullovers and other woollen articles.

Leeds adopted the destroyer *H.M.S. Leeds* as its mascot, and contributed to the comforts of the sailors. Many other institutes adopted a variety of the armed services funds as their mascot and held 'gift sales', 'bring and buy' events and so on to raise money for their special fund.

The British Deaf and Dumb Association selected the British Red Cross Society to raise funds for, and raised enough to purchase and equip two mobile physiotherapy units.

The Spurs Club in London raised the magnificient sum of £760 in three years for a variety of armed services' benevolent funds.

Deaf Prisoner of the Germans

David Cornish, a ship's stoker, was among the members of his ship's crew captured by the German raider *Manyo Maru* and was kept in the raider's hold for five weeks on black bread, ersatz coffee, fat, margarine and jam while the raider roamed the seas attacking fresh victims in the Indian Ocean.

He was eventually put ashore on the island of Emira where he had to live for six days on coconuts before being rescued and brought to Sydney, Australia.

Deaf Victims of the Blitz and Blackouts

A number of deaf people, including children, lost their lives during air raids by German warplanes on the British mainland, including a family of eight when a bomb scored a direct hit on their dug-out.

However, deaf people were in danger at any time during the blackouts. At least seven were killed by buses and trams operating in black-out conditions, and many were injured. One deaf electrician from Gillingham, Kent, a Thomas Pearce, was shot dead by a sentry in Southport, Lancashire, to which place he had been sent to do a job: he had failed to see the sentry in the dark and the sentry shot him after challenging him three times.

Although a number of deaf people, especially in London, Coventry and Southampton lost their homes, deaf institutes, churches and schools seem to have received more damage.

Deaf centres which were destroyed by enemy action included Southampton, Coventry, Clapham St Bedes, Great Yarmouth, Manchester's Roman Catholic Centre, and the premises of the National Deaf Club. Centres which received some damage included Norwich and Birmingham whilst in Bristol the square in which the deaf centre stood was reduced to rubble except for the deaf centre, which was unscathed except for blasted windows. In Manchester, the Church of All Saints across the road was reduced to rubble, whilst the deaf institute remained unscathed.

Perhaps the greatest amount of damage done to deaf centres in a short span of time occurred in the Baedeker Raids of May 1942 in South-West England.

The Baedeker Raids - May 1942
The South-West of England suffered in 1942 an intensive bombing campaign by the German Luftwaffe that really had little to do with the War.

The air raids were commonly known as the Baedeker Raids, after a publishing house that produced travel guides, because the Germans made a sudden switch from bombing major cities, industrial and military targets and bombed cities that did not have anything remotely possible connected with any major war effort. They were all 6 of them in fact what might be called tourist towns, like Torquay, Exeter, Bath, Weymouth etc. - the very towns which in fact had travel guides published by this firm. The firm itself was a casualty of the raids, and never published again.

There was first a minor raid on Exeter on a Thursday night, followed the next night by a much larger raid, which caused great damage to parts of the town. Amongst the buildings damaged was the Church Hall, where the deaf of Exeter met, and where the missioner had his offices.

Then the Germans left Exeter alone for one full week, during which they bombed, amongst other towns, Bath, Weymouth and Torquay.

Two views of Air Raid damage at Southampton Deaf Centre
Photos: Hampshire, Isle of Wight and Channel Islands Association for the Deaf

The Deaf Institute in Bath was totally destroyed, and all records were lost. Torquay Deaf Club suffered some minor damage, but nothing which could not be easily repaired.

In Weymouth, one of the casualities was the Toc H building, which amongst other things was home to the local deaf club. This building was totally destroyed, and the deaf of Weymouth were without a club for some months.

One week after the first raid on Exeter, the Germans returned in force, and devastated the centre of Exeter. Already previously damaged, the deaf centre was now made totally uninhabitable.

Another casualty of this bombing raid was the Royal West of England School for the Deaf at Exeter, which at that time had seemed a safe haven, not only for the children of the area the school served, but also for the 52 children and staff of the Anerley School for the Deaf, London, who had been evacuated there on 14th September 1939. Blasts from high explosives caused substantial damage to all the buildings of the school, and no room escaped damage. Fortunately, the tedious but sensible arrangement of sleeping all the children on the ground floor instead of in the bedrooms paid dividends; there were no serious casualties. Within four days, all the children had returned home, and the school was closed for two months to enable repairs to be carried out.

In these raids there were no human casualties in any of the deaf centres, although a few deaf families were made homeless when their homes were hit.

The deaf in Exeter occupied temporary premises for a few weeks, before settling into another building near the centre of the town, but not for very long. In early 1943, four Heinkel 111s made a low-level sneak raid on the town in broad daylight. The raid took less than five minutes, but the damage suffered by Exeter was greater than it had suffered in the Baedeker raids, and there was greater loss of life, over 250 people being killed. One of the buildings totally flattened was the new home of the deaf in the town, so for the second time within the space of one year, the deaf in Exeter had to find new club premises.

In the same 1943 raid, Torquay was also bombed again and the deaf centre escaped with minor blast damage when a bomb fell on the St. Marychurch building a few yards up the road, killing 18 children who were in the building.

Scene of devastation outside Bristol Centre for the Deaf
Bristol Deaf Centre took a very near miss when much of the square around it was reduced to rubble in a heavy air-raid. The local society later took the opportunity to build the new deaf centre on the bombed site.

Photo: Bristol Centre for the Deaf

The Bombing of Schools

The first bombs to fall on any British deaf school happened the day the war broke out at Margate on 3rd September 1939 when a number of incendiary bombs landed in the school grounds. This school was to be subjected to a number of air raid attacks, but the greatest loss the school suffered was when the Allen Homes were totally destroyed in 1942. These Homes were used to accommodate boarders at the school, and their destruction severely hampered the School's capacity after the war. The headmaster's house in the school grounds was also destroyed, and the main building hit.

Other schools which suffered wartime bomb damage included the East Anglian School at Gorleston-on-Sea which also had its headmaster's house destroyed, the Royal West of England School at Exeter as previously stated, and the Royal Cambrian School for the Deaf at Swansea. In London, the Old Kent Road and Anerley Schools for the Deaf which were both occupied by civil defence and military authorities at the time were also substantially damaged and needed major repairs after the war before they could be reoccupied.

The Allen Homes at The Royal School
for Deaf Children, Margate
Their loss caused severe accommodation difficulties for the school after being totally destroyed in the War.
Photo: Royal School for Deaf Children, Margate

In Manchester, the Clyne House nursery school, then occupied by the military authorities, was also severely damaged, and the main school building was hit by a bomb which went through its roof but which fortunately failed to explode.

Deaf People to the Rescue

During this war, the skies over Britain often saw a lot of aerial activity, and many planes fell to the ground damaged or in flames. On two occasions, deaf people were responsible for saving the lives of the pilots.

One July day in 1943 at Blaconsthorpe, Norfolk, a born-deaf farm labourer named Kenneth Andrews was walking home from work accompanied by his wife, and carrying his young baby when he saw a R.A.F. Typhoon fighter plane crash in flames. Quickly pushing his baby son into his wife's arms, Andrews ran to the downed plane and saw that the pilot was trapped in his cockpit.

Without any regard for his own safety, Andrews climbed onto a wing of the blazing plane, and kicked frantically at the toughened perspex of the cockpit canopy until it shattered, then dragged out the semi-conscious pilot. Seconds after Andrews had dragged away the pilot, the plane exploded, and was reduced to a smouldering wreck.

Andrews flagged down a passing vehicle, and saw that the driver would take the pilot to the nearest hospital, then calmly went home with his wife to have his dinner. When other people arrived at the scene, and saw that there was no-one in the burnt-out cockpit, they assumed that the pilot had bailed out. Only when the pilot recovered consciousness in hospital and informed the authorities of his rescue did the R.A.F. manage to track down Andrews, and make his bravery known.

The King's Commendation for Brave Conduct was gazetted to Kenneth Andrews on 5th November 1943.

Andrews himself was killed in a road accident in 1966.

In Swansea, John Roberts spotted a plane about to crash while he was travelling on a bus. Quickly getting off the bus, he ran to where the plane had impacted and dragged out the injured pilot who was covered in oil moments before the plane caught fire.

Alfred Reginald Thomson, R.A., R.P., (1894-1979)
- War Artist

All branches of the armed services at various times made appointments of official War Artists, who were commissioned to paint battle scenes or portraits for the armed services. In 1942 one such appointment was made of a deaf artist, Alfred Reginald Thomson, as official War Artist to the Royal Air Force.

A.R. Thomson was born in Bangalore, India, in 1894 and was educated at the Royal School for Deaf Children, Margate, in England before he went to study art at the London Art School, Kensington, and exhibited at the Royal Academy from 1920. He was elected A.R.A. in 1939.

The Royal Air Force always had two salaried artists at any one time, and one of these was a portraitist. In 1940, Thomson was considered as one of the portraitists, but his deafness was considered enough to disqualify him, and the post went to Eric Kennington who however resigned in 1942 over criticism of the 'violence' of his portraits, and now without an explanation for the change of heart over his deafness Thomson was appointed to succeed him.

Among the portraits which Thomson painted for the R.A.F. was one of Wing-Commander Leonard Cheshire, D.F.C. - later to be awarded the Victoria Cross and made Group Captain.

TWO PORTRAITS PAINTED BY A.R.THOMSON
AS R.A.F. ARTIST

**Dame E.Blair,
D.B.E., R.G.C.**
Matron-in-Chief,
Princess Mary's
R.A.F. Nursing Service
*Reproduced with the kind
permission of the
Royal Air Force Museum,
Hendon.*

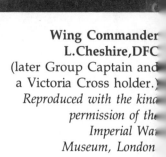

**Wing Commander
L.Cheshire,DFC**
(later Group Captain and
a Victoria Cross holder.)
*Reproduced with the kind
permission of the
Imperial War
Museum, London*

266

Chapter 17
The 1940s

**Christmas gathering at the Town Hall,
Leeds - 1949**
Photo: Leeds Centre for the Deaf

CHAPTER 17

The 1940s

Although other events of the decade were overshadowed by the Second World War, there were nonetheless a number of important milestones which saw the beginning of emancipation of the British Deaf Community from the shackles of paternalism and second-rate citizenship that they had been subject to since the International Congress of Milan in 1880.

There would still be a long way to go before deaf people could attain the rights, respect and responsibilities that were theirs in the late nineteenth century, but in the 1940s, the tiny seeds were at least sown to prepare the way.

The important milestones which sowed these tiny seeds were two Acts passed by Parliament in 1944 - the much-despised Disabled Persons (Employment) Act, considered by many disabled people, and not just deaf people, to be one of the most useless and degrading Acts ever passed by Parliament, and the Education Act.

One of the provisions of the Disabled Persons (Employment) Act, 1944, which disabled people disliked so much was that they should register as a disabled person for employment purposes. Most employers were required to reserve a certain percentage of their workforce for disabled people. In practice, the Act was unenforceable and unworkable, but it still remains law at the time of writing. It is often overlooked that this Act was designed to prevent the situation which occurred in the 1920s when unemployment was very high and thousands of deaf men (and other disabled people) could not get jobs, and, for that reason alone, it was an important milestone in the emancipation of deaf people.

The Education Act, 1944, which raised the age at which youngsters could leave school, contained many important provisions for deaf education which saw the standard of education slowly begin to improve.

Other important milestones in the 1940s were the founding of the National Deaf Children's Society (1944), the British Association of the Hard of Hearing (BAHOH) (1947), Mary Hare Grammar School (1946), the Cardiff Congress of the British Deaf and Dumb Association in 1947, the only one in that decade, and the National Assistance Act, 1948.

The founding of the National Deaf Children's Society and BAHOH were both important in that they brought to deaf emancipation the political muscle of two quite separate groups - the parents and the masses of people who had suffered hearing loss in adult life. This importance has not always been appreciated or recognised but nonetheless it is there.

The Cardiff Congress of the B.D.D.A. in 1947 was largely responsible for reinvigorating an organisation that had largely been stagnant in the 1920s, 1930s and during the war. The years following this Congress saw an uplift in membership, interest and activity that has been sustained to this day.

Mary Hare Grammar School

The founding of Mary Hare Grammar School was one of the most important milestones ever in deaf education, especially in the late 1940s now that the High School for the Deaf at Northampton was to close following Frederick Ince-Jones' illness and inability to continue with the school.

Not to have replaced the Northampton School with its fine academic record would have left a terrible vacuum in deaf education, but the founding of Mary Hare Grammar School avoided this, and gave more besides, since girls for the first time were to have the same opportunity of an academic education that had always been the privilege of boys at Northampton.

The First School, Burgess Hill
Photo: Sally Ellis

The school was named after the late Miss Mary Hare who had maintained an oral school in Burgess Hill for some years. Entry to this school was on the basis of selection following the results of an entrance examination, and Mary Hare Grammar was the first school in the country to provide the advantages of secondary education under the new Education Act, 1944, in a school set apart for that purpose.

Within a few years, however, it was evident that the homely atmosphere of Burgess Hill was not big enough - more and more deaf children of ability were coming forward and bigger premises were needed, so the school relocated to Arlington Manor, Newbury, Berkshire.

Other Schools
Two other important schools were founded in the years immediately following the Second World War - Hamilton

Lodge School, Brighton and Birkdale, Southport.

The oddity about these two schools was that Hamilton Lodge was founded as a direct result of the old Brighton Institution closing down to become Ovingdean Hall School for the Partially Deaf, which left the profoundly deaf in the South of England no school to go to except Margate which was having difficulties because of war damage. Birkdale School, on the other hand, was originally founded by the Liverpool School for the Deaf as a partially-hearing department before becoming an independent school for the partially-hearing.

Free Hearing Aids

One of the greatest legacies left to Britain by the post-war Labour Government of Clement Attlee is the National Health Service, and it was when the Bill for this was going through Parliament that the Duke of Montrose raised such a fuss over the fact that deaf people would be required to pay for hearing aids and batteries whereas other disabled people would be given what they needed free of charge, that the Government backed down and included free issue of hearing aids and batteries in its Bill.

The National Assistance Act, 1948

The National Assistance Act, 1948, made a number of provisions regulating the type of assistance which the State could or should provide for various classes of the British public.

It was probably one of the worst ever Acts of Parliament to be implemented by any government with particular regard to the welfare of deaf people. Of particular importance and concern to deaf people were Sections 29 and 30 of the Act.

Under the terms of the Act, local county councils and societies for the deaf were required to register schemes for the promotion of the welfare of, and provision of services for, deaf people. For the first time, deaf persons were to be part of a register which would entitle them to seek assistance, and to allow councils to assist.

The Act also empowered councils, societies and other suitably recognised voluntary organisations to appoint welfare officers for deaf people, who were to assist in the overcoming of disabilities, give such advice and guidance as might be required, and encourage participation in the activities of social centres and clubs for the deaf. In addition, the Act also empowered the provision of practical assistance in deaf people's homes; assistance in the obtaining of library and other recreational facilities; provision of lectures, games and other recreational facilities in social centres and outings; provision of religious services; assistance in travelling to and from participation in services in social centres or elsewhere, and to facilitate the taking of holidays by deaf people in holiday homes. The Act also empowered councils to provide social centres and holiday homes under any scheme set up.

The theory behind the implementation of the Act was well-intended but paternalistic, and the result saw deaf people in the 1950s and 1960s in the position of being cossetted and having everything possible being done for them, at the price of losing their independence. Many deaf people had no say in decision making - many things and services were provided on a 'take it or leave it' basis, irrespective of whether these were what deaf people actually wanted.

The worst aspect of the National Assistance Act, 1948, was that it engendered the 'gimme, gimme' attitude of a number of deaf people. Such an attitude was deeply disliked by those forward-thinking deaf people who were in the forefront of the struggle to shake off the yoke of second-class citizenship, and it was to take a long time to eradicate, and then, not completely.

Life and Death in the 1940s
In post-war Britain, as many institutes and centres struggled to repair their bomb-damaged premises, or find new ones like Bath, two new centres were opened, one at Basingstoke, and the other at Newport. The inspiration behind the latter was Gower Jones, the soldier of the 1914-18 war.

Elsewhere, throughout Britain, life for deaf people slowly began to resume some normality. Inter-institute sports matches picked up where they had left off at the outbreak of the war; club outings were once again the fashion, and the British Deaf Amateur Sports Association came out of its dormancy to prepare for the International Games once again.

Many familiar faces were, however, missing. Some had been killed in the war, others had died from natural causes. One of the latter was Robert Semple of Paisley.

Robert Semple (1874-1940)
Robert Semple was born in Paisley, Scotland, where he lived all his life, and devoted the whole of his leisure life to the services of his fellow deaf.

He founded the Mission to the Deaf in Paisley in a small room placed at his disposal by Canal Street Church, and he saw the work grow until the institute at Queen Street was built.

He was one of the original members of the B.D.D.A. which rewarded him for his services by electing him a Patron at the Torquay Congress in 1934.

People of Distinction
Among the deaf people who achieved distinction in the 1940s were a deaf woman who qualified as a doctor, an artist and a scenic artist working in films.

Ethel Sharrard (1918-)
Ethel Sharrard was born in Lincoln, and became deaf through meningitis at age 18 months. Despite this handicap, and her very poor speech, she attended a private school from age four to seven, then Lincoln High School from seven to seventeen.

During this period, she was helped by her mother who practised speech with her every day, and she learnt lipreading naturally, but was fortunate with friends at Lincoln High School who would take notes in lessons for her.

Her ambition was to become a doctor like her parents, and she passed the London Matriculation examination in 1937, obtaining entrance to Sheffield University. However, the University was reluctant to accept her due to her deafness - only the influence of her parents persuaded them to accept her.

In 1943, she passed her finals for Bachelor of Medicine and Bachelor of Surgery, and for her probationary training, she spent three months as house physican, and six months as house surgeon in Sheffield Royal Infirmary. All the time she was at University and in Sheffield Royal Infirmary, she had speech lessons with a teacher of the deaf.

D-Day saw her at work in the Emergency Hospital at Burntwood, near Lichfield where she had to deal with hundreds of war casualties. From there she went to the Maternity and Children's Hospitals in Birmingham, working long hours which contributed to a nervous breakdown.

She married a Philip Owston whom she had met at Sheffield University, in 1946 and retired from her career as a surgeon.

Ethel Sharrard is only the second deaf person ever to qualify as a doctor, and the first as a surgeon in Britain.

Roland Vivian Pitchforth, R.A., R.W.S. (1894-1982)
Vivian Pitchforth was born in Wakefield with normal hearing, and studied art at the Wakefield School of Art, thence the Leeds School of Art, leaving in 1915 to join the Royal Artillery with which he served in France until 1918.

He was demobilised from the Royal Artillery stone-deaf from the noise of the 60-pound guns he helped to fire, and for the rest of his life, he relied on lipreading which he learnt at classes for deafened soldiers and sailors at the Royal School for Deaf Children, Margate.

After four years at the Royal College of Art, he started to paint professionally, mostly in water-colour.

He was official War Artist to the Admiralty during the Second World War, when he painted many dramatic scenes.

He was a hard worker, and numerous works are held by

the Tate Gallery, Imperial War Museum and many other provincial galleries.

Roland Vivian Pitchforth
Photo: Old Watercolours Society

Hebden Bridge by Vivian Pitchforth
Reproduced by permission of Manchester City Art Galleries

Alexander Bilibin (1903-)

Born in Russia where he became totally deaf following a double mastoid operation, he was educated at the Northampton High School for Deaf Boys where from the outset he showed promise in Art.

Following his deaf education, he spent four years at the Royal Academy Schools, and also studied in Paris.

For a number of years from 1936 onwards, he was responsible for the scenic decoration of the famous Chelsea Arts Ball, and indeed, Bilibin's chief claim to fame is as a scenic artist in the film industry both in England and in Hollywood, and for his mural decorations in the old Cunard liner, Queen Mary.

Alexander Bilibin
Self-Portrait

Professional Boxer: Peter Livingstone (1910-1986)

Aberdeen boasts of two deaf men who were professional boxers. Henry Byres who was Scottish Featherweight champion from 1924 to 1930, and Peter Livingstone who boxed in the late 1930s, early 1940s.

The British Boxing Board of Control was not formed until

1929, when Byres had already been champion for five years, and it was then that professional boxers were required to hold licences.

Peter Livingstone was the first known deaf man in Britain to hold a B.B.B.C. licence, no. 27749 issued on 13.3.1940.

Peter Livingstone
Photo: Aberdeen & N.E. Scotland Society for the Deaf

Chapter 18
Literature, Theatre and Television

A scene from Robin Hood
(A School Play)

Photo: Royal Cross School, Preston

Literature, Theatre and Television

Publications for the Deaf: The British Deaf News
The earliest magazine for the deaf to be published in the United Kingdom was the *Edinburgh Messenger,* the first issue of which appeared in October 1843, but it had a short lifespan and the last issue to appear was No.12, January 1845.

The Edinburgh
QUARTERLY MESSENGER,
BEING A RECORD OF INTELLIGENCE REGARDING
THE DEAF AND DUMB.

"*Open thy mouth for the Dumb,*"—*Prov.* xxxi. 3.

No. I.   TUESDAY, OCTOBER 3d, 1843.   Price 1d. or
7s. per 100.

In thinking how the public might be induced more generally to espouse the cause of the Deaf and Dumb, a question has occurred:—How is it that there is no Periodical, besides annual reports of Institutions, put into circulation in behalf of Deaf Mutes? Other Societies have their "Missionary Magazines"—their "Church Missionary Papers"—their "Missionary Repositories"—and their "Home and Foreign Missionary Records" to communicate information regarding their objects: but no such vehicle exists to aid the cause of the Deaf and Dumb. To supply this want, this little periodical has been undertaken.

It will be our business to lay before our readers brief notices of the deplorable condition of untaught Deaf Mutes—to state the beneficial effects which education has upon them—to record interesting anecdotes regarding them: and to allow those of them who have been educated to plead the cause of their afflicted companions in their own simple and primitive style.

A portion of our pages will be occupied with accounts of Institutions established for their benefit,—their annual meetings, examinations, and other circumstances connected with their state and progress. These notices are not meant to be confined to the Institutions in Great Britain and Ireland, but will be extended to those on the Continent of Europe, and in the United States of America. The Statistics of the Deaf and Dumb, so far as they can be ascertained, will also be detailed, and every thing connected with them will be collected and put before our readers.

It is also our intention to point out the imperative obligations which are laid on all, to engage in assisting to procure education to a class of individuals who are the most ignorant of the human family—the Deaf and Dumb; and we shall especially urge the subject on the attention of those who profess to have imbibed the spirit of Him, who in the days of his flesh went about doing good,—making the Deaf to hear and the Dumb to speak.

The *Messenger* will be forwarded, as occasions present themselves, to the various Institutions for the Deaf and Dumb in this and other countries: and it will afford us much pleasure to receive from them (or other Friends to the Cause) such communications as can be embodied in it.

R. K.

Frontispiece of the First Magazine for the Deaf
Produced by the Institution for the Deaf and Dumb, Edinburgh
This magazine was published by the Edinburgh Institution for

the Deaf and Dumb, and produced by the pupils on the school's press. The editor was the headmaster, Robert Kinniburgh.

The next magazine to appear was *The Magazine for the Deaf and Dumb*, first published by the Association in Aid of the Deaf and Dumb (forerunner of the present day Royal Association for the Deaf) in July 1855, but only five issues were published, the last in 1857.

Genealogy of the British Deaf News

The present day *British Deaf News* can trace its origins back to 1873 when the Rev. Samuel Smith published *A Magazine Intended Chiefly for the Deaf and Dumb*. Then followed a bewildering succession of names as the magazine changed hands several times. In 1879, the magazine was called *The Deaf and Dumb Magazine*, and Mr. Alexander Strachern of Glasgow took over publication in 1881, gave it up in 1883 due to ill- health, and it was taken over by James Paul of Kilmarnock who continued it until 1885, when he handed over to Ernest Abrahams who renamed the magazine *Deaf and Dumb World*. The title was changed yet again in 1887 to

Deaf-Mute World, but only two issues were produced before Abrahams was forced to close down due to heavy losses.

Into the vacuum stepped *The Deaf-Mute* in 1888, published by a new organisation called The Deaf-Mute Association, brainchild of a J.J. Maclean and Francis Maginn of Belfast. However, proposals for the formation of a national association to be called the British Deaf and Dumb Association, together with a publication called *The Deaf and Dumb Times* meant only one issue was published.

From the appearance of the *Deaf and Dumb Times*, edited by Charles Gorham of Leeds, in 1889 the *British Deaf News* has an unbroken genealogy, although the magazine underwent a number of name changes and was merged with another magazine with a long lineage in 1955. The diagram opposite clearly shows the genealogy:

Although the first editor of the present *British Deaf News* was a hearing man, the majority of the editors of the *Deaf and Dumb Times, Deaf Chronicle, British Deaf-Mute, British Deaf Monthly.* and *British Deaf Times* were deaf men up to the death of Joseph Hepworth in 1921. In contrast, the *Deaf Quarterly News* (in its various names) was always edited by a hearing person, generally a missioner.

Apart from a brief period from 1962 to 1964 when the Rev. Mark Frame edited the *British Deaf News* no deaf person edited the magazine from 1921 to 1989 when Mrs Irene Hall was appointed editor - the first woman so appointed.

Deaf Humour
One feature of magazines for the deaf have been cartoons that illustrate deaf humour.

Other Magazines for the Deaf
Other magazines for the deaf exist, of which one, *Soundbarrier*, is probably the most commonly read by deaf people. It is published by the R.N.I.D. who have seen two other magazines *The Silent World* and *Hearing* go under due to financial problems.

Laugh with Len — *a special full length feature cartoon !*

Reproduced from the British Deaf News

One magazine, *Ephphatha*, the organ of the Royal Association for the Deaf, had a long history, being published for over 60 years, before it ceased publication with issue No. 200 in 1959.

The magazine or journal with the longest continuous existence under one title is *Teacher of the Deaf* which was first published in 1903. Other associations and organisations have their own magazines, for example *TALK (National Deaf Children's Society), HARK (British Association of the Hard of Hearing)* but few are read by deaf people.

Poetry of the Deaf

During the twentieth century, following in the footsteps of Harriet Martineau, there have been a number of deaf novelists and authors. The best known of these was Kate Whitehead, later to be the wife of Selwyn Oxley, who built up a huge collection of literature about the deaf. Other books written by deaf people have tended to be biographies, such as the highly humorous *Life among the Deaf* by Michael Jack.

Reproduced from the British Deaf News

However, there have been three people, David Wright, Dot Miles and Jack Clemo, who have had collections of poetry published as books, and who have earned part of their living as authors. As well as these three, one other deaf person, Frank Callaghan of Warrington, tried poetry and won second prize in a national poetry competition in 1985.

David Wright (1920-)

David Wright became totally deaf at the age of seven through contracting scarlet fever, and after a period of private tuition, was educated at Northampton High School for Deaf Boys, then at Oriel College, Oxford.

In 1950, he won one of the last Atlantic Awards in Literature, and has since published several books including *Monologue of a Deaf Man*, and was from 1965 to 1967 Gregory Fellow in Poetry at Leeds University.

Dorothy Miles (1934-)

Dot Miles, as she is more familiarly known, was born in Mold, North Wales, and became deaf at the age of 8 through meningitis while she was at the Christ Church Elementary School in Rhyl, North Wales.

Dorothy Miles

After an education at the Royal Schools for the Deaf, Manchester, and Mary Hare Grammar School she became a clerical assistant in a research laboratory library, then worked for a few years with deaf people in Blackburn and in Liverpool.

She then took the big decision to go to Gallaudet College in 1957 where she graduated with a B.A. in English with Distinction.

She married a fellow student in 1958, but was divorced in 1962, and became a naturalised American citizen, working in various fields including teaching and sign language research, but her first love was drama and poetry. When the National Theatre for the Deaf was formed in 1967, she was one of the early participants and was involved in every production from 1968 to 1973, before leaving to work in California.

Dorothy Miles returned to Britain in 1977, and has since been heavily involved in sign language teaching, video production, the Deaf Players Theatre, and also on several *SEE HEAR* productions.

She is probably the foremost signed poetry performer in the world, some of these performances being shown on television and to live audiences, and has had several poetry books published.

Jack Clemo (1916-)

Jack Clemo was born in 1916 in Cornwall, and started to go blind when he was five years old, progressing until he was completely blind when aged 39.

He also became totally deaf at the age of 19, and isolated from his neighbours in the Cornish clay community of Goonamarris, he turned to literature, more particularly poetry.

Goonamarris was also a deeply religious community, and Jack Clemo sometimes offended them with his own brand of view: that the way to a spiritual experience of God was through the communication of two people in sex, but as Clemo's literary efforts blossomed, the cottage at Goonamarris became a kind of literary Lourdes with people coming to see the writer.

Jack Clemo with his wife, Ruth

Jack Clemo married a Ruth Peaty when he was 52 years old, and went to live with her in Weymouth.

The Performing Arts

It is a common fallacy that deaf people do not enjoy the theatre, or even music; often this avenue offers a marvellous means for deaf people to express themselves in their own language. The main drawback has been that there has never been sufficient money or encouragement to enable deaf people to pursue careers or interests in the performing arts.

Just because deaf people cannot hear, it does not mean that they are impervious to music. Music does not depend on hearing alone, as some might think, but also on vibrations, and the majority of deaf people have a very acute feeling for noise through vibration, be it a metal wastebin being kicked accidently or stereo music - deaf people are often also wont to complain such noises are too loud whereas hearing people may feel the noises are nonexistent, in the background only, or reasonable; this is because the noises intrude on their world of silence.

As an illustration of how deaf people appreciate music, the sixth Duke of Devonshire - who was stone deaf - asked while on his death-bed for one final performance by his own orchestra.

There have been deaf musicians and composers, the most famous example being Beethoven. In the early 1980s, a young deaf girl triumphed over deafness to become a professional percussionist.

Evelyn Glennie, who lost her hearing at the age of six, was accepted into the Royal Academy of Music after a long struggle during which many professionals showed disdain for the ability of a deaf girl to become a professional percussionist, but the founders of the Beethoven Fund for Deaf Children supported and encouraged her to such an extent that she was able to graduate from the Academy with distinction, and give performances at the Royal Festival Hall and at many other concerts.

Evelyn Glennie
Photo: The Guardian

In the theatrical world, it is truly astonishing that there was no professional theatre of the deaf until 1967 when the National Theatre for the Deaf was formed in the United States. In Britain it was not until 1969 when the first semi-professional deaf theatre company was formed.

287

Drama has always been a favourite activity amongst deaf people since the first schools and social clubs came into being. In the 1890s, many adult deaf social programmes included regular dramatic performances in sign language. This continued through the early twentieth century, until in 1961 the Deaf Mime Group was formed by a few individuals who believed in the ability of deaf people to act and wished to provide those with the most talent with the opportunity of having professional tuition with the specific idea of appearing in BBC programmes for deaf children.

Even before then, the British Deaf Association were holding Drama competitions as a regular feature of their congresses.

In 1962, the R.N.I.D. took over sponsorship of the Deaf Mime Group who performed *Mario the Magician, Peter and the Magic Pears* - both in 1962 - and *The Waxworks Mystery* (1965) on BBC television, *Sganarelle*, and *The Pearl* at the Curtain Theatre in 1969.

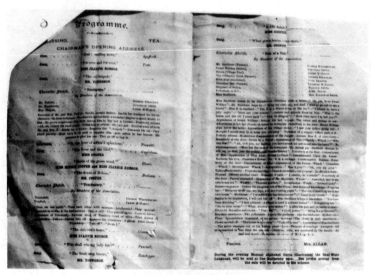

A Drama Programme
Aberdeen Institute for the Deaf - 1883

TWO PLAYS FROM THE 1940s

A Scene from 'Crystal Clear' by the Coventry Deaf Institute
Dramatic Society, 1947
Photo supplied by Carole Harris

A Scene from 'Meet My Grandfather' by the Spurs Club, 1948
Photo courtesy of the Spurs Club.

Drama Photofile

'Robin Hood' - 1938
*Photo: Royal Cross School,
Preston*

'The Mikado' - 1974
*Photo: Braidwood School,
Birmingham*

'The Three Swans' 1971
*Photo: Leicester Deaf Dramatic
Society*

**London Deaf Drama
Group 1980s**
Photo: British Deaf News

In 1969, the group was renamed The British Theatre of the Deaf, and performed at a number of theatres before going on a professional tour in 1974 supported by the Arts Council.

Since then a number of other theatrical companies have been developed starting with the Interim Theatre in 1979. A number of these are mainly educational, and the Theatre of the Deaf is now based at Bulmershe College of Higher Education, Reading.

This development has also meant that more and more deaf actors and actresses have come through the ranks to appear on television as well as in professional plays.

One such individual is Sarah Scott, partially-deaf elder daughter of comedian Terry Scott, who was for a time associated with the Interim Theatre, but who is now associated with a professional theatre which operates workshops and gives plays.

Sarah Scott in Signed Motion

The play *Children of a Lesser God* opened in Britain initially with American Sign Language and an American deaf actress, Elizabeth Quinn, in the principal role. Sarah Scott took over the role for a time at the Albery Theatre, London.

Children of a Lesser God proved to be an attractive play to a number of dramatic societies. For example, the Leicester Drama Society wished to perform it in one of their annual plays at the local playhouse, and through the local deaf society which had a long successful tradition of producing signed drama performances, they were able to recruit Jane Kilgour to play the principal role. It proved to be a very successful co-operation.

Jane Kilgour

Another deaf club with a long dramatic tradition, Coventry, was chosen for a special BBC *SEE HEAR* programme in which they performed their Old Tyme Music Hall dramatic show, with guest stars from the *SEE HEAR* programme.

Television

Considering the length of time that television has been with us, it is astonishing that there was no specific programme for deaf people presented by deaf people until the 1980s.

Through the 1960s and 1970s, programmes with sign language content were few and far between, and were mainly church services.

The first regular programme aimed specifically at deaf and hard of hearing people was a weekly review of the previous week's news, called *News Review*, shown on Sundays on BBC 2. It offered a weekly summary of the news by one of the BBC's newreaders in open subtitles, and once every blue moon, usually around Christmas, it deigned to provide viewers with some titbit of deaf activity.

Old Time Music Hall - by Coventry Deaf Dramatic Society
Shown on the *SEE HEAR* Programme, 1985
Photo: Carole Harris

It was highly unsatisfactory, and the almost non-existence of genuine deaf actors and actresses did not help improve matters when television programmes were made which had a deaf character central to the plot; hearing actors and actresses were used to portray deaf people, sometimes with disastrous results.

The BBC's *SEE HEAR* programme for deaf people was the first attempt to provide a regular series which deaf people could relate to. It is still the only main regular long-running series after 8 years of being on television, and for some years, the presenters have been totally deaf and users of B.S.L.

Rachell Bastilkar and Clark Denmark
Co-Presenters of *Listening Eye*
Channel 4 Television Programme for the Deaf

Channel 4 has shown several six-weekly series of a programme called *Listening Eye*, made by Tyne Tees Television using deaf presenters. This programme's format is fundamentally different from the *SEE HEAR* series in that it has current deaf affairs as its regular theme, and provides a valuable alternative to *SEE HEAR*. The same production team at Tyne Tees have also produced two documentaries, *A Language for Ben* and *Pictures in the Mind* which have earned praise from the deaf community and from the media generally. *A Language for Ben* was the Best Educational Production (Feature Length) in the American Television Movie Awards for 1985.

A number of independent television companies have also produced a series of deaf children's programmes, or regional news programmes for the deaf, but very few have actually used deaf presenters. One progressive station which does is Grampian Television which covers the north of Scotland.

At the time of writing, there is still no nationally-networked daily news programme in Britain which uses deaf people to present the programme. It is the avowed aim of the Deaf Broadcasting Council to secure this programme.

A scene from Pictures in the Mind
Photo: Tyne Tees Television Limited

Chapter 19
The 1950s

Annual Dinner Dance, 1954

Photo: The Spurs Club

The 1950s

The fifties heralded in the new Elizabethan Age, the Korean War, the beginning of the Space Age, the widespread use of television, and Teddy Boys.

Marilyn Monroe reigned supreme as the sex symbol of the decade, while Elvis Presley gave a new meaning to music; Roger Bannister smashed the four-minute mile barrier, and the Hungarians slaughtered England at football.

The Deaf World mourned the premature loss of Leslie Edwards, but saw important milestones in the founding of the B.D.D.A.'s Summer Schools, and of the Ernest Ayliffe Home at Rawdon, near Leeds. The first broadcasts on television about the deaf, including a church service, were made, and two secondary schools were founded - Burwood Park School at Walton-on-Thames and Nutfield Priory Secondary School at Redhill.

The B.D.D.A. Summer Schools
Much thought had previously been given to the desirability of higher or continued education for deaf people: schemes had been discussed many times, but never carried out and the intervention of the War did not help.

The main problem was that for deaf people, there was no opportunity in the present structure of education for them to acquire some form of higher or continued education, and in 1948 the B.D.D.A. grasped the initiative to establish one-week-long Summer Schools for deaf people.

The first was held in Edinburgh in the Summer of 1948 when only a few attended, but the summer of 1951 saw the B.D.D.A.'s summer school really launched at Ruskin College, Oxford. It proved to be enormously popular.

One of B.D.D.A.'s Summer Schools at Coleg Harlech
Photo: British Deaf News

In succeeding years the Summer School was held in various venues, the Coleg Harlech at Merioneth, Wales, being a popular venue, where it was held three times during the 1950s - the others being the University of St. Andrews and St. Luke's College, Exeter, (both once).

To this small beginning, the present B.D.A.'s extensive Further Education and Leisure activities owe their roots.

Centenarians

The summer of 1951 also saw that rarity in the Deaf Community - a deaf centenarian - when Laura Jane Smethurst of Oldham celebrated her 100th birthday on 1st August.

Only once before had any deaf person celebrated the century, a Miss Ann Cuttriss of Ely, Cambridgeshire, back in 1875.

Laura Jane had an especially busy birthday, with a large number of birthday cards, telegrams, flowers and presents, together with visits by civic dignitaries including the Mayor and Mayoress of Oldham.

Later, in 1962, a Miss Edith Lang of Newton Abbot, Devon, celebrated her 100th birthday on 30th October.

Mandy

In 1952 Ealing Studios took over much of the Royal Schools for the Deaf, Manchester, to make the film, *Mandy*, the story of a deaf girl who was played by Mandy Miller. The role of headmaster was played by Jack Hawkins, the well-known actor.

Some of the most memorable scenes from the film *Mandy* involved deaf children at breakfast. The top picture on the next page shows Mandy Miller reluctant to eat any breakfast, which is not surprising, as the bottom picture of an off-camera shot shows - the children had to have at least six helpings of porridge due to retakes. This was just too much for some!

The Ernest Ayliffe Home

This home for aged and infirm men was opened at Rawdon, near Leeds with funds raised almost entirely by members of B.D.D.A., and named after Ernest Ayliffe, President of the Association from 1920 to 1947.

The Deaf World Enters Television

In 1954 Birmingham Institute for the Deaf became the first deaf organisation of any kind to have a television programme made about it. It was transmitted on the B.B.C.

On 30th January 1955, history was made when the B.B.C. televised for the first time ever a full length church service for the deaf from St. Saviour's, Acton. The service was conducted by the Rev. Alan. F. Mackenzie, son of the late

The Breakfast Scene: Mandy
Photos supplied by Michael Davis

George Annand Mackenzie (q.v.), and was only made possible after hours of preparation in the church at Acton.

Around the same time, a remarkable gifted young deaf man named Stephen Skoyles, a former pupil of the East Anglian Schools for the Deaf, Gorleston, was making a career for himself at the B.B.C. as a caption artist, producing lightning sketches and cartoons which conveyed meaning without the need for words.

Stephen Skoyles
Photo: British Deaf News

Later, he was to produce films for deaf children of the 'Dick Barton' type.

Raising Money By Elephant
The ingenuity of deaf people to raise money to build their institutes is remarkable, involving a wide variety of methods. In St. Helens, Lancashire, they seized upon the opportunity presented by the arrival in their town of a circus to borrow an elephant to lumber round the town appealing for funds.

Educational Moves in the Fifties
In the 1950s two major boarding schools for the deaf were opened in Surrey. The first, in 1954, was the first Secondary Modern Boarding School for the deaf to be opened in Britain, and was established by Surrey County Council - Nutfield Priory Secondary Modern School, Redhill.

Nutfield Priory was set high on a ridge with extensive grounds in a building which was built in 1868 and acquired by Surrey County Council after the war. It was run on normal secondary modern lines. However, the growth of hearing-impaired units and the normal fluctuation experienced in all secondary schools saw a decline in pupils attending Nutfield Priory from 1984 onwards, and Surrey County Council took the decision at short notice to close the school in the summer of 1987.

Nutfield Priory School from the Air
Photo: Nutfield Priory School

The second school to open in Surrey was Burwood Park Secondary Technical School for Boys at Walton-on-Thames,

Surrey. This was a private school given by Lord Iveagh and Lady Patricia Boyd of the Guinness brewing family. Entry to this school was by the same entrance examination as that which was already in existence for entry to Mary Hare Grammar School. This was henceforth known as the Joint Entrance Examination.

There was, however, still no form of recognised higher academic education available to deaf people in Britain, and some went to Gallaudet College (now Gallaudet University) in Washington D.C., USA to acquire academic qualifications. One such person was David Anthony of Loughborough.

David Anthony (1931-)

David Anthony was born deaf of deaf parents, and after losing his father at age 3, he was educated first at the Royal School for the Deaf, Derby, then Mary Hare Grammar School.

David Anthony (front centre) with a group of international students at Gallaudet College
Photo: Gallaudet News

He left Mary Hare with a desire to become a teacher of deaf children, but no opportunity being available to him in Britain, what he became was a costing clerk with a Loughborough firm of crane manufacturers where he was deeply dissatisfied.

Denied the opportunity to acquire teaching qualifications in Britain, Anthony explored the possibilities further afield. Gallaudet College, with its degree and educational courses, could, he found, offer him that opportunity and eventually allow him to proceed towards his heart's desire.

In 1956, Sir Roger Makins, the British Ambassador to the United States, presented David Anthony with a bachelor's degree in education - the first deaf Englishman to receive a degree from an American college.

David Anthony is now a teacher of the deaf in Denver, Colorado, USA.

Mayor of Wembley: Arthur Edmond (1914-1982)
Arthur Edmond was educated at the Royal School for Deaf Children, Margate: in his final year, he was Head Boy.

Arthur Edmond
From a painting at the Royal School for Deaf Children, Margate

Showing great courage and dedication, he started his own printing business in a small garden shed, which grew into several shops. Always active in the affairs of his local community, he became Mayor of Wembley in 1954.

Arthur Edmond always had a deep love for his old school, and in 1964 accepted an appointment to become a Governor of the School, and was elected to the Committee of Management.

In 1973, he received what was probably his highest honour, his appointment as High Sheriff of Greater London by H.M. the Queen, and it was during his year as High Sheriff that he personally raised £100,000 towards his old school's costly rebuilding programme, a most remarkable achievement.

Besides these fund-raising activities, he found time to organise special tickets for the schoolchildren to attend the Lord Mayor's Show, encourage the Variety Club of Great Britain to donate video equipment to the school, and do a host of other things for his Alma Mater.

Arthur Edmond is the only known born-deaf person ever to be elected a mayor, and to be appointed a High Sheriff of Britain's capital city.

A Merchant Navy Engineer
Another ex-pupil of the Royal School for Deaf Children, Margate, was to become unique in another field.

Peter Roe
Photo: British Deaf News

Peter Roe of Gillingham, although totally deaf, carved out for himself a successful career as a ship's engineer officer in the Merchant Navy.

He qualified as a Chief Engineer after five years study, but his deafness debarred him from ever holding that position in Britain's Merchant Navy due to Ministry of Transport regulations, so he had to be content with the position of Assistant Engineer Officer.

Chapter 20
World Games for the Deaf

The British Team at Belgrade, 1969

Photo: British Deaf News

World Games for the Deaf

The modern Olympic Games were reconstituted in 1896 at Athens, and proved highly successful in forging sporting links between nations. Naturally, the deaf world too wanted to have the same opportunities.

In 1924 the French took the initiative and organised an International Games for the Deaf and Dumb, which was attended by deaf sportsmen from a number of mainly European nations. A team from Great Britain was organised under the auspices of the British Deaf and Dumb Association, and took part in athletics, swimming, diving, shooting, tennis and football competitions.

The Victorious British Football Team at Paris, 1924
Photo: Leeds Centre for the Deaf

Britain won the tennis doubles cup, the swimming relay race cup, and took prizes in diving and shooting (medals were not given until after the war). In football, Great Britain beat Belgium 4-1 in the final to win the cup.

2nd International Games - Amsterdam 1928
The 2nd Games at Amsterdam saw the participation of 11 nations, again mainly European.

Great Britain Football Team - 1928
Photo: Glasgow & West of Scotland Society for the Deaf

A feature of these early international games was that there was a points system in operation, and Great Britain finished 3rd overall, with firsts in the athletics 200 metres and 400 metres hurdles, plus several other placings. Great Britain also won the Ladies Doubles in tennis.

In football Britain retained the trophy that was won in 1924, this time beating Czechoslovakia 2-1 in the final. In previous rounds, Belgium were thrashed 12-0 and Holland 5-0.

3rd International Games - Nuremberg, Germany 1931
Held in the magnificent Olympic Stadium, Great Britain had a disastrous Games, failing to get a first in any athletic event,

and managing to be losing finalist in both the Ladies' and Men's Doubles.

George Scott, holding the Football Trophy after the win over Czechoslovakia in the Final of 1928
Photo: Glasgow & West of Scotland Society for the Deaf

To cap our misfortunes, Great Britain lost in a controversial fashion the football challenge cup that it had won in the 1924 Paris Games, and retained at Amsterdam in 1928. Drawn against Czechoslovakia in the first round, the same team that had been beaten in the final three years previously, the score was 0-0 at final whistle, so it was decreed that extra time be played.

Within two minutes of the start of extra time, the Czechs scored from a goalmouth scramble and the referee terminated the game. However, following a meeting at 2 am in the morning, the Games committee decided that full extra time had to be played first thing in the morning. Alas, nobody told the British team, although Czechoslovakia, Holland and France (who had also drawn, and had their game similiary stopped when France scored first) were told, and were on the pitch when the British team were still in their beds. As a result, Czechoslovakia were awarded the match only to be beaten by Germany who won the cup by beating Austria 4-1 in the final.

4th International Games - London 1935
The opening event was the 50-miles road cycling race near Reading, which was won by E. Coburn of Great Britain, followed home by a Frenchman in second place, and G. Kennington of Great Britain in third place, a splendid start for the British team.

The British Team in the 1935 Games, London
Photo: Betty Shrine

Alas, the British team could not keep it up, although they came first in the pole vault, the men's 800 metres, the women's 4x100 metre relay, and the men's 1,500 metres relay.

At tennis the finalists in the Men's Singles final were both

British, and Great Britain also won the Men's Doubles and the Mixed Doubles to finish the leading tennis nation. Britain did less well in swimming with no firsts.

At football, there was a new trophy to be won, given by the *Sporting Life* magazine. There were no mistakes made this time, and in the preliminary round France were dispatched 7-1, and the final, played at Highbury, Arsenal F.C.'s ground, was against Belgium who were beaten 4-2.

One feature of these Games was that England saw, perhaps for the only time, the marching of the German jackboots, the Nazi salute, and the flag with the swastika on public display.

5th International Games - Stockholm 1939
Fifteen nations took part in these Games, two of whom, Estonia and Latvia, would never again compete.

'England' as Great Britain in Stockholm, 1939
What happened to the Scots, the Welsh and the Irish?
Photo: Betty Shrine

These Games were notable for the supremacy of the Swedes in athletics and the Germans at swimming; both these nations almost swept the board in the events held in these competitions.

The only consolation for Britain was that, once again, they proved to be supreme champions at football, thrashing Rumania 7-0, and beating Sweden 2-1 in the final.

The British team and supporters had a hair-raising return from Stockholm over the period 2nd-4th Sepember, during which the Second World War broke out, and their ship was stopped and let go by a warship, and instead of arriving at Harwich, the ship went to Aberdeen.

VIth Olympiad - Copenhagen 1949
After a lapse of ten years due to the Second World War the international Games restarted at Copenhagen under a new title, the Olympiad.

This was the last Games when trophies were given instead of medals, and Great Britain brought home the Men's Singles and Men's Doubles tennis trophies, and the 96 km. road cycling trophy.

At athletics, our only winner was a Miss E. Horngold who won the 100 metres, breaking the World Record set in 1935.

Britain's football team had a tough time, playing Holland at 9 am one morning, then Denmark at 6 pm the same evening. They won both games 5-1 and 7-0. The next day Italy were the opponents in the semifinal, which went to extra time before Great Britain emerged 2-1 victors.

The final was against Belgium, the third time in six Games that these two nations had met in the final. At the final whistle, the score was 3-3, so extra time was again played before Britain emerged 6-4.

VIIth Olympiad - Brussels 1953
In this, the first Games to use gold, silver and bronze medals, Great Britain gained 6 golds, 3 silvers and 1 bronze - three of the golds coming from the tennis players who won

313

the Men's Singles, Men's Doubles, and provided both finalists in the Mixed Doubles.

Some of the British Team at Brussels, 1953
Photo: Betty Shrine

Nobby Clarke retained his 100 km. cycling title which he won at Copenhagen, whilst Nick Stovold was just pipped for third place, and at athletics Britain got golds in the men's 800 metres, and the 100 metres.

At football Britain failed for the second time due to misunderstandings when they were not informed of the new rule that corners conceded would count in the event of a draw, and thus lost the opening group match against France (1-1) although they thrashed Holland 9-0 and Sweden 3-2 in the other games. The final was won by Yugoslavia who beat Italy 2-1.

VIIIth Olympiad - Milan 1957
These Games saw the first entry of strong Eastern European teams like Russia and Poland since the war, and it showed in

the athletics where Britain could only win one silver medal. In football Britain lost a match for the first time by actual result (as opposed to misunderstandings in 1931 and 1953), Austria winning 3-2 after extra time in the opening match. Yugoslavia retained the title of Olympic champions.

Only in tennis did British players shine, dominating as they had done in the past whenever they had entered. Britain had finalists in all five finals, but only in the all-British Men's Doubles did Britain get a gold.

The final tally which Great Britain brought home from these games were therefore one gold, six silvers and two bronzes.

IXth Olympiad - Helsinki 1961
These Games in which 23 nations took part saw the poorest British performance since the start in Paris in 1924, winning only one gold, two silvers, and three bronzes.

Once again, tennis saw the best British performance with one gold, one silver and two bronzes. In athletics, D. Beech (who won the gold at Milan) could only manage second place this time, and the other bronze was won in the cycling 35 km. time trial.

At football, Great Britain made a great start by thrashing Turkey 13-1, but in the next round came up against the champions, Yugoslavia and lost by their heaviest score of any international Games, 0-5. Yugoslavia went on to complete a hat-trick of Olympiad championships.

Xth Olympiad - Washington 1965
There were twenty-seven countries taking part in these Games, and it had truly become more international with the participation for the first time of Iran, Australia, Japan, Argentina, India, Mexico and Israel. This was also the first time the Games had been held outside Europe, and the expense of sending a team to the U.S.A., plus visa problems, accounted for the absence of Czechoslovakia and Rumania.

Great Britain did much better in these Games than they

had done since 1953, winning three golds, six silvers and four bronzes. Two of the golds and one silver came from the brilliance of Malcolm Johnson in the cycling races. The other gold was won by our swimming team, their first since 1924 in Paris.

For the first time since the war Great Britain failed to win any tennis titles, the best they could do being losing finalists in four out of five of the finals.

The remaining silver was won by the football team, which was the best since 1949 at Copenhagen. They lost 1-3 to the Olympiad Champions, Yugoslavia in the final - Yugoslavia thus winning their fourth title on the trot.

XIth World Games for the Deaf - Belgrade, 1969

After the 1965 Games, the International Olympic Committee decreed that the word 'Olympiad' could not be used outside of the Olympics proper, so the title was changed to 'World Games for the Deaf , a title it retains to this day.

Great Britain only managed two golds (both in cycling), one silver (swimming) and one bronze (tennis), their lowest tally for many years.

The hero of the British team was, as in 1965, Malcolm Johnson with his superb cycling. If he had not had a fall and a puncture in his third race, he might have completed a hat trick of medals.

In football Great Britain was knocked out in the first round by Russia who were losing finalists, Yugoslavia winning for the fifth time since 1953.

XIIth World Games - Malmo, Sweden 1973

Once again British blushes were spared by the excellent performance of Malcolm Johnson who won two golds and one silver.

There was also a gritty performance by the swimming squad who returned with four silvers and two bronzes, the best British tally ever in this sport. The remaining silver and bronze medals were won by our tennis team.

Sports Photofile

British Medal Winners, Washington 1965 Games

Malcolm Johnson winning
the Gold Washington 1965

Winning again
Belgrade 1969

Photos: British Deaf News

317

British Team, Malmo 1973

Photos: British Deaf News

British Team, Koln 1981

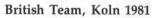

Medal Winners at Badminton and Athletics
Los Angeles 1985
Photos: British Deaf News

For British athletes and footballers, there was bitter disappointment - as one official said, 'We were not good enough'. Russia won the football final, thus ending the dominance of Yugoslavia, five times winners on the trot since 1953. They had to be content with a bronze.

XIIIth World Games - Bucharest, Rumania 1977
These Games saw the smallest British participation since they commenced in Paris in 1924; there were just four swimmers and two officials.

Lack of funds, disinterest, failure to meet qualifying standards all meant that, for the first time since 1924, Britain had no tennis, athletic or football competitors.

No medals were won.

XIVth World Games - Cologne, 1981
These Games were due to be held in Tehran, Iran, but due to civil disturbances and the likelihood of war conditions in the country, they were switched at the last moment to the German city of Cologne.

This enabled Britain to send a squad of 49 competitors, a vast improvement on 1977 when only 4 swimmers were sent.

The team returned home with one silver and six bronzes, mainly in swimming although David Robinson got Britain's first track medals since Helsinki 1961, winning the silver (200 metres), and bronze (400 metres).

In football Great Britain got to the semifinals for the first time since 1965 at Washington, and beat Sweden 5-1 for third place and the bronze medal.

These were the last Games held in Europe for ten years.

XVth World Games - Los Angeles, 1985
For the Fifteenth Games it was a return to the United States, this time in Los Angeles, only the second occasion when the Games had been held outside Europe. To many people, it was a mistake holding the Games in Los Angeles: too many events were held too far apart, and the urban sprawl of the

city meant that athletes often spent up to two hours travelling to venues.

For Britain, however, the 1985 Games were hugely successful, when five golds, eleven silvers and ten bronzes were won. The introduction of badminton as a sport saw a strong British entry, and resulted in three golds (Men's Singles, Doubles, Mixed Doubles), four silvers and three bronzes - in fact, the Men's Singles, Men's Doubles and Mixed Doubles were All-British finals, and the bronzes was also taken in the Mixed Doubles, making a clean sweep.

On the athletics track, Britain got its first ever athletic's gold medals since 1957 when Tim Butler won both the 5,000 and 10,000 metres. He also took the bronze in the 1500 metres. Two silvers were also won by David Robinson (400 metres hurdles) and the 4x400 metres relay team.

In swimming, there were exceptional performances by the British men, especially Alistair Johnson of Durham who broke the World Record in the 1500 metres freestyle yet still had to be content with a silver. In all four silvers and six bronzes were won by the swimming squad.

In football Great Britain thrashed Colombia 8-0, and beat Holland 4-2, but lost to Italy 1-2 in the final to take the silver.

XVIth Games - Christchurch, New Zealand 1989

Without any doubt, this was the costliest sports venture ever undertaken by the British Deaf Sports Council, who run the Great Britain teams, but the 42 competitors who went halfway round the world to represent Britain in Christchurch, New Zealand, did their country proud by winning twelve gold medals, eight silvers and six bronzes, the best tally ever by a British World Games for the Deaf squad.

Especially magnificient were the British swimming squad, particularly the men, who beat the USA - previously unbeaten over the past 20 years - in two relay races.

But there were heroes as well in badminton, athletics and football. For the first time since 1949 at Copenhagen, Great Britain's footballers won the final and the gold medal when they beat Ireland (who incidently had reached their first ever final).

The Great Britain Squad, Christchurch 1989
Photo: British Deaf News

World Games Summary - Great Britain

Venue & Year	Trophies won	Football team
Paris 1924	Men's Tennis Doubles Swimming relay	Winners
Amsterdam 1928	Ladies Tennis Doubles Firsts in athletic 200 metres 400 metres hurdles	Winners
Nuremberg 1931	None	Eliminated 1st Round
London 1935	Tennis : Men's Singles, Doubles; Mixed Doubles 50 mile road race (cycling) Firsts in athletics 800m; Women's 4x100m relay Mens 1500m. relay	Winners
Stockholm 1939	None	Winners
Copenhagen 1949	Tennis : Men's Singles, Doubles Cycling : 96km road race; first in athletics 100m	Winners

Medals Gained

	Gold	Silver	Bronze	Total	Football
Brussels 1953	6	3	1	10	Eliminated 1 Rd
Milan 1957	1	6	2	9	Eliminated 1 Rd
Helsinki 196	1	2	3	6	Eliminated 2 Rd
Washington 1965	3	6	4	13	Losing Finalists
Belgrade 1969	2	1	1	4	Eliminated 1 Rd
Malmo 1973	2	6	3	11	Eliminated 1 Rd
Bucharest 1977	0	0	0	0	Did not qualify
Cologne 1981	0	1	6	7	3rd Place
Los Angeles 1985	5	11	10	26	Losing Finalists
Christchurch 1989	12	8	6	26	Winners

Winter Games for the Deaf

The modern Olympic Games movement is not confined to 'summer' sports like athletics, swimming and the like, but also has a separate Winter Games for skiing, ice skating, ice hockey and so on.

The first deaf International Winter Games first took place after the Second World War, but Great Britain did not enter a team until nine Winter Games had been held, when following the increasing popularity of skiing due to exposure on television, a team of three was entered in the 10th Winter Games at Madonna di Campliglio, Italy, in 1983.

The team did not win any medals.

It was a different story in Norway in 1987. Crawford Carrick Anderson, a 16-year-old from Glasgow, exceeded all expectations to obtain Great Britain's first ever Winter Games medal when he took the silver in the Giant Slalom.

This young boy also took bronzes in the Slalom and the Parallel Slalom - a very creditable performance for someone in his first ever Games.

323

Top: The successful G.B. Swimming Team at Antibes 1983

Right: Crawford Garrick Anderson on the rostrum after receiving Great Britain's first ever Winter games Medal in the Giant Slalom in Norway, 1987
Photos: British Deaf News

European Championships
Various European Deaf Sports Championships were constituted in the 1970s for different sports, athletics, swimming, tennis and skiing.

Great Britain has not always participated in every championship, largely due to reasons of finance; priority has usually been given to fund-raising for participation in the World Games. However, in one sport, swimming, Great Britain has always participated due to the excellent efforts by parents and schools in helping to raise the necessary funds to send a team.

The first European Swimming championships were held in Kaposvar, Hungary, in 1975 followed by Hildesheim, West Germany (1980), Antibes, France (1983) and Crystal Palace (1986).

By the fourth Championship in 1986, Great Britain had established itself as the second-leading European nation in deaf swimming behind West Germany.

Medals Table

Venue & Year	Gold	Silver	Bronze	Total
Kaposvar, Hungary - 1975	6	4	2	12
Hildesheim, W Germany - 1980	11	2	2	15
Antibes, France - 1983	3	7	2	12
Crystal Palace, London - 1986	14	7	7	28

Note :- The success of Great Britain in many of the World Games and European Championships is due in no small measure to the dedication of volunteer officials of the British Deaf Sports Council who deserve the generous support of everyone in their efforts to raise funds to send sports teams to these Games.

Chapter 21
The 1960s

The British Deaf & Dumb Association's Yacht
Purchased for its Educational Courses
Photo: British Deaf News

The 1960s

The decade became known as the 'Swinging Sixties' in Britain as people began to enjoy the years of affluence and fun after the austerity of the post-war years and the 1950s.

Deaf people and deaf communities were no exception. New deaf institutes were opened in Leicester and Coventry incorporating every convenience, but St. John of Beverley in Green Lanes, London missed a great opportunity following a disastrous fire on the premises; Nottingham School for the Deaf moved out into its own premises after sharing the institute premises with the deaf society since 1931; the National Institute for the Deaf acquired the title 'Royal' to become henceforth known as the R.N.I.D., while the British Deaf and Dumb Association launched its educational and mountain venture courses and purchased a boat.

Later in the decade the Lewis Report was produced on the state of deaf education, and left things pretty much up in the air by making a number of conflicting recommendations.

The sixties were also the decade which sounded the death-knell for a number of proud old deaf schools and institutions. It was in the sixties that the crusade for integrating deaf children into ordinary schools instead of placing them in special schools for the deaf began to take off. Partially hearing units (PHUs) attached to secondary and primary schools began to spread throughout the country.

New Premises For Old Missions
Modernisation of our inner cities to include the provision of

327

ring roads and better road access in the 1960s meant that Leicester's Causeway Lane premises, and Coventry's Hill Street headquarters both had to come down. Consequently in both these cities the opportunity was taken to plan and build magnificent new centres for the local deaf incorporating all the modern amenities and games rooms as well as a small chapel.

Leicester's new centre was opened by H.R.H. the Duchess of Gloucester on 18th July 1961. She was accompanied by the Lord Bishop of Leicester who performed a dedication ceremony in the Church of the Good Shepherd attached to the new centre.

Leicester Mission for the Deaf
Photo: Author's collection

Coventry's Henry Fry Centre for the Deaf incorporating the chapel of St. John of Beverley was dedicated by the Bishop of Coventry in 1967.

Other cities and towns which built or purchased new centres included Bristol and Falkirk, but the London Centre of St. John of Beverley at Green Lanes appeared to miss a marvellous opportunity to do so when in 1960 a fire swept

Dedication Service at Coventry
Photo: Carole Harris

Falkirk's New Centre
Photo: British Deaf News

through the institute, destroying the games rooms and parts of the main hall. Only the church and one small lounge remained unscathed, and it was decided to continue with church services only for the time being while the social part of the centre was repaired, a decision that was later to be regretted.

B.D.D.A. Activities and Summer Schools

The British Deaf and Dumb Association's Summer Schools had proved so popular that in 1959 their leisure activities were extended to include Mountain Venture courses, and extended further still as part of the Association's Further Education programme to include such activities as ponytrekking, sailing and many other activities.

In 1963, for the first time, the Summer School went 'across the water' to Ballycastle in Northern Ireland.

The Summer School at Ballycastle, Northern Ireland
Photo: British Deaf News

Other Leisure Activities

Leisure activities were not, of course, confined to the

B.D.D.A.'s Further Education Service. Many centres for the deaf had their own sports and leisure activities, and of these, the centre at Hull must have been unique. In a town where the sport of Rugby League reigns supreme, Hull Deaf Club boasted what was probably the first and only deaf Rugby League team.

Ponytrekking
Photo: British Deaf News

Hull Deaf Rugby League Team
Photo: British Deaf News

331

Regional associations of the B.D.D.A. organised annual rallies which were much looked forward to by deaf members as a principal means of meeting old friends, and letting their hair down.

Dorothy Rait receiving the Ladies Individual Trophy
Photo: British Deaf News

Deaf motorists had their own club and association where they met to hold aptitude tests, and learn new skills, and at a time when ten-pin bowling was in fashion throughout the country, Aberdeen Deaf Club had their own team in the local league where they had some success; one of their ladies Miss Dorothy Rait won the ladies individual trophy for the highest score more than once. In 1966 their two teams came first and second in the League.

Deaf children also shone in leisure activities. Dennis Dashey, aged 9, of Barking, Essex, was judged the Sportsman of the Year at his local gymkhana, and only when it came to presenting him with his trophy did the judges realise he was deaf. Two pupils at the Royal West of England School, Exeter, Mervyn Frost and Lyn Rigler, won ballroom dancing awards; Mervyn the highest junior prize in Britain, the International Dancing Masters Association's Gold Award, Lyn the Association's bronze award.

At sport, the British Deaf Amateur Sports Association's various athletic, swimming and other sports championships were proving popular. One of the most popular was the innovative 5-a-side soccer championships which attracted large attendances.

Mervyn Frost & Lyn Rigler
Photo: British Deaf News

While sporting activities were the mainstay of British Deaf Community activities along with rallies and special events attended by hundreds of people, two young men were making their presence felt in another arena. They were wrestlers Mike Eagers and Harry Kendall. Before he turned professional, Harry had reigned supreme as undefeated British amateur heavyweight wrestling champion, and represented England at the Empire Games where he won two bronze medals. On the professional circuit, Eagers and Kendall formed a tag team called the Silent Ones.

In Scotland the Scottish Regional Council held an Arts and Crafts Exhibition which was extremely successful, and attracted a lot of entries. Photographic competitions were also in the fashion, and a number were held up and down the country.

Wrestler Harry Kendal visits a Deaf Club with Mike Eagers
Photo: British Deaf News

David Dashey with his Gymkhana Trophies
Photo: British Deaf News

Belfast Deaf Table Tennis Team
Photo: British Deaf News

One deaf artist who held regular exhibitions and who painted professionally was Robert Menzies Scott.

Robert Menzies Scott (1891-1977)

Robert Menzies Scott was born into a deaf family; his brother George was the captain of the 1928 Great Britain team which retained the football championships at the International Games for the Deaf in Amsterdam.

He was educated at Donaldson's Hospital School in Edinburgh, and began work as a litho artist in Glasgow, but never lost his love for art, always painting in both oils and water-colour. Many of his pictures reflected life on Glasgow's Clydeside industrial scene.

After his death in 1977, a special exhibition of over 200 oil paintings, water-colours, charcoal, pastel, pen, pencil and wash drawings was held at Hamilton District Museum as a memorial to him.

Scottish B.D.D.A. Regional Council's Arts and Crafts Exhibition
Photo: British Deaf News

Robert Menzies Scott at work as a young man
Photo: Glasgow & West of Scotland Society for the Deaf

Two paintings by Robert Menzies Scott
Reproduced by the kind permission of Hamilton District Museum

The Lewis Report, 1968

One report into the state of deaf education that had been long awaited came out in the summer of 1968. This was the Lewis Committee Report, a survey into deaf education by a Committee of 16 people headed by Professor M.M. Lewis, Emeritus Professor of Education at the University of Nottingham. Only one of those sixteen committee members was deaf. The Committee's terms of reference were 'to consider the place, if any, of fingerspelling and signing in the education of the deaf'.

The Report listed a total of fourteen recommendations, four of which suggested research activities directly connected with the use of sign language. However, there were also five recommendations which would tend to dampen such efforts, and two recommendations were injunctions to all concerned to improve the conditions for further oral advances. The other three were concerned with the need to improve school records, to remove the partially hearing from sign language research and experiment, and to define the aims of deaf education.

The overall impression given by the Report was that while the Committee were clearly impressed by the evidence submitted by advocates of sign language methods, they were unable or unwilling to give clear-cut advice as to the next step.

Earlier the same year a little known survey by the Department of Education and Science had been published, titled *Units for Partially Hearing Children*. This survey had looked at 74 of the 162 established P.H.U.s in Britain and was heavily critical of the standards. Only 15 out of the 74 were found to be satisfactory; 16 units had children who should have been referred to special schools; 11 units had children whose demands on teachers were too great for the system.

Twenty years on, with even more children in units and fewer in special schools which are consequently being closed, the postion remains unchanged.

Chapter 22
British Sign Language

**A Poster which typically illustrates the
liberation of Sign Language**
Reproduced with the permission of the Cheshire Society for the Deaf

CHAPTER 22

British Sign Language
Our Greatest National Heritage

George W. Veditz, the seventh president of the United States National Association for the Deaf, called sign language 'the noblest gift God has given to deaf people.'

The use of visual forms of communication is as much part of the natural heritage of human beings as is the spoken word. Gestures of the hands and arms, the face and body are in use in many everyday situations for emphasis, illustration, ceremony and signalling. They are in use in religious worship, in sporting situations, in certain occupations; they are in use for theatrical purposes, as in Far Eastern dance ceremonies, for the purposes of secrecy and silence, and also for the conveyance of lewd meanings.

Sign languages, which are not art forms but means of everyday communication independent of spoken language, have however, developed in several very different settings. The Australian aboriginal tribes, the Bushmen of the Kalahari Desert, the North American Plains Indians, all developed sign language for hunting, trading and storytelling around campfires. The presence of sign languages amongst these people would suggest that their use goes back to prehistoric man.

The Hebrew book, *Talmud*, records that deaf-mutes can hold conversation by means of gestures. This statement suggests that the rabbis who wrote the book had such conversations interpreted for them by hearing members of a deaf

340

person's family. This is the earliest recorded statement of any visual form of language amongst deaf people: it was, even then, probably a form of Yiddish Sign Language though not recorded as such. As it is, the earliest recorded use of sign language can be traced back to the religious order founded by St. Benedict (A.D.529). These monks were required to take vows of partial or perpetual silence, but although spoken words were considered unacceptable, signs were not, and so it came about that signs were created and passed down generations of monks. It was a Benedictine monk, Pedro Ponce de Leon of Spain, who is universally regarded as the first teacher of deaf pupils, and he used sign language to do so. This was *circa* 1550.

It was not until *circa* 1595 that the first recorded observation in Britain of sign language communication in use between two deaf people was made by Richard Carew of Edward Bone and John Kempe in Cornwall, but it is evident that the use of sign language by and amongst deaf people was well established by then. Scottish Court records indicate that Princess Jean, daughter of James 1, communicated by signs in the 1430s and King James 1 of England felt concerned enough soon after becoming King in 1603 to try to appoint a Professor of Signs in an attempt to make a detailed study of the sign language used by a deaf woman he met.

Certainly, the Gostwicke brothers and the Gawdy brothers who lived in the seventeenth century were fluent in sign language, and there is no doubt that John Bulwer who wrote the *Deafe and Dumbe Man's Friende* was influenced by the Gostwicke brothers, and we have Samuel Pepys' written evidence that at least one Minister in King Charles II's government (Sir George Downing) was a fluent interpreter of sign language.

From the day the first school for the deaf in Britain was established by Braidwood in Edinburgh in 1760, sign language amongst the pupils, if not amongst the staff, was in common use. Braidwood himself may have not at first known any sign language, but it is certain that he did later pick it up

One of the 1st Manual Alphabets
From John Bulwer's Deaf and Dumb Man's Friende,1648
Reproduced with permission of the British Library, London

from his pupils, and adapt his teaching methods accordingly to use a form of total communication (e.g. speech, writing, sign language and reading). The members of his family who carried on after his death, both at Edinburgh and then at Hackney, and at the newly-established schools in Birmingham and Edinburgh, all used sign language as a means of communication with their pupils. One person who trained under the Braidwoods, Robert Kinniburgh, was to become an interpreter *par excellence* in Scotland as he demonstrated on more than one occasion in a court of law.

Teaching methods in the early deaf schools in Britain placed a heavy emphasis on manual communication methods. The emphasis became more profound when these schools started to use pupil-teachers and junior teachers from suitable and gifted children who came through their ranks; people like Walter Geikie, the famous artist, and Edward Kirk, the headmaster of Leeds School for the Deaf, were pupil-teachers at their respective schools (the Edinburgh and the Yorkshire Institutions) before they moved elsewhere to carve out other careers for themselves. Practically all schools for the deaf prior to 1880 had deaf people on the teaching staff; often these outnumbered the hearing members of the staff.

This heavy emphasis on manual communication was one of the reasons that led to the establishment of pure oral schools in this country, starting with Arnold's school at Northampton in 1868. Some parents and educators felt that no effort was made, or little attention given, to the teaching of speech in these schools.

The spread of schools where pure oralism was in use forced the manual schools to respond by implementing a combined system, i.e. using articulation as well as manual communication, but the biggest change came after the Milan Congress of 1880 which voted to outlaw the use of sign language in the education of deaf children in favour of the pure oral method.

The Controversy Between Sign Language and Oralism

No history of any deaf community can, unfortunately, be complete without the mention of this controversy, or war.

Why? Many would ask, why the controversy? Why did deaf education and deaf children have to be blighted by such division? There is no simple answer, but perhaps one of the reasons is that deaf individuals look so ordinary; they look no different from other people until one tries to communicate with them, whereas other handicaps are visible.

Sadly the main blame and cause of the controversy lies at the feet of some professionals working with the deaf who influence hearing parents of deaf children. No parent wants to admit that their child is different from other children; parents usually tend to seek a cure for deafness, something which will make their child 'normal', they cannot accept, as deaf adults do, that their child is already 'normal'.

To this end, therefore, some parents are blind to reason. They embrace all that the oral philosophy offers to them in promising to make their child able to talk and lipread so well as to fit into the wider society without any difficulty; they reject the existence of a separate deaf sub-culture and heritage that can offer their child a full lifestyle. Teachers who embrace the oral philosophy do nothing to disillusion them; on the contrary, many encourage the parents to think in this way.

In consequence many parents do not find out until it is far too late that the pure oral method is a very rocky road indeed which preciously few deaf children succeed in mastering. Deaf people know this only too well, to their cost. Some even feel that to encourage parents to embrace an oral philosophy without detailing the possible consequences and giving equal opportunity to the benefits of other forms of education constitutes malpractice.

Be that as it may, this controversy over the best way to educate deaf children in this country has raged for many years. Hundreds of articles have appeared in print; salvos of criticism have been fired back and forth, claims and counterclaims made as to the effectiveness of the pure oralist method, or methods combining the use of sign language with speech.

Research findings and statistics were used by both camps in advocating the effectiveness of their methods, further confusing parents and other people who were unfamiliar with the terminology used.

The result was that deaf children who did not succeed in oral schools, and there were many of them, were labelled 'oral failures'; the standard of deaf education plunged. Those children who did get through an oral education often felt misfits in the wider society; many were so indoctrinated against going to deaf clubs or functions that they were psychologically damaged, leading lonely and isolated lives before they would 'discover' that the deaf way of life, the deaf sub-culture, was not as bad as it had been painted, that the deaf community and the deaf heritage were rich in opportunities for fulfilment.

Deaf adults themselves, as a whole, did not oppose the teaching of speech or lipreading. Many saw that the acquisition of those skills, allied to the use of sign language, as the ideal method to attain the highest measure of intellectual, social and moral happiness. But their views were never sought, and when expressed these views were totally ignored.

The oralist-dominated years that followed Milan, 1880, had a profound effect on deaf people, most of it negative. Parents would have nothing to do with deaf teachers, who vanished from deaf schools. Deaf education declined so much that by the 1960s, the average reading age of a school-leaver was 8 3/4. One has only to read magazines for the deaf from the 1880s to the 1960s to see how standards declined, as shown in Chapter 18.

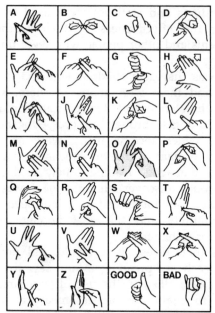

The present day Manual Alphabet
Reproduced with the permission of the British Deaf Association

Attempts to Suppress Sign Language
In a statement to the Royal Commission on the Education of the Blind, and the Deaf and the Dumb, whose report was published in 1889, Dr. David Buxton, a former headmaster of the Liverpool Institution for the Deaf and Dumb and a fervent oralist supporter, had this to say:

'I am so thoroughly in earnest in my advocacy of the superiority of the oral system, that I should be very glad to

see any other extinguished; but I know that must be a matter of time. The oral system is incomparably the best; it is not open to question at all, because it assimilates the deaf to the class with whom they live. If I want to communicate by signs to a deaf child I have to descend to his level, but by the oral I raise him to my level. For a time, perhaps, the combined system may struggle on; I think that is very probable. But that the sign system will last in itself, I have not the slightest expectation - I think sign language will die out.'

Many oral advocates held exactly the same view. Sign language was blamed for everything that was held to be 'bad' about deaf people - it was blamed for their lack of speech, for their poor grasp of the English language, for the high rate of intermarriage amongst deaf people. If anything was wrong with deaf people, sign language was the cause of it.

In order to suppress sign language, oral educators did everything they could to kill it. The co-operation of parents was sought, deaf teachers were refused employment, deaf children were told that using signs was bad and degrading. They were told that they would not grow up to be 'normal' people if they could not speak or lipread; many children were told that if they went to deaf centres, they were failures for deaf clubs were dens of depravity where sign language flourished.

Deaf adults like George Healey, James Paul, Francis Maginn and William Agnew, all highly respected pillars of the community, fought a tough, losing battle to stop this suppression. Agnew, in particular, was an extremely well-read and compulsive letter writer; he bombarded many influential newspapers and magazine about sign language. He drew tremendous pride from the fact that he could communicate as an equal with Queen Victoria.

Not even the British Deaf and Dumb Association could stop the tide. At its very first Congress in 1890, a resolution was passed that the Congress

'...indignantly protests against the imputation that the

finger and sign language is barbarous. We consider such a mode of exchanging our ideas as most natural and indispensable, and that the combined system of education is by far preferable to the so-called Pure Oral'.

It was to no avail as the oralist advocates began to implement their programmes with government backing. Some methods of suppressing the use of sign language were extremely harsh; punishments frequently included rapping children's hands with stiff sticks or rulers, tying up the children's hands behind their backs or in brown paper bags. Other forms included making them sit on their hands to keep them from going astray and forming signs; depriving children of amenities; making them write out 'I must not sign' repeatedly for up to an hour, or even more. Even natural gestures as innocent as describing, for example, the size of a fish incurred the wrath of the teachers.

All these attempts to suppress sign language only caused deaf people to defy them. Children would use it on the sly behind teachers' backs, or underneath desks, or in the lavatories. Unfortunately, such use also came to be associated with deceit, stigma and a negative, guilty attitude. It was like forbidden fruit, and visits to adult deaf centres by deaf schoolchildren became daring - children would in fact 'dare' each other to go, and those who would not were labelled 'chicken'. The deceit and the stigma slowly spread out amongst the general population who came to view deaf institutes and social centres as 'loony bins', and as such places to be avoided.

Abraham Farrar, regarded by the oralist advocates as their greatest triumph, became so concerned over the intensity of the moves to suppress and outlaw sign language that he counselled for '...tolerance over the use of sign language in education.' It would be, he stated in an article to a newspaper, a grave mistake to regard oralism as the vehicle by which all deaf people could make progress. Even he was contemptuously brushed aside; after all, when it really came down to it, Abraham Farrar was deaf too, and deaf people's views were of no consequence.

It was the gravest injustice ever done to deaf people.

Keeping the Spirit Alive

Fortunately for British Sign Language, there were a number of issues which ensured its survival despite all attempts to ruthlessly suppress it. First and foremost, it was that despite being taught by oral methods, and being forced to speak in schools, many deaf people left school with imperfect unintelligible speech, speech that was never going to be good enough to enable them to cope effectively in the wider society. In addition, many also had poor lipreading skills. For those people, B.S.L. was their most effective means of communication, and thus freed of the restraints that had blighted their youth, they began to use it in earnest. Research done at the University of Durham indicates that average British Sign Language users received as much of an education in the first twelve months of participation in deaf club activities as they received in all their school years.

Secondly the deaf community had, and still has, a very firm core which could never be eradicated by the oralists however hard they tried. This was the ten per cent who had deaf parents, for in such families, the use of British Sign Language was an everyday fact of life. Often, especially in rural areas, such homes of families were a substitute for deaf clubs; other local deaf people would gravitate to those homes so that they could have some means of communication. Deaf people would seek out other deaf people in the same way that Edward Bone would seek out John Kempe back in 1595.

Thirdly the British Deaf and Dumb Association despite its weak position and being practically taken over at the top and run by hearing people nonetheless managed to weld together a social, leisure, welfare and educational infrastructure which maintained a fabric out of which the Deaf Community could plan its resurgence.

These important factors were given a boost by developments in the United States in the 1950s when Dr. William Stokoe, a linguist, became fascinated by the language of signs in use on the Gallaudet College campus, and started his own research. He proved that American Sign Language had all the necessary ingredients that made up a language: the points of contrasts, the morphemes, the syntactical patterns. He was the first linguist to subject sign language to all the tests of a real language, and it withstood all the tests. However, when he published his initial findings in 1960, few people paid attention. He was nearly alone in his belief that sign language was a language in its own right.

Dr. Stokoe's research into sign language excited Allan Brindle Hayhurst, the Secretary-Treasurer of the British Deaf Association, so much that he started a project he was not to live to finish - a B.S.L. dictionary. Hayhurst's work on this project was eventually taken over by Durham University as agents for the B.D.A.

Perhaps more significantly, Stokoe's work also came to the attention of linguists and psychologists at Moray House College, Edinburgh, and at Bristol University. At Edinburgh Mary Brennan and at Bristol Dr. J. Kyle both formed teams to do research into British Sign Language. These teams both found that B.S.L. was indeed a language and one of greater complexity than ever had been suspected. By simply declaring that British Sign Language was a language people's perceptions changed.

Deaf people now officially had something positive and attractive which for them was a matter of pride, a priceless heritage, a thriving sign language, vibrant and moreover still alive a century after its death had been prophesied in 1889!

British Sign Language Today
Today B.S.L. is Britain's fourth indigenous language after Welsh and Scots Gaelic. These two minority languages, like B.S.L., have had a troubled history in that they have had to fight hard and long for their survival, and only in 1967, with the passing of the Welsh Language Act, did Welsh attain

equal status with the English Language - but only in Wales. Even then the battle has not been fully won in Wales because there is no right to use and learn Welsh, and to use Welsh in education, the courts and in financial institutions.

Evidence of official recognition of Welsh as a language can be seen most clearly in the extent to which the Government supports its promotion. The Government also financially supports Scots Gaelic-related educational and development projects, but Scots Gaelic is still not officially recognised in Scotland.

B.S.L. shares with these two other indigenous languages some evidence of official recognition, particularly in Government-sponsored projects, but desires the same official recognition as the other two in the arena where it matters most - in the educational battleground.

It is, and has always been since 1880, contested by the adult deaf community that failure to use the primary language of children in deaf schools has had disastrous educational results. Wherever Sign Language has been barred from schools, deaf school-leavers have emerged from their education academically deprived and condemned by their illiteracy to low career expectations, social exclusion and cultural deprivation.

At the end of the 1970s a small number of British schools for deaf children began to introduce Sign Language as part of the Total Communication approach that uses all the available means of communication according to the needs of the child. Success was such that nearly half the special schools in the country later followed suit as well as some Partially Hearing Units (PHUs) attached to mainstream schools.

However, many local education authorities still remain obdurate opponents of Sign Language, forcing parents to fight to get deaf children into Total Communication schools of their choice.

Ironically, these same local authorities' Adult Education departments have been deluged with people wishing to attend Sign Language classes as a result of being exposed to

its use on television, or as a result of social services departments' policies in encouraging staff to acquire sign language
communication skills in the furtherance of the rehabilitation
of their clients. As a consequence of this, there was a
national shortage of suitable deaf persons able to teach others
their language, and in 1985, the British Deaf Association
helped to establish with Durham University the British Sign
Language Training Agency (BSLTA).

BSLTA

The Certificate offered by the British Sign Language Training
Agency at Durham University - British Sign Language: Tutors
Course (Foundation Level) - was approved by the University
in early 1987, thus for the first time offering hearing people
the opportunity to be taught BSL by professionally qualified
deaf tutors.

**Clark Denmark, Research fellow British Sign Language
Training Agency University of Durham**
Photo: British Deaf News

One of the MSC-sponsored classes.
Photo: M.Cox

Members of the Foundation course on Graduation Day.
Photo: British Deaf News

The first 80 students were trained with funds raised through the Government-sponsored Manpower Services Commission (MSC), and contrary to expectations and the sneers of those who decried the qualification, the course is stiff, very demanding and not surprisingly, there were failures among the students. Both the University and the MSC demanded a high standard, and this was met.

Some of the first MSC-sponsored students on Graduation Day
Photo: Author's collection

There is still a long way to go before there will be enough tutors to cover the country, but in conjunction with the Council for Advancement of Communication with Deaf People (CACDP), which is also based at Durham University, the end result will hopefully see many hearing people proudly holding certificates to prove their competency in the use of B.S.L.

B.S.L. Interpreters
Deaf people accept that they are part of the dominant hearing world, and only ask for the right to participate in it. Because they do not live together in distinct or separate communities, they constantly need to communicate with English speakers and constantly require access to verbal or written information - at school, in job training, at work, on

television, in the health, welfare and legal services, at conferences and at social events. This would not be possible without interpreters.

Throughout history deaf people have usually had family members or friends to interpret for them, and once deaf schools became established, teachers commonly found themselves being asked to interpret at functions or services in the early nineteenth century. The first ever interpreter to be used in a court of law was a headmaster of a deaf school. Later, as more and more hearing people became missioners to deaf societies, these people often took on the role of interpreters. Later still, welfare officers, then social workers, fulfilled these tasks.

The above shows a form of interpreting equally as important as sign language interpreting, that of reverse interpreting when a deaf person chooses to use sign language to address a conference (in this case a political party conference) and uses an interpreter to do a voice-over
Photo: The Times

However, it was never a very satisfactory arrangement. Access to functions, events or information was very restricted, and there was no training system to give formal interpreting qualifications. Some hearing people working with deaf people became very proficient and professional interpreters, but too many were simply of a standard too low or do anything other than increase deaf people's frustrations at the lack of information they were being given access to. It was not uncommon for interpreters to censor the information being given to deaf people, sometimes with unfortunate results.

The situation became so bad in the late 1970s that moves were made to set up a register of interpreters, and to form an interpreters' association where guidelines were drawn up. Even so, because of the lack of training opportunities and professional status, it has been a long struggle to form a suitable cadre of interpreters, and it will be many years yet before sign language interpreters are around in sufficient numbers, and of equal status with foreign language interpreters.

Official Recognition of British Sign Language
The only way forward to overcome all these years of suppression, inadequacy, ignorance and to allow B.S.L. to flourish into a vital, vibrant, language is to secure official recognition of it as a language.

There is no doubt that the day will come; already in the European Parliament, a resolution has been accepted that each country's sign language be recognised.

Only then will the British Deaf Community be able to obtain a properly funded national interpreter service, and have B.S.L. widely used by hearing people as well as deaf people, and a respected culture with a most precious heritage.

Till then, British Sign Language needs to be exposed to the general public as frequently as possible, and one method of how deaf people and their organisations have been doing this is through holding Sign Language Marathons, which as well as being an excellent means of raising much-needed funds is also a means of providing wonderful opportunities to demonstrate its use in public places. The British Deaf Association in particular have organised a number of nationwide sign language marathons in which clubs and members have enthusiastically participated.

B.D.A. Poster advretising a National Marathon
Reproduced with the permission of the British Deaf Association

Sign Language Marathons

Top: BDA Awareness week at Redditch
Bottom: BDA Mini bus festooned with advertising
Photos: Redditch Deaf Club and British Deaf News

Sign Language Marathon at Northwich
Author's collection

Chapter 23
The 1970s

**The Bomb-damaged Ulster Institute for the Deaf
Victim of an I.R.A. Attack, Christmas 1971**
Photo: The British Deaf News

The 1970s

The 1970s were the decade in which deaf people began to get more involved in affairs influencing their own lives, when more deaf people began to stand up for their rights. In this they were indirectly helped by the Government in implementing Acts of Parliament which related to the definition of social work duties, and which regulated the re-organisation of local district and county authorities. These helped to release the stranglehold which missioners and welfare officers for the deaf had had for so long on their client group. Sometimes, however, these Acts worked to the disadvantage of deaf people especially in areas which were slow to recognise their needs, so that while the old societies or associations for the deaf went to the wall due to funds being cut-off at local authority level, there was no adequate provision made in Social Work departments.

In the long run, however, the local authorities' re-organisation provided the Deaf Community with the impetus it needed to shake loose the chains with which it had been bound since the early twentieth century. A new breed of professionals working for and with deaf people emerged as a result of this shake-up; professionals who had a totally different attitude and concept of deaf people in that they regarded deaf people as clients in exactly the same way as any other group of people were regarded, and not with the 'our poor brethren' attitude that had been so prevalent amongst the old-style missioners. It was, however, to take more than a decade for the Deaf Community to respond and produce the people it needed to take them forward.

One important milestone in the 1970s saw the British Deaf and Dumb Association's triennial Congress at Bournemouth in 1971 vote to change its title to the British Deaf Association, the word 'dumb' now taken to be offensive to the majority of people. Whereas in the past, the word had meant 'voiceless, unable to speak', it had now become so Americanised that besides meaning 'voiceless, unable to speak', it also meant 'ignorant, stupid'. While many deaf people were still unable to speak, they were definitely not ignorant and stupid.

Another important milestone was the creation of the Panel of Four - four organisations for and of deaf people, the British Deaf Association, the Royal National Institute for the Deaf, the National Deaf Children's Society and the British Association of the Hard of Hearing. This brought together for regular consultation and collaboration the four principal organisations with the Secretary of State to discuss many aspects of work amongst deaf people and to decide upon concerted action. Topics considered and discussed at these meetings were to range widely, and have included hearing aids, the training of social workers, special help for school-leavers, education of the public about and research into deafness, multidisciplinary assessments of deaf children.

The changing attitudes to deafness politically and in general may in no small way be attributed to a Member of Parliament named Jack Ashley who became deaf and brought deafness and its handicap into the House of Commons with great impact.

Jack Ashley (1922-)

Jack Ashley was born in Widnes and after being elected as Member of Parliament for Stoke-on-Trent South, he seemed set for high political advancement.

Tragedy struck, however, at the age of 45 when he got a virus infection following which he became totally deaf. His story since then has been a triumph of courage and perseverance.

He was successfully re-elected at every General Election

following his deafness, and managed to cope extremely well in the House of Commons, often with the best technological aids available, and became famous for his championing of disabled causes.

Jack Ashley
Photo: Royal National Institute for the Deaf

He was made a Companion of Honour in the 1971 New Year's Honours, became President of the Royal National Institute for the Deaf and became a familiar figure at many functions for deaf people. Possibly his most enlightening period of association with deaf people came at the Xth World Congress for the Deaf in Helsinki in 1987 where he spent ten days in his capacity as President of the R.N.I.D. and found it an experience never to be forgotten, given that he did not understand sign language.

He announced in 1989 that he would be standing down as Member for Stoke-on-Trent South at the next General Election, whenever that might be held. When he does, the Deaf Community will lose a much valued friend.

Other Events of the 1970s
The offices of the British Deaf Association were broken into,
and although nothing was stolen in this petty raid in 1971, a
real mess was made of the building with papers, files and
other items thrown about everywhere.

The same year, the oldest-ever British deaf person, Mrs
Annie Hutchinson McKee of Alloa, died aged 104. She had
lived in hospital for eight years and in that time had taught
all the nurses to fingerspell.

**Annie Hutchinson McKee cutting her cake on her 104th
birthday a few months before her death**
Photo: British Deaf News

At Christmas 1971 the Irish dispute between the I.R.A. and
the British Government affected the Ulster Institute for the
Deaf at College Square North when the I.R.A. planted two
bombs next door to the Centre and demolished the building.
The Church and the Hall at the institute were badly damaged
and had to be closed, forcing Christmas activities to be held
in another hall.

The winter of 1971/2 was, in Britain, memorable for the miners' and power workers' strikes which affected electricity supplies everywhere in the country. Power cuts of around two hours duration, sometimes more, were commonplace, and since most happened in the evenings, activities in deaf social clubs were badly affected. Amongst those affected were Birmingham - the A.G.M. being one of the casualties; Blackburn - which had also a central heating breakdown making it too cold to hold social evenings; Bristol; Bury - where the newly-installed gas fires proved to be a great boon; Carlisle - where the premises were burgled. Others affected included Chester, Coventry - where church services were held in candlelight; Leicester - where some church services and sports events had to be cancelled; Liverpool - where a sports match against Stockport was played in the freezing cold; Acton - bingo by candlepower. Clapham St. Bede's held a Candlelight Whist Drive. In fact, all over London and in many areas of the country, candlepower reigned supreme and most deaf people refused to be put off by the power cuts. Only the few deaf centres totally dependent on electricity suffered most, Bath being one of the unlucky ones when their annual Christmas Party had to be cancelled. In Scotland, Hamilton's Dinner Dance at the Commercial Hotel had to be cancelled at six o'clock when everyone was just getting there, and all had to go home bitterly disappointed. Dundee's A.G.M., like Birmingham's, was also cancelled. A few deaf people were casualties of the black-outs due to street and road accidents.

The B.D.A., which had for some years been supporting schools for deaf children in Jamaica and Ghana by giving sums of money to purchase equipment, was honoured in 1977 by the Council for Education in World Citizenship and the National Commission for UNESCO when it was chosen as one of the four recipients for awards made to those who had made a special contribution to UNESCO activities.

In 1978, the British Deaf Sports Council was honoured when the vice-chairman, Fred Broomfield, was awarded the

M.B.E. for services to deaf sport. Eighteen months later, in the Queen's Birthday Honours, the B.D.S.C. chairman, Dennis T. Harris also received the M.B.E., making it an unique double for deaf sport. Earlier in the decade, in 1971, a stalwart of the B.D.A., Cyril Robbins of Slough, had also been awarded the M.B.E.

**Two members of the British Deaf Sports Council
Chairman Dennis Harris** (Left)
Vice-Chairman Fred Bloomfield (Right)
who received M.B.E.s
Photos: British Deaf News

The changes in social work policies mentioned earlier had the unfortunate effect of causing the closure of the B.D.A's Ernest Ayliffe Home for Aged Deaf Men at Rawdon, Leeds, in 1978. As the policy was now to support elderly citizens in their own homes as far as possible, or in local authority homes in the area in which they lived, there had been such a decline in admissions to the Home that it was no longer viable. The closure was bitterly criticized in many quarters.

Rawdon was seen as a valuable asset which could be utilized for other activities, but at that time the B.D.A. Executive Council did as they felt was right.

The Ernest Ayliffe Home, Rawdon
Closed due to changes in Social Work policies
Photo: British Deaf News

Following its Congress at Ayr in 1974, where the theme was 'Spotlight on Communication', with lectures by Dr. Merrill of Gallaudet College, USA., and Dr. McCay Vernon of Maryland, USA., the British Deaf Association took the initiative to establish a Communication Skills programme which was funded for three years from 1977 by a Department of Health and Social Security grant. Out of these beginnings grew the Council of Advancement for Communication with Deaf People (C.A.C.D.P.) and the Register of Interpreters.

Two important educational implications occurred during the last two years of the decade in 1978 and 1979 with the first deaf student to enter Durham University, and the first ever fully comprehensive survey of deaf school-leavers' academic achievements published in a book called *The Deaf School Child*.

There had been up to then no university in Britain where support services could be given to deaf students. True a number of deaf people had gone through degree courses at various universities in Britain (and the choice still exists today), but they had to compete and study on the same terms as any other university student. Although some deaf people did complete their degree, others could not cope, and it was felt that the price was too high for deaf people. With the admission of its first student, Colin Dunlop, in 1978, the University of Durham embarked on a programme which was to see it develop into Britain's only University able to give to deaf students a support service which was aimed at making them more able to compete on equal terms with other students. In addition, one of the colleges of residence at Durham, the College of St. Hild and St. Bede, had a number of students' rooms specially adapted for the needs of deaf people.

Furthermore, as a result of the strong links forged between the University and the B.D.A., the University of Durham was to become a premier centre in Britain for other academic activities in the deaf field.

In June 1979 there was published a book *The Deaf School Child*, the result of a comprehensive survey into deaf school-children and school leavers by Dr. R. Conrad, of the Medical Research Council based at the Department of Experimental Psychology, University of Oxford. This research looked at the ability of deaf children to communicate verbally at the end of their school lives, and looked at what special schools for the deaf and PHUs had achieved. This research exploded all the myths that the majority of deaf schoolchildren were leaving school well educated with speech and lipreading skills good enough to cope in the wider world. It found that the majority of deaf schoolchildren were leaving school with an average reading age of 8.75 years, that most of them had poor speech and lipreading skills. It was a damning indictment of the failure of the oral methods which had been in use in deaf

schools since Milan, and vindicated all that had been pas-
sionately argued over nearly a century by deaf leaders like
Agnew, Paul, Maginn, Edwards. In the words of Conrad
himself, oralism's success was 'a fairy tale'.

Conrad's book coincided with the best educational material
ever produced for deaf people, the development of teletext
television services which enable subtitles to be obtained on a
few selected programmes and films. In 1985, 87% of deaf
people agreed that teletext television had enriched their lives
so much, and was to them of tremendous educational value,
although many admitted that sometimes they could not understand the language.

New Deaf Centres in the 1970s

In the short space of five weeks in February and March 1976,
the Duke of Edinburgh opened two new centres for the deaf.
The first took place on 13th February when the Duke visited
Leeds, and formally opened the new centre at Centenary
House, a former hospital.

The second opening took place on 20th March at Aberdeen
where the former All Saints Episcopal Church had been
purchased by the local society, renamed St. John's Church for
the Deaf, and had a massive three-storey building added
which housed a variety of lounges and games rooms.

Later in the year, in September, the new St. Vincent
Centre for the Deaf was opened in Glasgow by the Parliamentary Under-Secretary of State for Scotland, Frank Mc
Elhone, M.P. Costing over £200,000, the centre was custom-
built with all facilities including a Roman Catholic chapel to
cater for local deaf people.

Another deaf club which moved into new premises was
Chester who bought their first ever permanent building in
1975 after years of living in rented premises. Most of the
conversion and rebuilding needed at the old St. Oswald's
Church was done by deaf members themselves.

Two deaf centres visited by the Duke of Edinburgh
five weeks apart.
Top: Aberdeen Centre for the Deaf
Bottom: Leeds Centre for the Deaf
Photos: British Deaf News

Leisure Activities in the 1970s

The B.D.A's Summer Schools continued to be held in the 1970s but were now part of their Further Education and Youth Service programme, with courses where the accent was often on leisure activities such as flower arrangement, floral picture making, woodcarving as well as the traditional adventure and physical sports courses such as water-skiing, archery, canoeing and fencing. Some courses were designed to help deaf people to be aware of procedures, hence accountancy, current affairs, police work and fire prevention; committee procedures courses were also arranged.

Chester Members helping to build their new Centre
Photo: Cheshire Society for the Deaf

Summer schools had now been expanded into three categories - general, for families and for young people.

Drama courses and competitions were especially popular, and were always a feature of the Congresses held at Bournemouth, Ayr and Eastbourne. Also popular were motoring quiz competitions and skills courses.

**A youngster receiving Sailing Instruction on one of the
B.D.A.'s Further Education programmes**
Photo: British Deaf News

**Members of Warrington Deaf Quiz Team show their Medals
to the Mayor**
Photo: British Deaf News

Professionals with a Difference

While many deaf people pursued sedentary clerical or blue
collar factory occupations, four people were at the height of
their careers in fields not usually entered by deaf people.

Lester Piggott (1935-)
Lester Piggott has arguably been Britain's and possibly the world's best ever jockey, and is now a successful trainer.

His deafness was discovered at the age of 5, and had possibly been present since birth, Even at age 5, he was lipreading so well that his parents were shocked to discover he was deaf, and he never lost his lipreading skills.

Lester Piggott

He was, and remained so as an adult, extremely shy and a loner. He grew up on his father's stables where there were horses all round him, and he never lost his affinity with them, as he showed on more than one occasion on the nation's premier racetracks.

A much misunderstood man, the barrier created by his deafness being viewed by others as aloofness or taciturnity, Lester Piggott nonetheless was on good terms with the Royal Family, many of whose horses he rode to victory at Epsom, Ascot or Goodwood, and was awarded the M.B.E. for services to racing.

His life was shattered when, in 1986, he was convicted of

income tax fraud and sentenced to three years imprisonment, a punishment many people thought too harsh. In prison, his deafness did not help to make him acceptable to other prisoners, and he was badly hurt when the Queen stripped him of his honours. His hurt was not made any easier when his wife was seriously injured in a riding accident and for weeks hovered between life and death.

Despite these personal setbacks, Lester Piggott will always be remembered as a man who overcame a severe handicap to become a top class rider and give pleasure to millions of people.

Nina Falaise (1955-)

Nina Falaise was born in Skipton, Yorkshire, and, when it was noticed that her speech was developing late, she was taken to an audiology unit in London where it was found that she had a considerable high pitch hearing loss which had resulted from a shock at birth when the umbilical cord had wrapped itself round her neck.

Nina Falaise
Photo: TALK

She was educated in a small private school where it was found she had a very pronounced rhythmic sense of music

374

and movement, which resulted in her being placed in a ballet class in London at age 7.

She passed the entrance examinations to the Junior Royal Ballet Company school, but failed the medical examination on grounds of her deafness, so was thus debarred from attending that school.

In spite of this big disappointment, she performed at Sadlers Wells when aged 10, and was admitted to the Ballet Rambert School at age 14, and it was in Europe that Nina made her debut, with the Balletto di Roma, whose principal ballerina she was for three years. Since then, she has performed leading ballet roles almost exclusively overseas.

Nina Falaise relies on vibrations to feel the music, and although she can hear low-pitched noises, she is an excellent lipreader.

Martin Dutton

Martin Dutton was born deaf, and educated at the Yorkshire School for the Deaf where he developed a fine love of woodcarving in which he set up his own business in 1950.

Martin Dutton
Photo: British Deaf News

Dutton's skill at woodcarving was to earn him country-wide fame, and his carved figures are installed in a number of churches. His signature and trademark was a lizard, and one of his best works is a four-foot figure of St. Blaise, patron saint of woolcombers, which stands in a Roman Catholic Church in Bradford.

For a number of years, he helped to run the B.D.A's Woodcarving Courses at Danesmead School, York.

Alex Fraser (1920-)

Alex Fraser was born deaf, and attended Aberdeen School for the Deaf, before becoming a baker by trade.

He excelled at football, playing for Kilmarnock in the Scottish League, before taking up coaching. He was so effective that his team twice won the Scottish Amateur Cup.

However, his fame lies in the fact that he was the first deaf man ever to become a Scottish Football Association referee, and was in charge of the Scottish Junior F.A. Cup Final in 1959.

He was awarded the Norman Kirk Trophy for the Disabled Scot of the Year in 1971 for his services to football.

Alex Fraser
Photo: Aberdeen Press & Journal

Chapter 24
The Deaf Organisations

**B. D. D. A. Congress Dinner, Royal Venetian Chamber,
Holborn Restaurant, London - 1903**
Photo: British Deaf Association

B. D. D. A. Congress, Manchester 1909
Photo: Manchester Centre for the Deaf

CHAPTER 24

The Deaf Organisations

The British Deaf Association, or the B.D.A. as it is known, is
- after the Royal Association for the Deaf, an organisation for
deaf people rather than of deaf people - Britain's oldest
national deaf organisation, and owes its roots to the inspiration of James Paul of Kilmarnock who with several others
launched the short-lived National Deaf and Dumb Society
(N.D.D.S.) in 1879.

Internal bickering and strife - especially between those
members who lived in London under the auspices of the
Royal Association for the Deaf and Dumb (as it then was)
and others in the north of England and Scotland - was the
cause of the demise of the N.D.D.S. after an existence of
seven short years.

There were, however, a number of strong-minded and
far-sighted deaf people about, the most prominent of whom
was George Healey of Liverpool, who felt strongly about the
need for a national organisation of deaf people, and after
some considerable lobbying, a convention was held in Leeds
in 1890 which saw the birth of the British Deaf and Dumb
Association (the B.D.D.A.).

The first officials consisted of a President, Vice-President,
Secretary, Treasurer; not until later was the position of
Chairman created. The first President was the Rev. W.
Bloomfield Sleight, a hearing man, but the first secretary was
Charles Gorham of Leeds, a deaf man who was then the
editor of the *Deaf and Dumb Times*.

The Presidency has always remained the province of a
hearing person, and so has the Chairmanship until 1983, but

the secretary was always a deaf person until 1961 when Allan Brindle Hayhurst was appointed.

Headquarters of the British Deaf Association at Carlisle
Photo: Author's collection

The flaw in the constitution which enabled hearing people to be elected to the Association's Executive Council led, in the first 50 years of the twentieth century and well into the 1960s, to a situation where deaf candidates standing for election had to wear the label 'deaf' in the voting, and to a heavy dominance by missioners and welfare officers which left the B.D.D.A. a strangely ineffective force for all its national importance. Considerable criticism of the organisation in the 1920s and 1930s appeared in deaf magazines, and the B.D.D.A. was especially fortunate in having as secretaries at that time William McDougall and, from 1934, Leslie Edwards, deaf men of strong character, who could hold the association together during those turbulent times.

William McDougall (1865-1950)

William McDougall was born in Tillicoultry, Scotland, and became deaf through illness when aged 5. He was educated at Donaldson's School for the Deaf, continuing after school life as a pupil-teacher. Leaving temporarily, he went into partnership with his brother in a woollen mill, but returned to Donaldson's after a few years. He was the only deaf member of the teaching staff.

William McDougall
Photo: Deaf Quarterly News

In 1904 he was offered, and accepted, the post of Missioner at Carlisle which he was to retain until his retirement in 1935.

He became Secretary of the B.D.D.A. in 1906, a post he was also to hold until his retirement, a term of 29 years during part of which the post of Treasurer was joined to the Secretaryship.

Leslie Edwards (1885-1951)

Leslie Edwards was a rare breed in those years when deaf people were at their lowest ebb. He strode the world like a giant on his own terms.

As well as being Missioner to the Deaf at Leicester, he was also a lay preacher of some renown and an able cricketer who led Leicester Deaf Cricket Club to their first ever championship in 1927.

Leslie Edwards
Photo: The Deaf News

Appointed to the Secretary-Treasurership of the B.D.D.A. on the retirement of William McDougall in 1935, he was to hold the position throughout the difficult war years and was just beginning to see the development of the post-war B.D.D.A. when he met his untimely death in October 1951.

He was to be succeeded by the Rev. Mark Frame who was to hold the position for ten years before resigning.

The Tradition Goes

With the unfortunate death of Kenneth P. McDougall, son of William McDougall, the editorship of *British Deaf News* became vacant, and the Executive of the B.D.D.A. moved Frame across from Secretary to being the new editor of the B.D.N., and merged the Secretaryship once again with the Treasurer's post. Thus, in 1961 Allan Brindle Hayhurst became the first non-deaf person to be Secretary of the association, ending a tradition which went back to Charles Gorham in 1890, a move seen by some deaf people as further loss of control and destiny of their organisation, although Hayhurst was to bring to the B.D.D.A. a degree of professionalism it had hitherto not known.

The Congresses

The focal point of the British Deaf Association's activities have been its Congresses, starting with Leeds in 1890. Up to 1913, they were held every two years before the First World War put a stop to activities until 1920, but from 1922 onwards, the Congresses were held every three years except during the Second World War.

Perhaps the most important Congresses were Leeds in 1890 as the first, Cardiff in 1947 which saw the popularity of the B.D.D.A. start to grow dramatically, Plymouth in 1962 when a new Constitution was adopted and Bournemouth in 1971 which saw the title altered to the British Deaf Association.

The Congresses have been held as follows :

1890	:	Leeds	1931 :	Leicester
1891	:	Glasgow	1934 :	Torquay
1893	:	Swansea	1937 :	Isle of Man
1895	:	Dublin	1947 :	Cardiff
1897	:	London	1950 :	Aberdeen
1899	:	Liverpool	1953 :	Brighton
1901	:	Kilmarnock	1956 :	Blackpool
1903	:	London	1959 :	Edinburgh
1905	:	Windermere	1962 :	Plymouth
1907	:	Edinburgh	1965 :	Llandudno
1909	:	Manchester	1968 :	Scarborough
1911	:	Aberdeen	1971 :	Bournemouth
1913	:	Bradford	1974 :	Ayr
1920	:	Glasgow	1977 :	Eastbourne
1922	:	Birmingham	1980 :	Scarborough
1925	:	Southampton	1983 :	Torquay
1928	:	Belfast	1986 :	Rothesay
			1989 :	Swansea

Congress Garden Party, Botanical Gd'ns, Birmingham 1922
Photo: Birmingham Institute for the Deaf

Some of the delegates at the Torquay Congress, 1934
Photo: British Deaf News

A feature of the Congresses in the 1950s onwards was that they were of one week-long duration, with opportunities for the presentation of papers. The exception was 1989 at Swansea when Congress was over a weekend due to the proximity of the 1990 Centenary Year programme.

Another Break with Tradition
At the Torquay Congress in 1983, the B.D.A. made a break with nearly a century of tradition when Jock McD. Young, a deaf man from Glasgow, was elected Chairman. He was the first deaf person to hold the post.

The Princess of Wales Becomes Patron
Also in 1983 the British Deaf Association was honoured when Princess Diana, H.R.H. the Princess of Wales, consented to become Patron of the Association, and a Royal Visit was made to Carlisle in 1984 to cement the patronage.

B.D.A. Chairman Jock Young extends a warm welcome to H.R.H. the Princess of Wales on the occasion of her visit to Carlisle in 1984
Photo: British Deaf Association

Royal National Institute for the Deaf

The R.N.I.D., as the Institute is known, was originally founded in 1911 with the cumbersome title of National Bureau for Promoting the General Welfare of the Deaf. This title, however, still ably expresses the aims of the R.N.I.D.

The founder of the Bureau was a Mr. Leo Bonn, a wealthy merchant banker who had become deaf, and his family bank provided the early financial backing needed to establish the Bureau, and by 1924, recruit a small staff. The same year it was decided to reconstruct the organisation as the National Institute for the Deaf.

In 1928, the 'Counties Association for the Deaf' came into being; these have now been reconstructed as the Regional Associations.

In the period 1929-36, the N.I.D. began to establish homes and hostels for the deaf and to inaugurate lipreading classes which led to the establishment of the City Lit Centre for the Deaf in London.

The R.N.I.D.'s Rehabilitation Centre at Court Grange, Newton Abbott
Photo: Royal National Institute for the Deaf

Three views of Poolemead, the R.N.I.D.'s magnificent Home and Centre in Bath

Photos: Author's collection

In 1936 the institute was established at 105 Gower Street, where it still is today, and began to develop its technical department. Later the R.N.I.D.'s departments included the Library (the largest specialist library on deafness in the U.K.), research, community services, residential services as well as technical, scientific and environmental aids. There was also an information services department one of whose tasks was to produce the *Soundbarrier* magazine.

The word 'Royal' was included in the title in the Institute's Jubilee Year in 1961 by the approval of the Queen, and the R.N.I.D. maintains a number of hostels, homes and rehabilitation centres throughout the country, one of which, Poolemead in Bath, is the best of its kind to be found anywhere.

In 1986, the R.N.I.D. reorganised its services into six directorates: Community Services; Advocacy and Information; Residential Services and Employment; Financial and Administration; Fundraising; Communication Services. In doing so, a vigorous equal opportunities policy was pursued, including that of Director of Community Services. Doug Alker was the first deaf person ever to be appointed at director level in the R.N.I.D. or for that matter, the B.D.A., and much of this progressive attitude arose from the appointment of Mike Whitlam as Chief Executive in 1985.

Douglas Alker
Director of Community Services R.N.I.D.
Photo: Royal National Institute for the Deaf

The National Deaf Children's Society
This was founded in 1944, and was originally known as the Deaf Children's Society. The word 'National' was not added to the title until 1958.

Its primary objective when founded was to campaign to improve deaf education, and to sort out problems experienced by parents in bringing up deaf children.

Though its primary objectives still remain, the NDCS (as it is known) offers a wide range of educational, welfare, technical and information services to parents of deaf children and professionals working with deaf children, and has about 135 regional branches throughout the United Kingdom.

The British Association of the Hard of Hearing
Although social clubs for the Hard of Hearing were in existence as far back as 1918 at Edinburgh, what few there were were confined to large provincial centres and in London. In 1945, a Madeleine de Soyres, a French Canadian living in Welwyn Garden City, conceived the idea of a county organisation for people like herself who were hard of hearing and so the Hertfordshire League for the Hard of Hearing was formed, followed shortly by the Middlesex and Surrey League.

As more Leagues and Clubs began to form, Miss de Soyres in 1946 proposed the formation of a national body, and after a stormy inaugural meeting held at the National Institute for the Deaf in Gower Street, the British Association of the Hard of Hearing was formed in 1947.

BAHOH, as the association is known, had several objectives, the main being to foster the social and cultural activities of the Hard of Hearing, and to promote their interests. There are now numerous Hard of Hearing clubs throughout the country and BAHOH has a full-time office at 7 Armstrong Street, London.

Other Organisations for the Deaf
There are a number of other mainly regional or recreational

388

organisations for and of deaf people, but there are some that exist for specified aims and objectives. Those include SENSE - the National Deaf-Blind and Rubella Association, the Breakthrough Trust for Deaf-Hearing Integration, the Deaf Broadcasting Council, while an important recreational organisation is the Deaf Mountaineering Club.

The Deaf Mountaineering Club

While the D.M.C., as it is called, now comprises of a core of mountain enthusiasts who have settled into a well-established routine of Meets and one-week holidays, it was a different story in the beginning.

The D.M.C. is a direct result of the first British Deaf and Dumb Association Mountain Venture outdoor course arranged in October 1959 in conjunction with Cumberland County Council. This was so successful that a week long course was arranged at the same venue, (Keswick,) the following summer.

Rock-climbing
Photo: Mrs Irene Hall

In the 1960s, few people had cars and the D.M.C. represented to a lot of enthusiasts a feeling of adventure and achievement, particularly where difficult ascents were made.

Nowadays, the rock-climbing side has declined to the extent where fell-walking is the predominant activity of members at Meets.

Deaf Broadcasting Council

In 1979, a small organisation for the deaf, the National Union for the Deaf, launched an initiative and assisted in the production *Signs of Life* for the BBC's Open Door series of programmes, and as a result, there was convened the Deaf Broadcasting Campaign. It's original aim was to press for a weekly news programme using sign language, subtitles and voice.

Austin Reeves
Secretary of the D. B. C.
Photo: British Deaf News

Within a short period of time, however, the DBC (as it is known) had expanded its rôles and objectives into other areas of television to such an extent that it became a highly

390

respected umbrella consumer organisation representing most national deaf and Hard of Hearing organisations.

While it is impossible to pinpoint the exact impact the DBC has had on television media and authorities, it has undoubtedly been responsible for improving the quality of deaf people's lives to the extent that a positive attitude has been created amongst deaf viewers: they now feel they have the right to demand and expect from television an equivalent service to that which the general public accepts as the norm.

Members of the DBC. at one of their campaigns
Photo: Deaf Broadcasting Council

The DBC could not have achieved what it has without the considerable sacrifices made by its Secretary, Austin Reeves, a deaf man from Coventry. At the Rothesay Congress of the B.D.A. in 1986, the B.D.A. made one of its most popular choices when it awarded Austin their Medal of Honour for services to deaf television.

The Deaf Broadcasting Campaign changed the last word of their title to 'Council' in 1988 to reflect their increased status.

The Breakthrough Trust for Deaf-Hearing Integration

The Breakthrough Trust was formed in 1970 by a group of young deaf adults out of dissatisfaction with the then available outlets for deaf people and concern at the continuing isolation of the deaf individual from the rest of society.

In actual fact, an informal association known just as 'The Group' had existed for at least 10 years, meeting once a year at Easter.

A focal point was concern at the lack of a deaf contribution to society, to show what deaf people could do. For a variety of reasons, these opportunities did not then exist within the B.D.A. or the R.N.I.D., nor did an avowed aim of the Trust, free integration and communication between deaf and hearing people.

A Training Weekend in Telecommunications
Photo: The Breakthrough Trust

The main activity in the late 1960s and early 1970s was an annual Family Weekend at Thorpeness, Norfolk, where deaf and hearing families and friends came together to live together for a weekend. This manner of living together made everyone aware of the problems of communication between deaf and hearing persons.

From these humble but determined beginnings, the Breakthrough Trust has developed into a well respected organisation in the deaf world, with headquarters at the Charles W. Gillette Centre in Birmingham. It also has centres at Farnborough, Swindon and in London. At Swindon, the Roughmoor Centre is a well used activity centre immensely popular with all sections of the deaf community, especially schools.

Breakthrough Trust also specialises in awareness workshops, communication workshops, and has an active European section. One particular contribution that Breakthrough Trust has made to the Deaf Community is through its development and expertise in telecommunications technology.

Council for Advancement of Communication with Deaf People

In the late 1970s, the B.D.A. obtained the support of the Department of Health and Social Security in establishing a Communication Skills project which aimed to set standards of competence in sign language amongst learners, and to establish a register of interpreters.

By 1982, the project had developed to such an extent that it needed to stand on its own feet, thus the Council for Advancement of Communication with Deaf People was born. This cumbersome title has, with typical deaf characteristics, been abbreviated to CACDP, and awarded the sign for 'cap'.

It now organises a wide range of Communication Courses and offers assessments which lead to the awards of certificates at three levels. It works with the BSLTA although both are separate bodies.

In 1987, CACDP expanded into Northern Ireland and appointed John Carberry as its development officer for that country.

Chapter 25
The 1980s

**The 1980s: The Age of Information Technology
Members of a Deaf Centre Displaying
Minicoms Donated to them**

Photo: Redditch Centre for the Deaf

The 1980s

The 1980s were a most tremendous and exciting decade for deaf people in Britain. Although it could be called the Age of Information Technology due to the booming use of television teletext and prestel services, video projects and programmes, computer networks and telecommunications services by deaf people, there was so much more to the decade than just information technology.

The 1980s were the decade when deaf people rediscovered their pride, their culture and their heritage.

The International Year for Disabled People 1981 Symbol

Given a boost by the International Year for Disabled People in 1981, the decade saw the growth of political activity in campaigning for the rights of deaf people; the increasing deaf adult challenge to Britain's oralist education tradition; the retirement and early death of Allan Brindle Hayhurst which led directly to the expansion of the British Deaf Association which was subsequently followed by the Royal National Institute for the Deaf, in direct response to the needs and requirements of deaf people.

Unfortunately, amongst the great sporting achievements of British deaf athletes, the 1980s also saw internal strife within the British Deaf Sports Council when one regional association challenged the Council's constitution, a circumstance which eventually led to legal proceedings which severely damaged the Council's financial structure. The B.D.S.C. did remarkably well given this financial pounding to raise the status of British deaf sportsmen and sportswomen everywhere.

Important milestones in the 1980s were the appointment of H.R.H. Princess Diana, the Princess of Wales, as Patron of the British Deaf Association; the launch of the much maligned and misunderstood Sympathetic Hearing Scheme; the educational battleground involving the existence of schools for the deaf at Greenock, Manchester, Birmingham and a number of other localities; the formation of the European Community Regional Secretariat of the World Federation for the Deaf in which the B.D.A. took a leading role, and the recognition by the European Economic Community Parliament of member countries' sign languages.

Some milestones were not good news, particularly in 1987. This year saw the so-called Deaf Riots of Blackpool which were in reality more of a result of boisterousness on the part of hundreds of deaf people attending a rally, and misunderstandings by the local police, and journalistic sensationalism. The gutter-press headlines such as '1000 DEAF AND DUMB IN BATTLE WITH POLICE', however, did considerable damage to the reputation of deaf people, especially in Blackpool, which was difficult to repair.

The same year, 1987, also saw as a result of the formation of AIDS AHEAD - a consortium of organisations for and of deaf people and charities involved in combatting the spread of the Acquired Immune Deficiency Syndrome virus - a request for all deaf organisations to implement an equal opportunities policy. However, at the B.D.A's Manchester Delegates' Conference, a number of anti-gay motions were tabled which if passed would have left the B.D.A's own equal opportunities policy in tatters. After much heated debate, however, the motions were rejected.

The Political Battleground
The rise of deaf involvement in the modern political arena - apart from having Jack Ashley as a M.P. - could perhaps be traced back to the 1970s when the National Union for the Deaf was formed. Unfortunately although the N.U.D's membership included influential deaf persons such as Paddy Ladd, one of the early presenters on BBC's *SEE HEAR* programme, its membership remained small and insignificant largely due to the majority of deaf people being ignorant of it, and those who did know of it, were by and large not attracted to its politics, which tended to be extremely left-wing on some issues. Consequently, the N.U.D. never had any of the political clout that the larger organisations like the B.D.A. or the R.N.I.D. had, however little this was in some cases.

What the N.U.D. did achieve was, both directly and indirectly through other agencies, to instil in certain grassroots factions of the deaf community a sense of purpose and determination, which organisations like the B.D.A. were able to translate into action on certain issues, and to divert in other areas like, for example, attendance at political party conferences, and the launch of its manifesto. Also, for a brief period of time, a group of deaf activists within the B.D.A., mainly in the North-West of England, formed themselves into the Deaf Tribune Group on the same lines as one of the political party's inner groups.

Scenes of Political Lobbying by Deaf People at Parliament
Photos: British Deaf News

In other parts of the country, notably in Northumbria and in Scotland, workshops became the vogue where deaf people could get together, debate issues and sometimes translate them into action. Deaf people, generally, were able to look up to the Deaf Broadcasting Campaign as an excellent example of deaf political activity and achievement which was adaptable to similiar action on other issues.

Consequently when a Labour M.P., Robert Wareing of Liverpool West Derby, won one of the ballots which enabled Private Members' Bills to be introduced into the House of Commons, he chose to present an Anti-Discrimination (Disabled Persons) Bill which was scheduled for debate in the House of Commons on Friday 18th November 1983, Fridays being traditionally days when the Commons is almost deserted. The B.D.A. seized the opportunity to organise a lobby, using the sense of purpose and determination that had been instilled in the deaf community through its previous activities and that of the N.U.D.

Deaf people were urged to write to their M.Ps to support the Bill, numerous interviews were given on local radio stations and in local newspapers. Even more important, coach parties were organised from a number of regions and deaf people were urged to try and come to the Houses of Parliament to show their support.

The ground swell was such that the day exceeded everybody's expectations; at least 500, maybe 750, deaf people turned up at Westminster along with assorted smaller numbers of blind people, people in wheelchairs, and people with other disabilities, and by 10 a.m., the Great Hall at Westminster Palace was jam-packed with disabled lobbyists. Wheelchairs, guide dogs for the blind, and sign language interpreters were everywhere.

The Government, who did not wish to see the Bill passed on the grounds that there were already adequate moves towards giving disabled people rights and that a Disablement Commission would be unworkable and too expensive to run, was confronted with a totally unexpected situation and faced defeat. In desperation, they ferried in their supporters and Ministers from wherever they could be found, causing severe disruption to long-arranged meetings and functions for that day. The Anti-Discrimation (Disabled Persons) Bill was defeated by 210 votes to 164, the highest turn-out in the House on a Friday for many years.

Although deaf people, along with other groups of disabled people, were disheartened by the defeat of the Bill, they drew satisfaction from the fact that never again would the Government ignore them.

The political activity resulting from the lobbying in favour of this abortive Bill set the tone for further lobbying and political activity in the future, both at the Houses of Parliament where another massive 1,000-strong lobby took place in April 1987 to press the Government to implement the Disabled Persons Act, 1986, as well as a number of other smaller lobbies elsewhere, notably at the International Congress on the Education of the Deaf at Manchester in 1985.

The Congress of 1985 saw a most remarkable challenge from the adult Deaf Community to educationalists, organised jointly by the B.D.A. and the N.U.D., whose leaflet Campaign for Deaf Rights in Education, was widely distributed. There was remarkable support for the British from the Swedish and American deaf delegates, who were there in considerable force, as well as from other European delegations. Their co-operation resulted in a gauntlet being thrown down to the Congress Committee in the form of eight resolutions aimed at increased deaf participation.

A feature of the 1985 International Congress was the fringe meetings organised by the B.D.A. and the N.U.D., which were often much more stimulating and interesting than the main Congress programme, which was an attempt to provide a showcase for the oral-only view of deaf education. It did not succeed, and many delegates went home with great respect and admiration for the well-orchestrated work done by deaf organisations and delegates.

Deaf people's efforts in other political arenas also attracted wide publicity and notice. In 1983, the British Association of Teachers for the Deaf for the first time ever allowed deaf delegates; Christine Reeves addressed the Liberal Party Conference in Sign Language in October 1984 in which she pleaded for greater access to political debate by deaf people through interpreters. Three years later, at the same party's 1987 Conference, Peter Jackson addressed the Conference on the subject of A.I.D.S. and the needs of disabled people and ethnic minorities in direct government funding.

Christine Reeves
Addressing the Liberal Party Conference, 1984
Photo: British Deaf News

In South Wales, Richard Williams campaigned for local government election as a Plaid Cyrmu candidate. He was already a councillor on the Tonyrefail Community Council, and was seeking election to the larger county council.

The Educational Battleground
Deaf people's increasing political activities were not solely

confined to the purely parliamentary, conference or local election arena, but also in particular to the educational battleground arising from the implementation of the 1981 Education Act which gave the green light to local education authorities to rationalise their educational provision to children with special needs, including those with hearing loss.

Richard Williams on the election trail
Photo: British Deaf News

Some education authorities took the Education Act too literally and decided to close schools for the deaf.

The first school to be affected was Greenock's Garvel Centre for the Deaf which had a staff of seven catering for 65 children based in a building only opened in 1968. Parents, teachers and local deaf people joined forces, and saw the decision of Strathclyde Regional Coucil to close the school reversed.

The next fight took place at Manchester in the autumn of

1983 when the local education committee announced the closure of its two day schools for the deaf, and immediately, Manchester's deaf community, aided by members of the Deaf Tribune Group, B.D.A. Headquarters staff, and other activists, launched a campaign to prevent mass integration. Over 200 people packed Manchester Deaf Centre's hall one September evening which was attended by local education officers, and at the end of the meeting, it was pledged that one school would be retained - a partial victory.

Elsewhere, however, the battle was not always being won. School after school closed down due to falling numbers of pupils and to integration policies. Sometimes the fight to save schools did not even get off the ground as local authorities learnt from Greenock and Manchester, and simply did not re-open after summer holidays. Perhaps the saddest closure was Birmingham's Royal School for Deaf Children at Edgbaston which had been established in 1812.

The Schools Today

Today few of the great institutions from the 1800s remain - these are the Royal School for the Deaf, Derby; Royal School for the Deaf, Exeter; Royal Schools for the Deaf, Manchester; Royal School for Deaf Children, Margate; the Royal Cross School, Preston; The School for the Deaf, Stoke-on-Trent; Yorkshire Residential School for the Deaf, Doncaster; St. John's School, Boston Spa; Northern Counties School, Newcastle; Aberdeen School for the Deaf; Donaldson's School, Edinburgh; Glasgow School for the Deaf. As this book is being written, the Royal Cross School is fighting closure plans.

Many of these schools have further education departments, Doncaster College for the Deaf being established on the Yorkshire Residential School's campus. One, the Royal Schools for the Deaf at Manchester, now caters only for multihandicapped deaf children.

Other schools can trace their ancestry back to the old institutions, but today operate under other names. These include Elmfield School for the Deaf, Bristol; Beverley School for the Deaf and Partially Hearing, Middlesbrough; Alice Elliott School, Liverpool; Ovingdean Hall School, Brighton; Elmete Hall School, Leeds; Braidwood School, Birmingham; Ashgrove School for the Deaf, Penarth, South Wales; Garvel School, Greenock; Jordanstown Schools, Newtownabbey, N. Ireland.

The Mary Hare Grammar School at Newbury remains still the only non-statutory grammar school for deaf children in Britain, with about 200 places. It has the largest number of secondary school deaf pupils in this country, and contrary to fears, the relaxation of its no-signing rules outside of the classrooms and abandonment of its Speech Trophy has not led to any decline of its high academic standards.

Burwood Park School at Walton-on-Thames still remains the only secondary-technical school for the deaf in the country, but now has Norfolk College for the Deaf attached to it.

Principal secondary schools for the deaf in London are Newham School for the Deaf, Oak Lodge Secondary School, and the Winston Churchill Schools for the Deaf.

Other principal schools for the deaf and hearing-impaired include the Penn School, High Wycombe; Newbrook School, Manchester; Thomasson Memorial School, Bolton; Heathlands School, St. Albans; Tewin Water School, Welwyn Garden City; Birkdale School for Hearing Impaired Children, Southport; Hamilton Lodge, Brighton; Longwill School, Birmingham; Thornpark School, Bradford; Gateside Centre for the Hearing-Impaired, Paisley; St. Francis de Sales School for Hearing-Impaired Children, Belfast.

A number of schools cater only for primary deaf schoolchildren, and operate a peripatetic service, thus in effect being a resource centre for the deaf and hearing-impaired, or they operate as a unit attached to a main secondary/high school - Heston School for the Deaf in Hounslow is a good example.

A majority of the present-day schools use Total Communication methods; only Birkdale School, Ovingdean Hall and St. John's at Boston Spa are exclusively oral in and out of the classroom, while Mary Hare Grammar School, Burwood Park School and a few others operate an oral-only classroom policy.

An increasing number of schools are using deaf people once again in the classrooms, but only about half are qualified teachers. Some deaf people are also used in hearing schools as communicators.

Judith Collins was appointed a classroom assistant by Kirklees Education Authority as a communicator in a primary school for a deaf child. This was made the subject of a television documentary. *A Language for Ben* which won an international award for Tyne Tees television.
Photo: British Deaf News

Hamilton Lodge in Brighton is unique in that for the first time in the twentieth-century, a deaf person was appointed Deputy Head of a deaf school. Mabel Davis had been a teacher at the Alice Elliott School in Liverpool before she was appointed on merit to the Deputy Headship in 1987.

With Anthony Boyce being appointed Head of Applied

before a deaf person is appointed Head of a deaf school, thus completing the educational revolution.

Mabel Davis
Speaking with passion at the 1985 International Congress
Photo: British Deaf News

The 1982 Working Party Report of the National Study Group on Further and Higher Education for the Hearing-Impaired, formed to consider the position of hearing-impaired people wishing to teach, went a long way towards helping to regulate and underline the importance of deaf teachers of the deaf, and there is no doubt that in time, many more deaf people will come through the ranks.

Support Services for Young Deaf People
The increase in the provision of further education departments at some schools for the deaf did not solely come about because schools needed to take a look at what resources they could provide to counter falling school numbers. It was also due to the requirement of young deaf people to acquire further education in an environment better suited to their needs.

There was, however, another area where young deaf people were being denied further education opportunities, and this was where they were being employed full-time and this was where they were being employed full-time under the Government's Youth Training Scheme. Part of all YTS schemes involved the trainees being given opportunities to acquire skills in different work settings, some of which necessitated in-college training, and deaf people were getting into difficulties because of communication problems.

**Computer course at
Doncaster College
for the Deaf,
Yorkshire**
Photo: Doncaster College

In 1986 the Manpower Services Commission agreed with the Panel of Four to establish a Communication Support Services which would provide BSL/SSE interpretation, language training and note-taking services as well.

Allan B. Hayhurst Research Fellowship

To commemorate the work and interest of their late Secretary-Treasurer Allan B. Hayhurst, the B.D.A. instituted a research fellowship at the University of Durham. The fellowship aimed to provide an opportunity to a prelingually deaf person to undertake academic research in a university setting on certain deaf subjects dear to the heart of A.B. Hayhurst, the deaf community, its language, culture and/or deaf children and their education.

The first recipient of the fellowship was Peter Jackson.

Two views of schools from the air.

Yorkshire Residential School for the Deaf, Doncaster
Photo: School Archives

Royal Schools for the Deaf, Manchester
Photo: R.S.D., Manchester

Rebuilding work at the Royal School for Deaf Children, Margate showing the old school in the background
Photo: Royal School for Deaf Children, Margate

Burwood Park School, Walton-on-Thames
Photo: Author's Collection

Northern Counties School, Newcastle.

Royal School for the Deaf, Derby.

Photos: All from the Author's Collection

410

Top: Donaldson's School for the Deaf, Edinburgh.
Middle: Royal Cross School, Preston.
Bottom: Royal West of England School for the Deaf, Exeter
Photos: All from the Author's Collection

Leisure Activities in the 1980s

Even now, in the 1980s, new deaf centres were being opened, mainly in rural areas where deaf clubs had not hitherto existed. New clubs opened in the 1980s included Vale Royal in Cheshire, Eastbourne, Redditch, March (Cambridgeshire), Ashford (Kent).

However the days of philanthropy were long over, and many centres and clubs for the deaf had to resort to a variety of innovative methods of raising funds to keep their clubs going. These included sponsored swims, pram-pushes, pub crawls, cycle rides, snooker and darts marathons.

Pram Push (Vale Royal)
Photo: Author's collection

In 1984 the British Deaf Sports Council joined the act, and organised a John O'Groats to Land's End Relay Run Marathon. It took a team of 13 runners, two minibuses and a lot of hard work and 8 days to complete the 1,000-mile route, most of it in a mini-heatwave. It was well worth the effort, raising over £2,000 for the World Games Fund.

In sport, there were first ever football and cricket tours oversea by national teams. The B.D.S.C. football team made a tour of the Middle East, playing in Qatar, Bahrain, Arabia and Kuwait, while a British deaf cricket team toured Denmark in 1981, playing five matches against strong opposition and losing them all, and in Barbados and the islands of St. Vincent and Bequia in 1983. Earlier, in 1980-1, West London Deaf C.C. had become the first deaf English team to make a cricket tour of Australia.

John o'Groats to Lands End Marathon Run
(British Deaf Sports Council)
Photo: Geoffrey Eagling

To show that deaf people were no different two young profoundly deaf men, Gerry Hughes of Glasgow and Matthew Jackson of Birmingham, sailed completely round the British Isles in a yacht, taking 23 days to complete the trip. In doing it, they did without any form of communication with other vessels or land; no shipping forecasts were available, and no radio direction equipment could be used; all navigation was by dead reckoning.

Elsewhere, a number of deaf sportsmen and sportswomen were also making their mark in hearing-dominated activities. Alan Kilby of Sheffield followed in the footsteps of the brilliant wrestlers Eagers and Kendall, becoming British professional champion at his weight in the process. In the little-known sport of trampolining, Mike Hawthorne of Essex, a former pupil of Woodford School for the Deaf, was selected

St. Trinian's Cycle Ride (Hartlepool);
Pub Crawl (Bury St. Edmunds): Parachute Jump (Plymouth)
Photos: British Deaf News

Snooker (Huddersfield)

Lancaster (Sponsored Walk)
Photos: British Deaf News

to represent Great Britain at international level, the first deaf person ever to compete at this level anywhere in the world.

The British Deaf Cricket Team in the West Indies
Photo: Author's collection

Gerry Hughes and Matthew Jackson after their round Britain trip
Photo: British Deaf News

In another little-known sport, the National Riding and Driving Event, (pony and carriage riding), a disabled deaf girl

Erica Cox from Wales won several honours and competed at the national championships at Windsor where she came second. A young girl from Hamilton Lodge School, Brighton, named Sarah Jane Cooke, became so proficient a cricketer that she was selected to tour Denmark with the England junior squad. She was also selected to play for the Women's Cricket Association in a quadrangular tournament in Ireland involving Ireland, Holland, Denmark and the W.C.A., and was selected for Young England to play against India, but was unable to play. She is in the national squad of 22 players who undergo regular training.

A regular feature of early summer activities organised by the B.D.A. and a number of regional associations has been Gala Weekends held at various holiday camps owned by Pontins or Butlins throughout the country where fun and games are the order of the day.

Egg-Throwing contest at one of the B.D.A.'s Gala weekends
Photo: British Deaf News

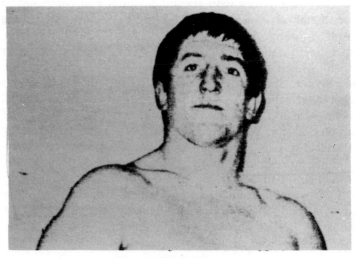

Alan Kilby
Photo: Who's Who in Wrestling

Mike Hawthorn
Photo: British Deaf News

418

Erica Cox with Prince Charles
Photo supplied by Mrs.P.K.Wrighton

Sarah Jane Cooke
Photo: Evening Argus

The general increase in leisure time brought with it the importance of developing more programmes for deaf youth, but a shortage of suitably trained deaf youth leaders hampered progress and created a vacuum in the provision of services for the deaf. An organisation called the Friends of the Young Deaf became the first to develop extensive programmes for deaf youth with the emphasis on integrated activities. However, in 1987, the British Deaf Association obtained from the Department of Education and Science a grant of £26,000 to provide a course for deaf people which would lead to a Part-Time Youth Worker's Certificate.

Training Courses
The B.D.A.s grant of £26,000 enabled it to develop jointly with the City of Salford Youth Service and the Greater Manchester Youth Association a project which was the first of it kind in Britain, a training course for deaf youth leaders leading to a qualification.

Participants on the B.D.A.'s Youth Leadership Course
Photo: British Deaf News

The project was devised because many profoundly deaf children were missing out on the facilities of the statutory youth service and were unlikely to attend mainstream youth clubs, a situation which was made worse by the critical lack of trained deaf youth leaders due to the unsuitability of mainstream youth leadership training courses for deaf people.

The Youth Leadership Project was not the only course to be put on to resolve a critical shortage of suitable trained deaf people within the deaf community. The spread of the most serious scourge of the century, A.I.D.S., highlighted another desperate shortage within the deaf community, that of suitably trained deaf counsellors.

The formation of AIDS AHEAD, mentioned earlier, was originally based on the need to provide deaf people with the same sort of health education and advisory services being promoted by the Government to the general public. Unfortunately, the project could not stop there as it became apparant that trained deaf counsellors were also desperately needed to support deaf people with HIV infection or with A.I.D.S.

Hitherto, deaf people had never been specifically trained to be counsellors of any kind, except insofar as this formed part of mainstream social work training provision, and AIDS AHEAD succeeded in securing a substantial grant to lay on a number of counsellor-training courses. The co- operation of the deaf gay community, which although well- established had only recently come out into the open, was sought and their assistance was extremely invaluable in the project.

The success of these two projects has enabled other training projects to be developed, notably in journalism and in video/television work, and no doubt will be extended into other areas as more and more deaf people discover opportunities to develop and broaden their skills through courses based on the use of B.S.L. as a communication training factor.

People on the 1980s

The 1980s were the decade in which deaf people achieved status that for many years had been denied them. Deaf people became television presenters, researchers, deputy head teacher, principal officers within organisations for and of deaf people.

Murray Holmes (1946-)

Born in Greenock, Scotland, Murray Holmes became deaf through meningitis at the age of 5, and he was educated in classes for the deaf in a local school where strict oralism was enforced and which he left with no academic qualifications whatsoever.

Murray Holmes
Photo: British Deaf News

His educational experiences have left him a strong advocate of Total Communication for which he has constantly campaigned.

He was elected to the Executive Council of the B.D.A. in 1976, and became Vice-Chairman in 1981, and in 1983, was elected to the Bureau of the World Federation of the Deaf (W.F.D.).

At the W.F.D. Cogress in Finland in 1987, Murray Holmes was elected one of the four Vice-Presidents.

Father Peter McDonough(1955-)
One sunny summer's day in 1982, history was made when Pope John Paul held an open air Mass at Heaton Park, Manchester. It was attended by an incredible number of people, at least 250,000 minimum, probably more. Millions more people watched the event on television.

Before all these watching millions of people, Pope John Paul ordained some priests, one of whom followed the service through a sign language interpreter. That man was the first deaf person in this country to become a Roman Catholic priest, and probably the first ever to be ordained by a Pope.

Father Peter McDonough
Photo: British Deaf News

Father Peter McDonough was born deaf of deaf parents, and has a sister who is partially deaf. After a mixed primary education in partially hearing units and in ordinary state schools, his parents at last won their battle to send him (and his sister) to St. John's School for the Deaf, Boston Spa.

After leaving St. John's, he attended Salford Polytechnic where he got his engineering diploma, then decided to study Electronic Engineering at Sheffield University. However, during his first year at University, his mother died, and he got a sudden calling to be a priest.

After a series of interviews, he was sent to the English College in Valladolid, Spain, where in the company of 30 other English students he studied for the priesthood.

Father Peter McDonough is now parish priest at St. Mary's Oswaldtwistle, Lancashire, and is also Chaplain to the Deaf in the northern part of the diocese in which he is based.

Other Success Stories

The 1980s also brought to the fore other success stories of deaf people, in particular two connected with education of the deaf, Mabel Davis and Christopher Jones.

Mabel Davis, who became deaf at age 7 through meningitis, was educated at Mary Hare Grammar School before becoming a librarian. She was spurred to take up teaching as a career when she took evening classes for deaf adults with low literacy levels. This made her determined to become qualified as a teacher of the deaf. Through grit, she achieved her qualification, with the B.D.A. providing interpreter support for important lectures, and started work as a teacher at the Alice Elliott School for the Deaf, Liverpool where she was widely respected by colleagues, pupils and parents. This respect was to stand her in good stead when the Deputy Headship of Hamilton Lodge School for the Deaf, Brighton, became vacant. She applied for, and got the position to became Britain's first deaf deputy head for many decades.

Christopher Jones was also educated at Mary Hare Grammer School, and became a laboratory technician on leaving school. At the age of 28, he became persuaded by a professor in the Department of Psychology at the University of Hull to go for a degree. By then, he was already campaigning for better education of the deaf, having become appalled, like Mabel Davis, at the low literacy of orally-educated school-leavers.

He is now a research psychologist at Donaldson's School for the Deaf in Edinburgh, the only deaf person in the country, and he has pioneered a system of education based on Interactive Video. It has proved so successful and innovative that Christopher Jones has acquired the nickname 'The Interactive Kid'.

Christopher Jones
Photo: British Deaf News

Deaf art, which had contributed so much to the advancement and status of deaf people through the centuries, still maintains a presence through the work of Trevor Randall, who became the first deaf student to graduate with a masters degree from the Royal College of Arts.

Trevor Randall at one of his exhibitions
Photo: British Deaf News

Randall is probably Britain's only deaf professional artist who paints for a living and exhibits regularly.

He lives in London.

Princess Diana and Deaf Children
In her capacity as Patron of the British Deaf Association, H.R.H. the Princess of Wales, Princess Diana, takes time to meet and try to sign to deaf children whenever the opportunity arises.

**The Princess of Wales
at the Northern Counties School, Newcastle**
Photo: Northern Counties School

And Here's to the Next Hundred Years!

Meeting deaf children and parents at Leeds
Photo: Leeds Centre for the Deaf

Advertisement for the B.D.A.'s Centenary Celebrations 1990
Reproduced with the permission of the British Deaf Association

427

Bibliographical Notes and Sources:

A Brief History
Royal Residential Schools for the Deaf, Manchester 1958.
A G.P.'s Progress to the Black Country
D.H. Crofton. *Volturna Press, Hythe, Kent 1984.*
A History of the Centre for the Deaf, Bristol 1884-1984
Daphne Outhwaite. *Deaf Information Project, Bristol 1985.*
American Annals for the Deaf
Vols. 25,26,27,28.
Deaf Heritage, A Narrative History of Deaf America
Jack R. Gannon. *The National Association of the Deaf, Maryland, U.S.A. 1981.*
Anecdotes and Annals of the Deaf and Dumb
Dr. David Buxton. *W. Fearnall & Co., Liverpool 1854.*
Ancient and Modern Denbigh
John Williams. *John Williams, Denbigh 1856.*
Annual Report 1986
Nottingham and Nottinghamshire Society for the Deaf.
A Review of the R.N.I.D. 1911-1979
Royal National Institute for the deaf, 105 Gower Street, London.
Arnold's Education for the Deaf
A. Farrar. *Simpkin, Marshall & Co, London 1901.*
A Sketch of the Sixth Duke of Devonshire
Sir A. Clifford. *Published privately by Chatsworth Trustees.*
A West Country Family: the Pophams from 1150
F.W. Popham. *Olivers Printing Works, Battle, Sussex 1976.*
Bath Guide 1818-1831
Bedfordshire Historical Records Society
H.P.R. Finberg. *Vol. XXXVI, 1956.*

Breakthrough Trust
Review 1987; Review 1988.
First Decade Report 1971-1981
Breakthrough Trust Deaf-Hearing Group.
British Artists in India
Sir W. Foster. *Walpole Society, Vol. XIX.*
British Deaf Monthly
Nos. 1,5.
British Deaf Mute & Deaf Chronicle
Nos. 1,3,5,9,10,14,17,19,23,39,41.
The British Deaf News
Vol. 1, Nos. 1,2,4,5,9,10,11.
Vol. 2, Nos. 1,3,4,5,7,8,11.
Vol. 3, Nos. 4,6,7,8,9,10,11.
Vol. 4, Nos. 3,4,7,10.
Vol. 5, Nos. 1,2,3,4,7,8,10.
Vol. 6, Nos. 1,3,4,5,6,8,11.
Vol. 7, Nos. 7,8.
Vol. 8, Nos. 2,3,4,6,7.
Vol. 9, Nos. 5,10.
Vol. 10, Nos. 1,5,8,9,11.
Vol. 11, Nos. 3,4,7,10.
Vol. 12, Nos. 3,4,6,7,10,12.
Vol. 13, Nos. 1,2,3,4,5,6,7,8,9.
Vol. 14, Nos. 1,2,5,6,8,9,10.
Vol. 15, Nos. 1,3,6,7,8,10,11.
Vol. 16, Nos. 1,3,4,5,7,8,10,11.
Vol. 17, Nos. 1,3,6,7,8,9,10,11,12.
Vol. 18, Nos. 1,2,4,5,6,8,9,10,11.
Vol. 19, Nos. 1,3,5,7,8.
Vol. 20, Nos. 2,3,4.

British Deaf Times
Vol. 1,2,6,9,10,11,14,15,17,19,22,23,28,30,40,42,55,73,75,77,78,
84,85,88,90,93,95,100,103,183,189,225,229,231,235,241,245,257,
341,375,399,
409,563,597,611.

British Miniaturists
Raymond Lister. *London 1951.*
British Sign Language, a Beginners Guide
Dorothy Miles. *BBC Books 1988.*
Burke's Extinct and Dormant Baronetcies
Burke's Peerage (Genealogical Books) Limited 1841.
Catalogue of Paintings
Walker Art Gallery, Liverpool. *Merseyside County Council 1982.*
Chatsworth
Derbyshire Countryside Ltd, Derby 1988.
Chosen Vessels
George Firth. *Papyrus Printers, Exeter 1988.*
Chirologia
John Brewer (1644). *British Library, London.*
Correspondence: P.K. Wrighton re Erica Cox.
Correspondence: Sarah Jane Cooke.
Copies of Correspondence: British Embassy, Washington D.C. and Dr. E.M. Gallaudet.
Courtesy of Jack Gannon, Gallaudet University, Washington D.C., U.S.A.
Coventry Deaf Chronicle
Coventry and Warwickshire Association for the Deaf 1965.
Deafness, a Personal Account
David Wright. *Allen Lane, Penguin Press, London 1969.*
Deaf & Dumb Magazine
Nos. 1,2,3,8,19,22,25,26,33,34,35,36,39,43,48,53,56,63,66,69,71.
Deaf & Dumb Times
Vol. 1, Nos. 1,3,4,6,8,9,10,12.
Vol. 2, Nos. 1,2,3,4,7,8,9,10,11.
Vol. 3, Nos. 1,3,4.
Deaf Quarterly News
Nos. 46,75,90,91,92,93,96,98,100,103,111,121,123,127,131,140, 141,142,143,144,145,148,149,150,151,152,153,154,155,156,157,15-8,159,160, 161,162,163,164,165,166,167,168,169,170,171,172,181.
Dictionary of British Animal Painters
J.C. Wood. *F. Lewis, Publishers, Leigh-on-Sea 1973.*

Dictionary of British Artists Working 1900-1950
Grant M. Waters. *Eastbourne Fine Arts, Eastbourne 1975.*
Dictionary of British Artists 1880-1940
Johnson & Grentzner. *Antique Collectors Club 1952.*
Dictionary of British 18th Century Painters
Ellis Waterhouse. *Antique Collectors Club 1981.*
Dictionary of British Historical Painters
Frank Lewis. *F. Lewis, Publishers, Leigh-on-Sea 1979.*
Dictionary of British Landscape Painters
M.H. Grant. *F. Lewis, Publishers, Leigh-on-Sea 1952.*
Dictionary of British Marine Painters
Arnold Wilson. *F. Lewis, Publishers, Leigh-on-Sea 1967.*
Dictionary of British Miniature Painters
Daphne Foskett. *Faber & Faber, London 1972.*
Dictionary of National Bibliography
Vol. III, XIII, XVIII, XXI, XXII, XXXV - 1888 edition.
Dictionary of Painters of Miniatures
J.J. Foster. *Philip Allan Co., London 1926.*
Dictionary of Scientific Biography
Vol. V, *Charles Scribner's Sons, New York 1972.*
Dictionary of Victorian Painters
Christopher Wood. *Antique Collectors Club 1971.*
Dorothy Osborne's Letters
British Library Collection.
Edinburgh Congregational Church for the Deaf
Edinburgh & East of Scotland Deaf Society 1930.
Edinburgh and East of Scotland Society for the Deaf: 150th Anniversary
George Hagan. *Greig Bothwell, Edinburgh 1985.*
Egerton MSS
British Library Collection.
Encyclopaedia of Boxing
Goldsworthy: 7th Edition, *Hale (London) 1983.*
Ephphatha
Nos. 1,6,200.
Etchings Illustrative of Scottish Character & Scenery
W. Geikie 1841.

Everyone Here Spoke Sign Language
Nora Ellen Groce. *Harvard University Press, Cambridge,·
Massachusetts 1985.*
Fifth Annual Report, 1938
The Sussex Diocesan Association for the Deaf & Dumb.
Freeford Manor Records, Lichfield.
Gallaudet Encyclopaedia on Deafness
Gallaudet University Press, Washington D.C., U.S.A.
Gentlemen's Magazine
November 1883.
Annual Report, 1875
Glasgow Society for the Deaf.
Hearing
No. 32, 1977.
Hist. MSS. Comm. Rept.
British Library Collection.
**History of Northern Counties School for the Deaf,
Newcastle 1838- 1988**
Robin W. Herdman. *Northern Counties School for the Deaf.*
**History of the Ulster Society for Promoting the Education of
the Deaf and Dumb and the Blind**
J.G. M'Clellard. *Jordanstown Schools for the Deaf.*
A Historical Survey 1823-1923
Royal Residential Schools for the Deaf, Old Trafford,
Manchester.*Taylor, Garnett, Co., Manchester 1923.*
Historical Survey 1826-1976
Royal West of England School for the Deaf, Exeter.
Index Card Catalogues
    Cambridge University Libraries.
    Central Public Library, Manchester.
    National Galleries of Scotland.
    National Portrait Gallery, London.
    Public Records Office, London.
Information Pamphlets
    British Association of Teachers of the Deaf.
    British Association of the Hard of Hearing, 7-11
    Armstrong Road, London.

National Deaf Children's Society, 45 Hereford Road, London.

Royal National Institute for the Deaf, 105 Gower Street, London.

Inscription on Memorial
East Anstey Parish Church.

Journal for the History of Astronomy
Vol. 10.

Journey into Silence
Jack Ashley. *Bodley Head, London 1975.*

Lester
Dick Francis. *Michael Joseph, London 1986.*

Listening Eye
1988 Series. *Tyne Tees Television, Newcastle.*

Logbook of the Hugh Bell School, Middlesbrough.

Knights of England, Vol. 2
William A. Shaw. *Shaw, London 1906.*

Magazine for the Scottish Deaf
Oct-Nov 1929, Dec-Jan 1931.

Margery's Son
Emily Holt. *J.F. Shaw & Co., London 1879.*

Members List, Edinburgh Deaf & Dumb Congregation Church, 1830-?

Milan Congress Report
A.A. Kinsey.
National Deaf Club Historical Records (Courtesy of M. Napier).

Newspaper Articles
Aberdeen Press & Journal, 2.12.1987, plus several undated cuttings.
Bath Chronicle, Dec 1791; Oct 1792; April 1794; May 1794.
City News, Manchester, November 1880.
Daily Mail, 11th May 1982.
Daily Telegraph, December 22nd 1878.
Evening Argus, 21.7.1983.
Glasgow Evening News, 20th November 1891; 21st August 1906.
Glasgow Evening Times, 12th October 1889; 19th November

1891; 26th July 1892; 30th May 1893; 9th November 1897.
Glasgow Herald, 20th November 1891.
Glasgow Mail, 1890.
Greeley (Colo.) Tribune, 18th December 1979.
Greenock Telegraph, 16.3.1976; 21.3.1980; 8.10.1982.
Leicester Mercury, undated newspaper cutting 1988.
Liverpool Post, 3rd August 1943.
Liverpool Review, 9th April 1887.
Somerset County Gazette, 4th November 1899.
Somerset County Herald, 5th January 1889.
The Christian Leader, 4th March 1890.
The Denver Post, 10th July 1977.
The Evening Star, Washington D.C., 28th May 1956.
The Guardian, 29th June 1982.
The Northampton Independent, 19th March 1927.
The Times, 14th May 1986.
Washington Post, 26th April 1905.
West Somerset Free Press, 12th January 1935.
Norfolk Records Society
Percy Mulligan. *J. Goose & Son, Norwich 1939.*
Notable Deaf Persons
Guilbert C. Braddock. *Gallaudet College Alumni Association, Washington D.C. 1975.*
Nutfield News, Summer 1987
Nutfield Priory School, Redhill.
Official Records and Archives
   Bedfordshire Records Office
   Cambridgeshire Records Office
   Cheshire County Records Office
   Cornwall Records Office
   Kent Records Office
   Norfolk County Records Office
   Northamptonshire Records Office
   Public Records Office, London
   Scottish Records Office
   Somerset County Records Office
   Staffordshire County Records Office

434

The Royal Humane Society
Old Watercolours Society Club
Vol. 43, 1968.
On the Marriage and Intermarriage of the Deaf and Dumb
David Buxton. *W. Fearnall & Co, Liverpool 1857.*
Past, Present and Future, the Story of a School
G.W. Montgomery. *Donaldson's School for the Deaf, Edinburgh 1988.*
Peeps into a Deaf World
W. Roe. *Published Privately (1916).*
Philocophus, or the Deafe and Dumbe Man's Friende
John Brewer 1648. British Library Collection.
Popham MSS
Somerset County Records Office.
Prophecies of the Brahan Seer
A. MacKenzie. *Constable, London 1977 edition.*
Queen Alexandra
Georgina Battiscombe. *Constable, London 1984.*
Questionnaires: Responses from:
    Aberdeen and North East Scotland Society for the Deaf
    Acton Deaf Club
    Ashford Deaf Club
    Ashgrove School for the Deaf, Penarth
    Basingstoke Deaf and H.O.H. Club
    Braidwood School for the Deaf, Birmingham
    Bromley Deaf Club
    Bryn Glas School for the Deaf, Mold
    Burnley Deaf Group
    Bury St. Edmunds Deaf Club
    Bury Deaf Welfare Society
    Chesterfield Deaf Club
    Coventry Deaf Club
    Durham Deaf Club
    Edinburgh and East of Scotland Society for the Deaf
    Ely Diocesan Association for the Deaf
    Exeter Deaf Club
    Garvel Deaf Centre, Greenock

Glasgow & West of Scotland Society for the Deaf
Hamilton Lodge School for Deaf Children, Brighton
Harlow Deaf Club
Jordanstown Schools, Newtonabbey, N. Ireland
Lewisham Deaf Club
Linfern School, Kilmarnock
March Deaf Club
National Deaf Club
Neath Deaf Club
Newham School for the Deaf, London
Newport Deaf Club
Northern Counties School for the Deaf, Newcastle
Nutfield Priory School for the Hearing-Impaired, Redhill
Peterlee Deaf Club
Plymouth Deaf Club
Royal Cross School, Preston
Royal School for Deaf Children, Margate
Royal School for the Deaf, Manchester
Royal School for the Deaf, Derby
Royal West of England Residential School for the Deaf, Exeter
St. Giles School & Service for the Hearing-Impaired,
Edinburgh
Salisbury Deaf Club
Sefton Deaf Club
Southampton Deaf Club
The Sixty Six Club
The Spurs Club
The Sussex Diocesan Association for the Deaf, Brighton
Thomason Memorial School, Bolton
Vale Royal Deaf Club
Warrington Society for the Deaf
Record of One Hundred Years' Work 1812-1912
The Royal Institution for the Instruction of Deaf and Dumb
Children, Edgbaston, Birmingham.
**Report of the Royal Commission on the Education of the
Blind and the Deaf and Dumb**
H.M.S.O. 1889.

Report of the Working Party
Higher Study Group on the Further Higher Education for the Hearing Impaired (1982).
Royal School for Deaf & Dumb Children, Margate
The School Press, Margate 1938.
St. Andrew's Church, Walberswick, Suffolk: Graveyard Inscriptions & Parish Notes.
School Brochures:
    Aberdeen School for the Deaf
    Ashgrove School for the Deaf, Penarth
    Burwood Park School, Walton-on-Thames
    Donaldson's School for the Deaf, Edinburgh
    Doncaster College for the Deaf, Doncaster
    Norfolk House College, Walton-on-Thames
    Royal School for the Deaf, Manchester
    St. John's School, Boston Spa
Seaforth MSS
Scottish Records Office.
Scottish Painting
James L. Caw. *Redwood Burn Ltd., Trowbridge 1975.*
Sorinia Reserata
J. Hacet, 1693. British Library Collection
Spurs Club Records. (Courtesy of R.A. Goulden, historian).
TALK
Summer 1972 No. 64.
Telegraph Sunday Magazine
11th January 1987.
The Art of Instructing the Infant Deaf and Dumb
John Pauncefort Arrowsmith, 1819. British Library Collection.
The Deaf American
January 1972.
The Deaf News
No. 186, 1951.
The Deaf of Other Days
Selwyn Oxley. *Ferrier & Co., London 1921.*
The Dukes
Brian Masters, *Blond & Briggs, London 1980.*

The Edinburgh Messenger
No. III December 26th 1843.
The History of Lichfield
Rev. Thos. Harwood. *Cadell & Davies, London 1806.*
The History of the Association
Hampshire, Isle of Wight and Channel Islands Association for
the Deaf 1979.
**The History of The Yorkshire Residential School for the
Deaf Children 1829-1979**
A. Boyce. (In course of print, 1989).
The House - A Portrait of Chatsworth
The Duchess of Devonshire. *Papermac 1982.*
The House of Commons 1754-1790
Lewis Namier & John Brooke. (London 1964) Vol. III.
The House of Commons 1790-1820
Roland Thorne. (London 1986) Vol. IV.
The Loyal and Ancient City
Howard Clayton. *J.M. Tatler & Sons, Derby.*
The Man Who Loved to Draw Horses
A.D. Cameron. *Aberdeen Univ. Press 1986.*
The Quiet Ear
B. Grant.
The Royal School Magazine, Margate
Nos. 65,66.
The Siege of Lichfield
Rev. W. Greasley. *Constable, London 1923.*
The Silent World
Vol. 8, 1954, 1956.
The Teacher of the Deaf
Vol. 1, 1903, No. 44, 1946, 1956. Vol. 6, No. 33.
Tonkin's MSS
Cornwall Records Office.
Transcript of 50th Anniversary Dinner Speech, M. Webster
(Bedford Deaf Club).
Typewritten Notes, Anerley Deaf School & The Old Kent
Road School.
Typewritten Notes, *British Theatre for the Deaf*, R.N.I.D.

Typewritten Notes, *"Deaf Burke"*, R.N.I.D. Library 1968.
Typewritten Notes, *Drama & the Deaf*, R.N.I.D.
Typewritten Notes, Deaf Mountaineering Club, I.G.M. Hall.
Typewritten Notes, Northampton School, F. Ince-Jones - Northampton C.R.O., ZAB799.
Typewritten Notes, *The Story of a School*, Ashgrove School for the Deaf, Penarth.
Units for Partially Hearing Children
H.M.S.O. 1972.
Unpublished Thesis, Colin M'Dowell.
Volta Review
May 1933; March 1948, 1946, Vol. 48.
Walpole Society, Vol XVII
Basil Long.
Annual Report, 1919
Warrington and District Society for the Deaf.
Who's Who in Wrestling
D'Orazio and Edwards. *Paul, London 1971.*
Woman
28th May 1982.